Study Skills for Health and Social Care Students

Study Skills for Health and Social Care Students

Claire Craig

Los Angeles | London | New Delhi
Singapore | Washington DC

SAGE Publications Ltd
1 Oliver's Yard
55 City Road
London EC1Y 1SP

SAGE Publications Inc.
2455 Teller Road
Thousand Oaks, California 91320

SAGE Publications India Pvt Ltd
B 1/I 1 Mohan Cooperative Industrial Area
Mathura Road
New Delhi 110 044

SAGE Publications Asia-Pacific Pte Ltd
33 Pekin Street #02-01
Far East Square
Singapore 048763

Library of Congress Control Number: 2009920464

British Library Cataloguing in Publication data

A catalogue record for this book is available from the British Library

ISBN 978-1-84787-388-0
ISBN 978-1-84787-389-7 (pbk)

Typeset by C&M Digitals (P) Ltd, Chennai, India
Printed and bound in Great Britain by TJ International Ltd, Padstow, Cornwall
Printed on paper from sustainable resources

Dedication

I dedicate this book to Carol and Nicola – the two greatest friends a girl could have

Contents

Acknowledgements

This book would not have been possible without the help and support of my many students who have so generously given their time and shared their ideas and experiences. Particular thanks to Angela Bedson, Helen Brown and Helen Saunders for their enthusiasm, wisdom and for transporting me back to my student days.

Thank you to Chris Glover from the Learning and Teaching Institute at Sheffield Hallam University and occupational therapist Janet Ulman, who gave up their time to read through and comment on drafts of the text, and to Patrick Brindle from SAGE for all his help, encouragement and for turning the dream into a reality.

I would like to reserve a special thanks to my amazing husband Neil, who has patiently navigated this journey with me and has shared his creative talents, providing the illustrations that accompany this book. And to Eddie for patiently foregoing many walks while I was sitting at the computer.

Part I Introduction

1 In the beginning...

This is the book I longed to read when I was a student many years ago. Although I had studied for a degree before, I did not find the transition to being a student in health and social care an easy one to make. I struggled to see the links between what I learned in the classroom and what I would be doing in practice. Sessions in academic or key skills left me cold as I really could not see the point of learning how to take notes or write essays. 'After all', I told myself 'when did writing an essay help a patient?' I was desperate for placement and the opportunity for hands-on experience.

Yet placement came as a shock. I found it hard to manage my time, prioritise whom I should see and when I should see them. Being part of a team also brought its own challenges. The hardest part, though, was getting to grips with the vast quantities of reports, records and notes I needed to keep. Needless to say, I scraped through, but only just.

Then on my second placement I had a breakthrough. I had inadvertently brought my academic skills folder with me and with little to do in the evenings I started to read it. As I did I suddenly realised that the steps to writing assignments, taking notes and giving presentations at university were surprisingly similar to the skills required to write reports, keep records and share information at the many case conferences on placement. The only real difference was the context. This was a light bulb moment. As soon as I understood the relevance I applied myself to these so-called academic skills and saw the marks I gained for assignments and on placement improve on a meteoric trajectory.

Things have travelled full circle. I now help my students make the links between academic skills and the core skills and competencies required for placement. I listen to their 'ah ha!' moments as they begin to relate the two.

I hope that you will enjoy reading this book, that it will result in your own 'ah ha!' moments and help you to place academic skills in their widest context, leading to every success at university, on placement, in practice and beyond.

2   How to gain the most from this text

Congratulations. In choosing to pursue a career in health and social care you are embarking on an exciting journey that will stretch you to the limit and lead to an extremely rewarding future.

This book will provide you with the necessary underpinning skills to ensure that you gain the most out of your course. You will learn how to read ruthlessly, think, structure your ideas, write well, develop techniques to cope with pressure and find ways to manage your time. As a result this book will:

- Help you to make connections between what you learn in the classroom and what you learn on placement

- Prepare you for practice experience

- Enable you to understand who you are, the skills you already have and how to hone these

- Demystify some of the language you will inevitably encounter

- Ground your learning through case studies and examples

- Make learning into a fun and enjoyable experience

Finding your way around the text

The book looks at the main academic skills required by all student health and social care practitioners. It starts by putting these skills into their broadest context and helps you to understand how skills developed in the classroom relate to placement and vice versa.

This is followed by a quick 'survival guide' to get you through the first few weeks of university life, describing some of the things you may encounter. The book is then divided into three broad sections:

- **Organising your learning**. This section focuses on the self-management skills that will underpin your personal and professional development, with tips about how to set and achieve goals, ways to manage your time, techniques you can use to cope with anxiety and the wider support mechanisms you may need to tap into.

- **Building and developing skills**. Here the focus is on the academic skills you need to succeed. From how to research information to expressing your ideas in writing, this section contains it all.

- **Planning and preparing for the future**. This final element of the book helps you to move beyond university. It offers advice to help you gain your dream job and describes ways to engage with a lifelong learning process.

Navigating the text

Each chapter contains a number of ingredients including:

JARGON-BUSTING

where key words are demystified and technical terminology translated into English.

 ### AT A GLANCE

a quick (and often humorous) way of deciding whether the chapter is relevant for you.

STARTING POINTS

a series of self-tests, quizzes or questionnaires to help you recognise your skills and identify gaps in your knowledge.

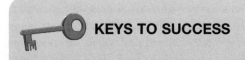 ### KEYS TO SUCCESS

tools, rules and techniques required to unlock your potential and succeed in your studies. Case studies, student narratives and model answers provide concrete examples of how to apply your learning.

SKILLS IN PRACTICE

this section moves away from the classroom to show you how to develop and apply your skills on placement.

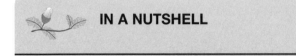 **IN A NUTSHELL**

a summary of the information contained in the chapter.

 References and signposts to further reading and resources

offering links to further resources you may find useful.

Who is this book aimed at?

This book is relevant for students undertaking programmes of study or courses related to health and social care practice, including general nursing, mental health nursing, midwifery, paramedic practice, operating department practice, radiography, occupational therapy, physiotherapy and social work.

It recognises that you are bringing with you a unique set of skills based on your previous experience and that a number of different pathways and routes of study lead to qualification. The book is relevant for students on full-time or part-time courses, can be used in work-based learning contexts and is suitable for individuals studying to diploma or degree level.

A website accompanying the book can be found at www.skills4health.co.uk. This contains a wealth of additional materials, including two-minute tutorials, links to further resources and a number of quizzes to help test your skills and further broaden your understanding. It also includes a template for a personal and professional development record. This will enable you to evidence your learning, track your progress and document your achievements in a format that you can take with you to interview and beyond.

A note about terminology

Your university will have its own way of describing the roles that practitioners play in your education, including clinical tutors, practice teachers, supervisors, placement educators. For the purposes of this book, I have used the word 'educator' or 'placement educator' to describe the person who educates you in practice. Likewise, you will hear the people you work with described in various ways, including patients, clients and service users. I have tried to reflect this and have used these terms interchangably depending on the examples described.

Gaining the most from the text: you do not have to eat the whole elephant at once

Remember, it is unnecessary to know everything straight away. The one sure way to feel completely overwhelmed and bored by any text is to try reading it from cover to cover in one go. Some parts will not be relevant or may not make any real sense until you are putting a particular skill into practice as part of your course.

In order to gain the most from the book it is probably best to dip in and out of it as you go along. Buy your own copy so that you can use it as a workbook, complete the 'self-test' exercises, work through the activities and as you do, identify where you need to focus your attention. Draw, doodle, add your own notes as this will help you to interact with the book, remember what you read and make connections with your work. In a sad way, come to regard the book as your friend and companion as you journey through your course and your career (but when someone asks you if you have made any new friends at university do not include this book among them!).

Oh, and if I have not said this already. Good luck. Enjoy…

Let's begin by looking at the bigger picture. The aim of your course is to equip you with the necessary skills to be a competent and confident practitioner. What does this mean exactly? What does this future look like? For a moment, zoom forward to your first day of work. Use the space below to make a list of all the skills and competencies you will ideally possess to enable you to perform your role. You could do a mini sketch of yourself if you find this helpful.

This book suggests that the skills and attributes you have just listed bear an uncanny resemblance to those you require to study. If you find this hard to believe, consider the following, which are taken from a range of job specifications for posts in nursing, midwifery, occupational therapy, physiotherapy, social work, operating department practice and paramedic practice.

- Ability to prioritise work and keep calm under pressure

- Good personal organisation skills

- Demonstrates clarity in written and spoken communication

- Confident in following written and verbal instructions

- Documentation written to a high standard and in accordance with standards set down by the Trust

- Contributes to the maintenance of up-to-date service information leaflets

- Group work skills

- Team player – able to work collaboratively with others

- Capacity to work effectively in multi-professional teams

- Contribute to research activities being undertaken in the service area

- Demonstrates skills in researching information

- Ability to reflect and critically appraise own performance

- Commitment to personal and professional development

- Understanding of continuous professional development (CPD) requirements of the profession

If you looked beyond these at three key national documents which cumulatively list the skills and attributes required by all health and social care practitioners, you would see a very similar picture. Links to the following documents are available on the website if you would like to find out more.

- The Standards of Proficiency (Health Professions Council)

- The Standards of Proficiency (Nursing and Midwifery Council)

- The National Occupational Standards for Social Work

Clearly each profession has a core of specific knowledge and a set of competencies unique to that area of practice. These might relate to an ability to understand anatomy or legislation, to perform specific clinical procedures, undertake therapeutic techniques or work with particular media and technologies. However, in addition, there are a range of generic skills required by all practitioners. The main difference is the context in which they are used. As you can see from the above examples, these can be broadly divided into the following areas:

- Self-management: an ability to organise your time, manage stress

- Communication (verbal and written)

- Working with others

- Research: delivering evidence-based practice and ability to keep up to date with the most current practices

- Reflecting on practice

- Engaging in a process of personal and professional development

Mastering these skills effectively offers you the key to unlock potential knowledge and enhance patient care. For instance, the listening and communication skills you develop in the classroom could form an integral part in your ability to form therapeutic relationships or to put carers at ease. Your experience of working in a project group will inform your ability to work within a multidisciplinary team and facilitate your own groups in practice.

You heard it from the students

Here, students reflect on this experience and the relationship between the different elements:

My supervisor commended my ability to help the group relax. I did not have the heart to tell her that all the techniques I shared were those I had learned to manage my exam nerves!

I am currently on placement in a service working with people who have complex communication needs. Two years of lectures have taught me the art of listening. I can read silences, pick up on cues and concentrate on the real message. It has all been worth it just for this.

Before I started my course I found speaking in front of other people really difficult. In view of all the presentations I have given in class, feeding back to the multidisciplinary team now is a piece of cake!!

If we begin at the end point, the dream job in your chosen career, you have a vested interest in developing these skills and in evidencing how you have used and applied them during your course. This book allows you to do both. Each chapter contains a series of activities to try and questions on which to reflect. Use the templates on the website to evidence your learning and as you progress through your course build a portfolio to demonstrate your skills and record your personal and professional development.

   Now let's turn to the first stage of this process and look at ways to survive the first few weeks of your course.

4 Getting started: a survival guide to the first few weeks of your course

Countdown to study...

8 weeks to go: successful results. Mood elation. Cannot wait to start my course.

7 weeks to go: mood still elation. Handed in my notice at work/returned from my holidays, it is all happening.

6 weeks to go: reading list arrives. It looks long and the books look expensive. Less elation, reality dawns.

5 weeks to go: still no timetable. Worried about what is going to happen during the first few weeks.

4 weeks to go: heard from one of the second-year students on the course. Bursary forms came through and accommodation confirmed. Super-elation.

3 weeks to go: still not started on the reading list. Feeling concerned.

2 weeks to go: what should I wear? Will I make any friends? Will my family cope? Anxiety levels high.

1 week to go: not sleeping. Excited. Feel sick most of the time.

   Lift off...

JARGON-BUSTING

Induction: An orientation process to help you take the first steps to beginning your course.

Reading list: A guide to books, journals and other types of information relating to the subjects you are studying.

Enrolment: Largely an administrative and form-filling process required before you can begin your course.

Fresher's fair/New Starters week: A social event where university societies, clubs and associations show you the range of activities on offer and try to persuade you to sign up.

(Continued)

(Continued)

CRB: Short for criminal records bureau check. This is a formal process where your name is checked against existing criminal records (if you have any known convictions, you are required to declare these beforehand). This is a legal requirement and needs to be undertaken before you are able to work with vulnerable people.

Bursary: A means-tested grant open to students studying on some health and social care courses.

 **AT A GLANCE**

This chapter is for you if

- You are about to start your new course
- You started your course a few weeks ago and are still struggling to find your way around
- You are part way through your course and would like to re-live those first few weeks for nostalgic reasons

The longest journey starts with a single step

The weeks leading up to your course can feel like an emotional rollercoaster, veering from excitement and elation to fear and trepidation as the day draws closer. Starting anything new is taking a step into the great unknown. Even if you have studied for a degree beforehand, a course leading to professional registration will contain a number of subtle differences.

One of the first challenges you will encounter is managing the transition from university to practice. Just when you feel confident in the classroom, then you will be thrust on to placement. Here you will need to get to grips with a new learning environment. This chapter is a guide to surviving the first few weeks of university life and the first weeks on placement. It shows you some of the simple steps you can take to ensure that your anxiety levels are kept to a minimum so that you can make the most of these new and exciting challenges.

STARTING POINTS: READY TO ROLL OR READY TO RUN?

Try this activity to see how prepared you are to begin your course. For each question, choose the sentence that best relates to you – (a) – (d).

Question 1

(a) You have read and digested every piece of documentation that contains a university hallmark.
(b) Letter? You vaguely remember receiving something but you would struggle to place where you last saw this.

Question 2

(a) You have already memorised the train/bus timetable.
(b) You have a vague idea of where the bus stop is.

Question 3

(a) You own every book on the reading list.
(b) You plan to own every book on the reading list.

Question 4

(a) You know the name of the building and the number of the room where your first lecture is going to be held.
(b) You have an idea of what the building is called and plan to follow anyone who seems to know what they are doing.

Question 5

(a) You know the name of every tutor who teaches on your course.
(b) You know your name and the name of the course.

Question 6

Read the following terms and place these in order of formality:

(a) Tutorial
(b) Seminar
(c) Lecture

Question 7

Which is longer?

(a) A semester
(b) A term

(Continued)

TVII784

(Continued)

Question 8

Induction means:

(a)   A term used in midwifery meaning to artificially deliver a baby.
(b)   A term used in education meaning introduction.
(c)   None of the above.
(d)   Both of the above.

To find the answers, read on…

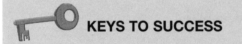 **KEYS TO SUCCESS**

These are the keys to a stress-free first few weeks at university and on placement:

- Be proactive: check out the practicalities
- Get to grips with terminology
- Manage expectations
- Tune into how you learn
- Adjust your attitude
- Recognise your strengths and be open to learning about your needs

Be proactive: check out the practicalities

The motto for the first few weeks is 'Be Prepared'. A couple of weeks before you begin you will receive a letter describing what you need to bring with you, the time to arrive and where you need to go on your first day. Start to put these things together, dig out your certificates, arm yourself with passport photographs and avoid the frantic last-minute dash. If nothing has arrived two weeks before the course it is worth getting in touch with someone in the university administration office just in case the letter has gone astray.

As the time draws near, start to think about transport. Make sure you know where you are going, plan a route and have a contingency plan. Transport can be stressful at the best of times, especially during the first few weeks of a university term where countless other students are all fighting for a limited number of parking spaces.

It is worth seeing if the timetable is available beforehand, particularly if you are planning childcare and trying to juggle a busy home life. You will probably need to monitor minor changes online throughout the year but this should not be too much of a problem.

If you are living in halls of residence, check what you need to bring. Some halls have a communal kitchen where utensils are provided. It is worth confirming how big your new home will be as this will help to determine how many belongings to pack into the car/suitcase/train.

The final issue to think about at this stage is finances. Many health and social care courses are funded by the Department of Health and you may be eligible for a small means-tested bursary. You will not be looking at millions of pounds, but when you are a student every penny counts. The university will be able to advise you regarding this and provide information relating to other grants and loans you may be entitled to apply for.

Here students share some of their top tips to managing finances:

I bought all the books on the reading list. It was a big mistake because I've not even opened some of these. Buy one book from the key reading and then add to this once you know what is relevant.

Do not forget that the University Library will also stock the books on your reading list so it can be worth using some of these to start with. Once on the course, if you are constantly reviewing a particular book, then you probably need to buy yourself a copy.

I car-share with a friend. It's nice to travel into uni with someone and it saves on petrol.

Before you come, set up your direct debits, buy a TV licence and see which banks are close to your halls of residence. The closer they are the better since the last thing you want to do is to have to trek half way across town every time you need money.

I was worried about money and whether I could manage a part-time job to tide me over and make ends meet. I managed to get a job in a care setting. This looks good on my CV as well as my bank balance.

Whatever job you get, make sure it doesn't clash with placement.

Bring a packed lunch. Food can be expensive and the queues during the first few weeks were horrendous!!

This final point about food is well made. Much socialising will be done over lunch, coffee and tea (with the obligatory bar of chocolate). Universities have food outlets but these can be expensive if they are not subsidised. Say, for example, you drink two cups of coffee a day at £1.50 a cup. In a 40-week academic year this would add up to a whopping £600 a year and £1800 over the three years of your course. A flask of tea or coffee and a nice packed lunch might not look as glamorous as a cappuccino but it would stop you from burning a hole in your pocket.

Get to grips with terminology

University is full of jargon, to the point that it can sometimes feel as though you are in a foreign country where everyone speaks a different language. You will need to spend time orientating yourself. If you are unsure about what something means, ask. The chances are everyone else will be wondering about this too. The following guide to university language will kick-start the process.

Enrolment	A form-filling process where you sign up to the course. The equivalent of a contract.
Module	A unit of learning. Some courses are divided into modules. Each module will focus on a particular topic.
Semester	A division of the university year (one semester = six months).
Term	A division of the university year. Shorter than a semester (one year = three terms).
Level 4, 5, 6	Year one, year two, year three.
Enquiry-based learning	A form of self-directed learning where you are given a challenge or a stimulus to act as a springboard for learning.
Problem-based learning	A form of self-directed learning where you are given a problem or a case study to kick-start the learning process. Very similar to enquiry-based learning.
LLRC	Library, learning and resource centre.
VLE	Virtual learning environment: a space on the computer where tutors will communicate with you, where lectures will be posted and where you can have an online discussion with your peers.
Blackboard	An example of one of the virtual learning environments.

Manage expectations

What is it like being a student? Do you envisage friends, all-night parties, having the space to sit in and work in a library where you can absorb information away from the demands of the family?

Keep going back to this image as the course progresses and monitor your expectations. Everyone will have some kind of a idea about what student life as a health and social care practitioner will be like. For some this is very much an idealised picture. They imagine George Clooney from *ER* or Florence Nightingale when the reality is nothing like this. They dream of perfect ivory towers for learning where things run seamlessly, whereas the reality is that lectures will be cancelled at a moment's notice and from time to time mistakes will be made. If the gulf between the ideal and the reality is too big, then you will quickly become disillusioned and will struggle to cope. You therefore need to be very clear about your expectations and to ask whether these are realistic.

A good starting point is to recognise the difference between health and social care courses and other degrees. If you imagine that being at university is one big party, then you are in for a bit of a surprise. Students on health and social care courses study far longer than their peers on other arts or humanities programmes. This is because your course needs to take into account the 1,000 or so placement hours required. While your flat mates may be thinking 'Can I really be bothered going to that lecture?', you have little choice. Your learning has a direct impact on client care and failure to attend sessions will prevent you from progressing. This makes complete sense. Imagine how you would feel if you went to a GP and he said 'Sorry, I can't help you. I missed the lecture about how to treat eczema'! When you signed up to the course there was the expectation that you were agreeing to behave in a professional manner, attend lectures and take responsibility for your own learning.

This all sounds very dark and serious. It is not meant to be. Your student life will be incredibly rewarding and great fun, but perhaps not in the way that you might expect. Always hold on to the bigger picture: the rewards of working in your chosen field and beginning a lifelong career are immeasurable.

A minority of students, however, find that this is not the right course at the right time. Realistically, you will not know this until you have been on placement. Do not make any rash decisions. Even if you transfer on to another course, you will usually be able to take a number of credits with you.

Finally, expect great things of yourself but remember it is not necessary to know it all straight away. Students are incredibly hard on themselves, expecting to gain the highest marks from day one. Remember, if you knew everything on your first day then there would not be a need to study.

Tune in to how you learn

Understanding how you learn is one dimension of managing your expectations. When students think about learning they tend to see it in the following way:

Teacher = distant expert
Student = passive sponge, soaking up the knowledge

This can be useful for learning facts but by the same token it is quite passive. Health and social care practitioners need to think on their feet, respond to new information and work quickly with little guidance. Most courses will therefore use a model where you are encouraged to learn more actively, within this model:

Lecturer = resource providing learning opportunities
Student = active partner, exploring, challenging, developing and testing out ideas

This model is far more collaborative and focuses on an equal relationship. Learning is an active process where you take responsibility. How you learn is seen as being as important as what you learn. Does this sound scary? There is no need to panic as you will not be plunged straight in at the deep end. Instead you will take part in a number of different learning opportunities, ranging from very formal lectures which tend to be led from the front by your lecturer through to problem-based learning seminars where you direct your own study. Here is a quick resumé of some of the different ways you will learn.

Key to interactivity rating

*	Low
**	Medium
***	High
****	Very high

Lectures

Purpose: Provides you with an overview of the subject area. The main function of a lecture is to impart information and outline key concepts.
Numbers: Large: often to the whole year group
Length of time: 1–2 hours
Interactivity rating: *

Workshops

Purpose: To enable you to explore a subject. The focus is on experiential learning. These are often quite practical, with an element of 'doing' as well as discussion.
Numbers: Smaller, probably a maximum of 20 students
Length of time: 2–3 hours
Interactivity rating: ***

Practicals

Purpose: These are 'hands-on' sessions where you have the opportunity to put your skills into practice.
Numbers: Again small, 10–20 students
Length of time: 1–2 hours
Interactivity rating: ****

Problem-based and enquiry-based learning seminars

Purpose: To promote the sharing of skills and learning from each other. You will be given a learning trigger or stimulus and then work together to research information around this.

Numbers: small, 8–10
Length of time: 1–2 hours
Interactivity rating: ****

Anatomy laboratories

Purpose: To learn anatomical terms and gain a good understanding of how the body functions.
Numbers: Vary – sessions can be delivered very formally to large numbers or can be based on more interactive learning opportunities with small groups of 10–15 students
Length of time: 1–2 hours
Interactivity rating: Variable from * to **

Tutorials

These are focused pockets of learning, usually with a specific purpose. There are two types of tutorials:
Academic tutorials: Where your progress is reviewed or feedback on a piece of work is given.
Personal tutorials: Where wider issues impacting on learning are discussed.
Numbers: Very small, can be one to one
Length of time: Varies. Tends to be negotiated with your tutor. No more than 1 hour
Interactivity rating: ***

Self-directed learning

Purpose: Where you are given a topic to research and are expected to set your own learning objectives and organise your study time in such a way as to meet these.
Numbers: Depends how you organise your study time. It could just be you or you might decide to team up with a small group of other people and work together
Length of time: Unlimited – as little or as much as you want to put into it
Interactivity rating: ****

Seminars

Purpose: These are organised teaching sessions where you are expected to present information or actively contribute to the discussion.
Numbers: Small, usually 5–8 people
Length of time: Usually 1–2 hours
Interactivity rating: ****

Adjust your attitude

Mark on this self-belief cup how confident you are in your ability to succeed on your course.

Is your self-belief cup half full or half empty?

Successful study is not necessarily about intelligence or experience: much can depend on your attitude to learning. Take three students, for example: Mark, Fran and Pete. All three manage to scrape a pass on their first assignment.

Mark is the least confident of the three. He does not feel as though he is 'good enough' to be there. He does not tell anyone this outright, but inside he feels a fraud and is convinced that the reason why he gained a place is because the Admissions Tutor confused him with someone else. When he receives his mark his worst fears are confirmed and he sees this as evidence that he should leave.

Fran is quite the opposite. She feels that she is ready to do the job now and sees all this studying as a waste of time. When she receives her mark, she screws up the feedback sheet and throws it in the bin. Clearly, her tutor has no idea about what she is talking about and is wrong. Interestingly, she does not do too well on the next assignment or the one after that.

Pete would be the first person to say that he is not the most academic student in the world but he is confident about who is and knows that to have been offered a place means that his interviewer recognised his potential. He is pleased that he passed his assignment and very much sees this as a learning opportunity. He is only at the beginning of his course and he wants to develop his skills to gain a good result. He therefore arranges to see his tutor to discuss her comments in more detail. He acts on this advice and it pays off. The mark for his second assignment is much higher.

These students all possess the same level of ability but the distinguishing factor is their attitude. Mark left the course not because he was unable to do it but because he believed he was unable to do it. Fran, on the other hand, was so convinced that she could do it that she failed to see the evidence presented before her and to act on this. Pete did exceptionally well. Not because he was the brightest or most talented of the three but because he held on to a realistic picture of his skills, did not expect to know everything and was open to learning. Learning is not comfortable. It is not meant to be…

Recognise your strengths and be open to learning about your needs

How well do you understand your strengths and recognise your learning needs? Try answering the following questions.

- Where do you learn best?
- How do your learn?
- What was your most positive learning experience?
- Your biggest academic flop?
- A turning point in your studies?
- Someone who has inspired you?
- Would you learn best from listening to a person telling you something, from looking at a picture or from trying something out?
- Are you confident about speaking in front of others?
- How do you rate your essay-writing skills?
- What is your best personal characteristic?
- What is your worst personal feature or characteristic?

In answering these questions you have just taken the first step to finding out what really makes you tick.

When you begin a course in health and social care practice, you do not start with a blank canvas. You will bring with you a range of skills and understanding that will be highly relevant and will have a direct application to your course. You may have acquired relevant theoretical knowledge and study skills during your A levels or on your access course. Further skills could relate to practical experience gained through paid or voluntary work, or as a result of caring for a family member.

Draw on this knowledge and experience and make connections with your previous learning. Use the exercises in each of the chapters in this book and the resources on the accompanying website (www.skills4health.co.uk) to explore your strengths and identify your learning needs.

Skills in practice

Over the duration of your course you will be expected to undertake a specified number of placement hours. The exact number of hours will be set down by your professional body and these will be timetabled accordingly, usually in blocks of between 6 and 12 weeks at set periods.

Placements are undoubtedly the best part of your course. They provide you with the opportunity to put your skills into practice and to gain a feel for what it will be like once you have qualified and are 'out there' doing the job. They are organised in such a way as to offer you a range of experiences in a number of areas of practice at different levels so that as you move from placement to placement you are given increasing amounts of responsibility and are expected to perform more complex tasks until, by your final placement, you are ready to take the final step that will see you move from student to qualified practitioner.

Possibly the most challenging thing about going on placement is the process of constantly switching from university to placement mode. This is particularly true of your first experience. Just as you have started to feel comfortable at university, you will need to get to grips with a different setting, new terminology and different systems. You are away from friends and with a completely new staff group. The good news is that you will be able to apply a number of the same steps you used to success-fully negotiate the first weeks of your university course.

Be proactive: check out the practicalities

Once again, the key here is to be proactive. Your university placement tutors will make sure that you are well briefed. You will be allocated a placement educator in the clinical area who will act as your supervisor/tutor for the duration of the placement and the steps you need to take beforehand will be discussed in a preparation session and possibly outlined in a handbook. These may include some or all of the following:

- Send a CV to your placement educator outlining previous placements undertaken and the breadth of your experience
- Make contact with your placement educator to introduce yourself
- Arrange a pre-placement visit to meet with your educator and gain an overview of the placement
- Identify training required (e.g. manual handling)
- Identify pre-reading to help orientate you to the client group and the setting

Remember, first impressions count and your aim is to demonstrate that you are organised and enthusiastic. Before you go on your placement you therefore need to check that you are clear about:

- What time you need to arrive on the first day
- The date of your first day
- Where you are going and how you get there
- Parking arrangements
- Contact names and numbers

- Whether you need to wear a uniform and, if not, what is the accepted dress code

- Policies about hair, nails, make up and body piercing

- Whether you need to provide evidence that you have had the appropriate inoculations/ CRB checks

Here placement educators share what they are looking for in the first meeting with a student:

As an educator I am looking for someone who is enthusiastic and interested. I do not mind if the student has not worked in the area before just so long as they are committed and are willing to learn. I love it when a student is organised and they arrive on the first day with a clear idea about what they hope to gain from the placement and with the necessary documentation which, as their educator, I am required to complete. The ward is busy and if I can see that they are taking responsibility at this point then I know that things will go well.

When a student takes time to write and send a CV describing their experience it means that I am able to think about what experiences they will benefit from and before they set foot in the hospital, I can tailor the placement to meet their needs.

Things I look for in a student: smartly dressed, someone who is able to listen and a person who has taken the time to find out a little about what the placement entails beforehand. Pet hates are students who arrive late, who have not taken the time to find out about our dress code and who basically look incredibly bored.

Get to grips with terminology

If you thought that the terminology at university was confusing, then prepare to be completely bamboozled on placement. You will encounter a wide range of alien terms, from medication to instrumentation. Here are some less specialist phrases you will come across:

Placement educator	The clinician responsible for your placement learning experience.
Link tutor	Usually a university tutor who acts as a bridge between your course and the placement.
Handover	The process of passing information about a patient to another member or members of the multidisciplinary team in order to ensure continuity of care. This may occur at points of staff change-over (e.g. nursing shifts) or when an intervention ends and another member of staff takes over care.
Referral	Document used to refer someone to a service. It will include space to detail the presenting problem and the reason why they have been referred to a service. In some settings, referrals may be made verbally.

PMH	Past medical history
Discharge	The end of a treatment or intervention.
MDT	Abbreviation for multidisciplinary team. This is the name given to the team of health and social care professionals you are working alongside.
ADL	Abbreviation for activities of daily living. These are activities associated with looking after yourself: cooking, cleaning, home management.
PADL	Personal activities of daily living. These include dressing, washing and bathing.
Home visit (HV)	Assessment performed in the person's home.
Ward round	Meeting of the members of the multidisciplinary team to discuss a person's progress.
Off-duty	Staffing rota: a term often associated with nursing.

It can be useful to purchase a small exercise book that will fit into your tunic or trouser pocket. Use this to record unfamiliar terminology as you progress through your placement. As you move from setting to setting you will build up quite an extensive vocabulary.

Manage expectations

You will arrive on placement with a range of expectations, each of which will play a part in your overall experience. These might relate to your expectations about:

- Your chosen profession

- What it means to be a professional

- The patient group you are working with

- What being a student on placement involves

- What you are expected to know

- What you are expected to do

Add to this an entirely different level of expectations from the perspective of your placement educator and you begin to grasp the complexities of emotions and practicalities you need to grapple with and resolve.

It is worth taking time to explore what these expectations are because:

- If the reality equals your expectations or better, the result will be increased motivation and a positive placement experience

- If your expectations are greater than the reality, the result will be disappointment and despondency

Activity

1 List the main reasons that led you to choose this particular profession. Tick any of the following if they apply.

- Personal experience
- Career
- Previous work
- Observations in practice
- Caring for someone
- Other

2 What are your main motivations for choosing your profession?

- Altruism (to help others)
- Money
- Having a career
- A vocation
- Working in a hospital
- Gaining a diploma or degree
- Other

3 Use the space below to describe what you imagine a typical day on placement will be like.

4 Describe or, if you are a more visual person, draw your ideal supervisor.

5 Imagine that you are your supervisor. Describe or, if you are a more visual person, draw your ideal student. How do you compare?

This exercise is a good starting point to refer to as you progress through your placement. Use it to create a baseline against which you can compare your experience. As you grapple with any emerging challenges do not forget that you have a range of resources at your fingertips, including:

- Your university tutor

- Other students

- Documentation relating to your placement

More information about the range of support mechanisms is provided in Chapter 8 of this book. If you have any concerns, speak to your placement educator. Discuss what is expected of you and seek regular feedback on your progress.

Remember that every placement experience will be different and some placements will be more closely in line with your ultimate career aspirations. However, this is not an excuse to dismiss other areas of practice. All placements offer rich learning opportunities and prospective employers are frequently looking for students with a breadth of practice experience. Moreover, many of my students, who have often arrived at university with very fixed ideas in terms of the area in which they hope to work, have changed direction as a result of very positive placement experiences in different specialisms.

Finally, if you are a student on a work-based learning programme, one of the challenges you may encounter is if you are given a placement where you currently work. It is important that you somehow distinguish this experience from your usual work role as colleagues may find it difficult to see you in this new light. If this situation arises, make sure you speak with your university tutor.

Tune in to how you learn

A key to succeeding on placement is to take steps to tune in to your learning. Learning on placement is not like learning in the classroom. With the exception of specific sessions offered through in-service training or tutorials, it is less formal, extremely practical and hands on, and you will need to rely on your observational abilities. Here you will need to identify and 'tune in to' possible learning opportunities and, on occasion, make your own. The following quotes are from students who describe some of their experiences on placement.

On my first placement my educator arranged for me to visit a number of departments in the setting. It was really helpful to gain an overview of how our work fitted into the patient journey. (Chloe, diagnostic radiography student)

I was working in an acute mental health setting and I mentioned to my educator that I would like to understand more about the role of the community psychiatric nurse (CPN). He was fantastic and arranged for me to spend the day shadowing the CPN. This gave me a real insight into what they do. (Ying, mental health nursing student)

When I am on placement I actively seek out key reading and resources. It is always good to have something to hand if my educator is writing up her notes and it helps me to consolidate my learning. (Clare, student in learning disabilities)

I tend to learn best by doing. When I am on placement I always try to create a resource or something I can offer back to the team. On my last placement I made a board game relating to home safety. (Frank, occupational therapy student)

Placement offers an amazing opportunity to observe specialist procedures or see specialist equipment in use. In one setting, we splinted in theatre. It was quite an experience but it helped me to understand about working under pressure. (Sue, occupational therapy student)

Again, it is worth reflecting on the types of learning opportunity you would find beneficial before you go on the placement and to keep a record of these as your placement progresses.

Adjust your attitude

Placement offers you the opportunity to develop a broad range of practical skills and to gain a sense of how it feels to work within your chosen profession. However, while at university the emphasis is completely on you and your needs, as soon as you step into the practice environment the focus changes. Here your needs are still very important but in this busy environment, where your educator may be dealing with life and death situations, the client has to come first. On placement, you will need to learn how to take responsibility for your learning and, no matter how you feel, to behave in a professional manner. Again, do not expect to know everything. In fact, being over-confident can act as a barrier to your learning and prevent you from gaining the most from the experience. Rather, build on your learning, share your skills and make sure you are a team player.

Recognise your strengths and be open to learning about your needs

The act of physically being on placement in an unfamiliar setting and with a client group with whom you have never worked before can feel quite daunting. Just orientating yourself to this place will take time and your learning curve will feel pretty steep. As well as learning about various techniques and procedures, it is possible that you will also have to confront things on a personal level about who you are, the values you hold, about how you respond to particular situations and cope under pressure. It is completely natural to feel overwhelmed, tired and out of your depth at times. However, do not feel disheartened. Various support mechanisms exist and the relationship you have with your educator will be key. Amidst all this new learning you must not forget your strengths and the skills and knowledge you bring with you to that situation. This may relate to learning at university or it might be in relation to work or practical experience you gained before embarking on your course, whether in a paid or unpaid capacity. For instance, this may relate to a time when you cared for family or friends or when undertaking voluntary work as part of a school project. The key here is to recognise your strengths and find ways to relate these to the placement setting. As you move from placement to placement build on these, actively request feedback so that you can identify the gaps in your skills and understanding, and seek out new learning opportunities in order to address these areas for development.

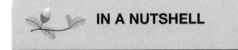

IN A NUTSHELL

Any change, even when it is an extremely positive one, can be stressful. Embarking on a course in health and social care is exciting and fun, but it will also bring its own challenges and frustrations. In order to ensure that you are ready for this experience you need to:

- Ensure your expectations are realistic

- Reduce your stress levels by making sure that you are clear about the practicalities

- Orientate yourself to the new language you are encountering

- Prepare to move outside your comfort zone

- Do not expect to know everything from day one

- Relax and enjoy the experience!

References and signposts to further reading and resources

Drew, S. (2001) 'Student perceptions of what helps them learn and develop in higher education', *Teaching in Higher Education*, 6(3): 309–31.

Healey, J. and Spencer, M. (2008) *Surviving Your Placement in Health and Social Care: A Student Handbook*. Maidenhead: Open University Press McGraw-Hill.

Honey, P. and Mumford, A. (1992) *The Manual of Learning Styles*. Maidenhead: Peter Honey.

Yorke, M. and Longden, B. (2007) *The First-year Experience in Higher Education in the UK*. York: Higher Education Academy. Available at: www.heacademy.ac. uk/resources/publications (Last accessed 26/04/09).

Part II   Organising your learning

5 Setting and achieving goals

 **AT A GLANCE**

This chapter is for you if

- The last goal you successfully achieved was on a football pitch

- You have grand ideas but find it difficult to work out how to fulfil these

- You find it difficult to concentrate on any one thing

- You have always wanted to write a SMART target

- Learning goals or outcomes on assessments seem to be written in Mandarin

Life would be extremely dull if you did not have something to work towards. Identifying and working towards goals can offer a direction and provide a sense of meaning and purpose so that you are focused in your studies. Goals come in all shapes and sizes and may focus on long-term aspirations or on more concrete tasks that need to be achieved in the short term. For instance, at university a short-term goal might be to pass a module or a piece of coursework by a set date, whereas a more long-term aspiration could be to gain a certain classification of degree or a level of mastery in a skill. As you move beyond university you will continue to set and work towards goals that relate to your career progression and your continuous professional development. This process will enable you to maintain a clear focus, work in a systematic way, monitor your progress and keep you motivated.

Goal setting goes hand in hand with action planning. Once a goal has been defined, the process of action planning enables you to map out the practical steps required to reach this and the resources you will require on the way. If you imagine that the goal is a destination on a map, the action plan represents the route you will take to get there.

Writing goals and developing action plans is a real art form. This chapter will help you to identify what you hope to achieve on your course, develop clear targets and create action plans to maximise your chances of success. It then looks at ways of applying these skills on placement both in terms of developing and writing your learning objectives and also in collaborative goal planning with clients.

STARTING POINTS: GOAL-SETTING – HIT OR MISS?

Think back to the last goal you set yourself (this could be a New Year's resolution, something you wanted to learn or achieve, or even a financial target you decided to work towards). For each question below, choose the statement that best relates to you.

Question 1

(a)   When it comes to goal-setting my motto is 'Reach for the stars'. Aim big, fall hard.
(b)   I like to aim high but I recognise the need to break larger goals down into smaller, more manageable steps.

Question 2

(a)   Why bother writing down your goals when they are all in your head?
(b)   I find it useful to write down my goals. The process helps me to clarify my thinking and decide exactly what it is I am working towards.

Question 3

(a)   A SMART target describes a goal that is clever.
(b)   A SMART target describes a goal that is specific, measureable, achievable, realistic and time-limited.

Question 4

(a) If I don't achieve a goal that I've set myself, I tend to block it out. There is no use dwelling on failure.

(b) If I don't achieve a goal that I've set myself, I revisit the process and use it as a learning experience.

Question 5

(a) Action plan: isn't that a toy most little boys play with?

(b) Action plan: is a comprehensive strategy that identifies the steps required to achieve a specific goal.

Question 6

(a) I don't bother setting goals. I prefer to drift through life.

(b) I find that goals offer me a direction and a focus.

Question 7

(a) I regularly set goals but I find it hard to meet them, mainly because I lose motivation.

(b) I recognise that in order to meet my goals I need to build in small steps of things I can easily achieve. This boosts my confidence and keeps me motivated.

If you answered mainly (a), this chapter is definitely for you. You may not see the importance of setting goals but then experience problems in achieving these because you struggle to maintain motivation.

If you answered mainly (b), great. You sound like an experienced goal-setter. You recognise that goals provide a focus for you to work towards and that if you want to achieve these you need to follow a clear process. This chapter will provide you with the opportunity to hone your skills.

Thinking about your long-term goals

Spend a few moments thinking about your long-term goals. What are you ultimately working towards?

- A good degree
- A successful career
- A well-paid job
- A good social life with lots of friends
- Something else

What would you ultimately define as success?

- A management post in the hospital or community
- Being a senior member of staff
- A PhD or other higher qualification
- A settled family life with a part-time job doing what you really enjoy
- A specialist post
- Something else

Jot down your own ideas.

My long-term goals are:

If these are your long-term goals, what about more short-term goals? Make a list of things you hope to achieve in the next:

Hour

Day

Week

Month

We will return to these a little later in the chapter.

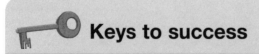 **Keys to success**

Our ability to achieve the goals we set will depend on many factors: how realistic these goals are, how much we want to reach them, the resources that are available to help us. The process of writing these can help us to understand what we really want to achieve and create a focus where we can channel our energies. Consequently, the very act of writing a goal will increase the likelihood of success – particularly if we have included an action plan because it means that we have spent time thinking about what we really want to achieve and how we are going to do this.

Goal-setting is a useful skill to develop in the first few weeks of your course as you will use this as you approach your work and placement. The ability to success-fully achieve your goals is underpinned by the following skills:

- Identify your goal
- Put the goal/objective in writing using SMART terminology
- Develop an action plan which includes the range of resources you can draw on
- Reflect on the experience

Identify your goal

This is more challenging than you think. Broadly speaking, you will encounter two types of goals:

1. **Process- or task-orientated goals.**   These tend to refer to tasks to be achieved, e.g. finishing an assignment by a particular date, or passing a particular examination.
2. **Aspirational goals.**   These relate more to aspects of competence or mastery, e.g. 'My goal is to achieve a mark of 50 or above in the next anatomy exam'.

These can be subdivided into:

Long-term goals: things you would like to achieve in the more distant future (months, years, decades)

Short-term goals: things you need to achieve more immediately (hours, days, weeks)

Go back to the exercise at the beginning and look at the goals you identified. These were quite focused on goals relating to your career or education. To add balance, you also need to think about things you would like to achieve on a personal level. Once you have decided these, record them in the grid below.

	Goals at university (these could relate to health, lifestyle, family, friends, hobbies and interests)	Goals relating to my career (classification of degree, specialism, mark for a particular assignment)
Long-term		
Short-term		

This is a useful exercise to do as it highlights any potential conflicts. For instance, if a long-term goal is to gain a first and your short-term goals all relate to building friendships and having a good social life, you may have to rethink one of these.

Put the goal/objective in writing using SMART terminology

Recording your goal in writing will provide you with a clear focus and will increase your chances of success. You need to think very carefully about how you phrase this:

In order to...

My goal is to...

What (verb)...
Increase...
Develop...
Reduce...
Complete...

To what extent (a specific measure)...
By ten marks
By one hour a day
By a half, a quarter

When...
Date

Are you SMART enough?

This is not a personal question. To maximise your chances of success your target should be SMART. This doesn't mean it has to think for itself. SMART is an acronym for goals that are:

Specific
Measureable
Achievable
Realistic
Time-limited

Imagine someone identifies that their goal is to run ten miles. This may initially sound impressive but if you begin to unpick it slightly ... ten miles at once? Ten miles running one mile a week? Ten miles in a lifetime? Ten miles in the next ten years? The more woolly the goal, the less chance you have of achieving this. Therefore once you have written down your goal you need to interrogate it using a series of questions.

Specific: what is it you want to do exactly? Why?	Is my goal clear? Would a stranger reading this goal understand what I hope to achieve? If it is a large area, do I focus on one aspect (e.g. in communication skills, do I mean verbal, written, non-verbal communication)? Am I referring to a general skill or one for a particular situation (e.g. one-to-one communication or communicating with a certain group)?
Measurable: by how much?	Is it quantifiable, does it include a numerical value? Can I measure this? Are there any woolly terms? Improve by how much? Develop in what way? If I have used the word 'increase', do I attach a number to this? How will I know when I have succeeded?
Achievable/attainable: is it feasible?	Can this be completed within the time? Can this be completed in terms of the resources I have? Is this ambitious enough? Is this over-ambitious?
Realistic: is it reasonable?	Is the gap between my starting point and the end point too large? Have I done anything similar? Are there barriers beyond my control that could prevent this from happening?
Time-limited/timely: by when?	Do I include a date or a time frame? How focused am I?

Here are a few examples:

My long-term goal is:

To gain a 2:1 classification in my social work degree.

To gain a mark over 60% in my final radiography examinations at the end of next year.

To work in the specialism of respiratory medicine within two years of qualifying as a physiotherapist.

My short-term goal is:

To verbally share my answer in front of my enquiry-based learning group on Friday.

To gain a mark over 60% in the anatomy examination on Tuesday.

To complete and hand in my psychology assignment on Thursday.

To critically examine the use of electro-convulsive therapy in the treatment of depression and to present these findings to my seminar group on Tuesday 1 December.

It will take time to get into the habit of writing SMART targets. Do not lose heart as many qualified practitioners still struggle with this.

Top Tips

Here are a few top tips of ways to write SMART targets as shared by students.

When I write goals I try to picture what the end point will look like and jot this down. The next key heading for me is the time limited part and this is what I focus on. I might have great hopes but I need to 'get real'. I simply use this as my starting point. 'If that is my end point what can I achieve by…'. I therefore begin by writing: By x date I will… I want to succeed and this means that my goals suddenly become very specific.

I focus on the measurable part. I used to write things like 'increase understanding' but then trying to measure this was impossible. Now the first question I ask is 'How will I know that I have succeeded? Is it possible to measure what I want to measure? Increase/decrease etc. is always followed by the word 'by'.

I like to imagine goal-setting as a journey. I jot down the answer to three questions: Where are we going? When will we get there? How will we know that we have got there?

Develop an action plan which includes the range of resources you can draw on

It is fine to decide what you want to achieve but you also need to be clear about how you are going to get there. It is a bit like going on a long journey – you will need a map with landmarks to guide you. The process of mapping out the steps and working out the resources that can help you is called **action planning**. This will also help you decide if you are actually going to enjoy the journey. Sometimes, mapping out like this helps you reach a deeper self-understanding. It can increase your motivation because you realise that the steps along the way are going to be really enjoyable or it can even help you come to the realisation that you need to adjust the goal.

Here is a worked example of this process.

When it comes to giving a presentation Carla really struggles. This is the one area she really needs to improve on. She has an assessed presentation coming up in six weeks' time.

The first thing she does is to decide her goal. Her long-term goal is to express her ideas confidently in oral presentations to groups of over ten people. She gained 42% in her last one when the pass mark was 40. She wants her short-term goal to be specific and measurable, so she writes it in the following way:

> I will gain a mark of over 50 in the assessed oral presentation on attitudes towards disability in six weeks' time.

She would ideally like to get a first, which requires a score over 70, but given her last mark was 42% and she only has six weeks to plan she also wants to be realistic and doesn't want to set herself up to fail. If she says a mark 'over 50', this is a sizeable improvement but it doesn't stop her from reaching the really high scores either. Also note the positive way she frames this using the words 'I will'. It is always better to write a goal that focuses on the positives rather than the negatives (it is better to say I will eat more healthily rather than I will not eat chocolate).

The next questions you ask yourself when action planning are: How am I going to do this? What steps do I need to take? What methods will I use?

Carla decides to break down the task into manageable chunks. From her experience she knows that the presentation requires her to:

- Research the subject

- Make notes

- Plan the presentation

- Assemble the PowerPoint slides

If her goal had been a process- or task-orientated goal 'to give a presentation', the above steps would be sufficient. However, she has aspirations to gain a particular mark. She therefore needs to include some element of evaluation to prevent her from making the mistakes she made before. Thinking back to her last performance she realises that she failed to leave herself enough time to practise, receive feedback and develop a polished presentation. She therefore builds in two additional steps:

- To practise the presentation in front of a 'critical friend'

- To make adjustments to the presentation based on their feedback

The next stage of action planning is to identify the resources that can help you. These can include people, organisations, literature and equipment. Carla decides that she will draw heavily on the written feedback that she received from her tutor following the last assignment and will invite her closest friend from university to listen to her and to give feedback one evening.

The very process of thinking this through then provides her with a clear picture of the timescales and timings she needs to work to. If you are following this process you might find it useful to record the stages in some way. Sue Drew and Rosie Bingham recommend that you use a grid format as illustrated below (Drew and Bingham, 2001: 242).

Goal			Deadline	
Task	Methods	Resources, help, support	Start date	End date

You write the main goal in the box at the top and then record in more detail the stages you should go through, along with the various timescales for their completion. Here is an example Sue and Rosie provide (ibid.).

Task	Methods	Resources, help, support	Start date	End date
Devise new filing system	Sort notes under headings Create a list of topics/files Make new files	Chapter 'note taking' Filing cabinet Files, File dividers	1 November	20 November

I would add a further column to show date achieved. This will help you to monitor your progress and allow you to make small adjustments as necessary.

The above example is quite detailed. Sometimes your tutor will ask you to develop an action plan for the year containing a whole series of goals. Here you will not have the time or space to record the specifics. In this instance, a grid like the one below will be more appropriate.

Goal/target	Priority	By when	Specific action/ resources needed?	Date achieved

When this is marked, your tutor will be looking at:

- Your level of insight (How have you identified a particular goal? Have you picked up on a genuine need or aim?)

- How realistic your goals are in terms of whether they are achievable and whether they are sufficiently demanding

- Whether your goals are SMART or not

- Your ability to prioritise

- The range of resources identified

- Your timeframes for achievement and whether these are realistic

Reflect on the experience

This is not the end. The final stage comes at the point where you decide whether or not you have been successful. Reflecting on the factors that helped or hindered you enables you to turn this into a learning process. We can all think of goals that we have failed to meet – most people's New Year's resolutions are a classic example. However, if you are to succeed in the future, it is imperative that you step back and look at the process as a whole and pick out exactly what it was that allowed you to meet your goal or not, whatever the case may be. Here are a few things you may need to take into account.

Problem	Result	Possible solution
Your goals were over-ambitious	You felt overwhelmed	Set smaller more bite-sized goals
Goals were under-ambitious	You felt bored and unmotivated	Set more challenging goals
You failed to take into account wider factors	You were taken by surprise	Think more broadly and abstractly about possible issues
You did not make full use of resources	You struggled to find information	List possible resources before you begin
Too much to do within the set timeframe	You failed to meet the deadline	Check how realistic your goals have been
No defined end point	You were unsure whether you met the goal	Always ask yourself 'How am I going to show I have achieved the goal?'

Skills in practice

On placement you will be expected to set and work towards a series of goals that you have identified and negotiated with your placement educator. These goals, sometimes called learning objectives, will help to frame your learning experience and determine your focus for the placement. The second part of the chapter looks at how to translate the steps to success in goal-setting to the context of practice placement. Initially, in terms of your own aspirations, and then in terms of those of your clients as you engage in the process of collaborative goal-setting.

The process of setting learning goals or objectives on placement is pretty much the same as the process you have already engaged in at university with two small exceptions:

• The placement context will determine the type of goals or objectives you identify

• Your learning goals/objectives will be negotiated with your placement educator

Like all modules on your course, the placement will carry a set of overarching learning outcomes set down by your professional body which you have to meet. These will assess particular competencies which contribute to your fitness to practise. Your individual learning objectives will be additional to these and enable you to personalise your learning. They allow you to identify areas for personal and professional development and offer clear parameters in which to work. Because they are negotiated they provide a vehicle for your educator to communicate his/her expectations and at the same time offer you a way to demonstrate that you have insight into your particular learning needs and are working towards these.

The keys to success still stand:

• Identify your goal/objective

• Put the goal/objective in writing using SMART terminology

• Develop an action plan which includes the range of resources you can draw on

• Reflect on the experience

Identify your goal/objective

The first stage is to identify your goal/objective. What is it you would like to achieve from the placement? You may base this on:

• Your previous experience of placement

• Comments made by placement educators about areas for development

• Feedback from tutors

• The new learning opportunities or particular specialisms the placement presents

Broader criteria may guide you and if you are strategic, you could link these to overall learning objectives. Here are a few broad areas you may wish to consider

Communication	Communication with team members, external agencies, carers, clients, communication with individuals with complex communication needs, one-to-one communication, answering the telephone, interviewing, expressing ideas in front of others, adapting communication style, non-verbal communication, written communication (reports, notes), awareness of a range of communication aids
Teamworking	Identifying roles of individual team members, working with the team, liaising with external agencies, statutory and non-statutory organisations, working with support staff, considering team dynamics and your impact on these.
Written communication	Report writing, notes, client leaflets, minutes from meetings
Self-management	Coping with challenging situations, planning, managing your caseload, using your initiative, time management, recognising boundaries and limits to skills
Skills relating to the placement	Understanding how a condition impacts on a person, developing your therapeutic relationships with clients or your

particular therapeutic style in collaboration with your educator, undertaking particular assessments (initial interviews, home visits, grip strength, range of motion, mood, pain, vital signs, assessing for a wheelchair), using a piece of equipment, understanding a range of financial benefits a person can claim), performing a particular procedure under supervision

Here are some learning objectives set by students on placement:

- To independently lead a group-work session for clients in week 3 of the placement.

- To evidence a literature search of occupational therapy (OT) practice in cardiac rehabilitation. To produce a written summary of this by week 5 of the placement.

- To co-facilitate a 'hand-class' with my supervisor by week 6 of the placement.

- To undertake procedure X with minimal supervision by my educator by 10 January.

- To articulate the reasons for using approach X of practice over approach Y to the wider team at the meeting on Friday.

Use the space below to write your own learning objectives.

Put the goal/objective in writing using SMART terminology

Given that placements are time-limited and you will need to demonstrate that you have made good progress towards particular goals, it is even more important that these should be SMART.

Specific: Make sure you are focused here – the broad areas of assessment or communication are too big. Bury right down to get the specifics. The strength is in the detail.

Measureable: Be clear about the level you could be expected to achieve when taking into consideration the length of the placement and the time available.

Attainable: Will your placement allow this to happen? (For example, is undertaking the particular procedure or intervention with minimal supervision acceptable in this setting and at your point of training?)

Realistic: Again, is it realistic within the confines of the placement, the resources available, the level you are expected to work at and the length of the placement?

Time-limited: State when you will achieve your objectives by. (Try not to focus all your objectives on the end of the placement. It is really good practice to build in more short-term objectives that can be achieved daily, weekly or fortnightly, so that you can demonstrate the progress you are making.

If you struggle to pitch these at the right level, Joan Healey and Margaret Spencer (2008: 47–8) offer an excellent framework for writing placement objectives, and identify terms and phrases that reflect what is expected of you at the various stages of your course. Here are a few examples taken from that framework:

Year one	Year two	Year three
Explain	Examine	Teach
Identify	Analyse	Critically evaluate
Describe	Compare and contrast	Judge

As your course progresses, you will be expected to perform at an increasing level of complexity. Margaret Spencer and Joan Healey (2008) emphasise the need to develop learning objectives that reflect the level that you are working at. It would be inappropriate, for example, if you are a final-year paramedic to include a learning objective that refers to carrying out a very basic procedure or undertaking an assessment that would be expected of a student in the first year. Equally, it is important not to set yourself up to fail by pitching your objectives at too high a level. Gaining the right balance can be challenging and your placement educator will be able to guide you and offer advice.

Develop an action plan which includes the range of resources you can draw on

All that remains is to use the skills developed in the classroom to create your action plan, making sure that you identify the resources available with key milestones so that you can demonstrate your learning. It is also useful to leave a space to record when you have achieved your goal/objective and to reflect on your experience, identifying further areas for development based on this. Here is an example of a plan developed by a third-year occupational therapy student.

Target/goal	Priority	By when	Specific action needed?	Resources	Date achieved
Reflection By the end of the placement to demonstrate my ability to engage in reflective processes	High	15 May	Maintaining a reflective journal. Maintaining a portfolio to address and evidence continuing	Template Website	

Target/goal	Priority	By when	Specific action needed?	Resources	Date achieved
within the team to enhance evidence-based approaches.			professional development. Using supervision as a reflective approach to team process. Visiting websites such as the 'Cochrane Library' and 'OT Seeker' to stay abreast of evidence in practice. Reading health-related and profession-related journals.	Supervisor/ colleagues Medical library Learning centre/ journal club	

As you can see, the main difference between the action plan you develop at university and the one you develop on placement will be the range of resources that you tap into. Here are a few examples of additional resources you may find on placement:

- Your placement educator

- Colleagues

- Other students

- Clients and carers

- Medical library

- Clinical documents (using these as a model on which to base your own note-writing process)

- Your university practice placement supervisor or link tutor

- Observations you may make

- Case presentations

- Training opportunities (including in-service training)

- Journal clubs

- The workplace resources file

Add to your own as you go along.

Reflect on the experience

Your ability to record and articulate your thoughts and reflections on the process will demonstrate to your placement educator that you are able to take responsibility for your learning. If you do experience problems on the placement, it can provide additional support to evidence the breadth and depth of skills you have developed. Use the action plan as a working document during supervision sessions as a focus to discuss your progress, possible barriers that may be preventing you from meeting your objectives and further resources that you require to meet your needs. This provides more evidence of your ability to solve problems.

It is good practice to look at ways to adjust your goals and to be completely honest if something is not going to plan. It is highly likely that your placement educator will already know this and it demonstrates that you have insight and can take the initiative.

Goal-setting: the added dimension

Placement offers you a rich learning opportunity to develop your skills in identifying, writing and recording goals. This will serve you well throughout your career as you engage in a process of continuous professional development and lifelong learning. However, the setting of personal goals and learning objectives on placement not only relates to your personal aspirations. Indeed, goal-setting is a key element of the treatment planning process.

When working in health and social care practice this same process of goal-setting with clients will define the purpose of your intervention and ultimately shape the treatment you implement. In this way, goals provide a focus, give direction, and enable the patient or client to monitor their progress.

Goal-setting with clients is usually a collaborative process where the individual's needs and wishes are given priority. Its purpose is to:

- Clarify the direction of the intervention

- State the expected results and the timeframe for achievement

- Identify the resources required to accomplish the goals

Goals may be broken down into:

Long-term goals (the ultimate aim of treatment). For example:

- Client X will be able to walk independently without the use of walking aids

- Client Y will return to appropriate supportive accommodation

Short-term goals, which describe outcomes of treatment that will be achieved during a more immediate timeframe. Where these short-term goals are very specific, they are sometimes also described as objectives. When writing these, make sure you are clear in terms of who you are referring to, what they will achieve (e.g. will they be able to perform the task or activity independently or will they need some form of assistance) and make a note of the timeframe by which they will achieve this:

- In one week's time client X will be able to independently cook simple warm snacks on the ward

- On Tuesday 1 August client X will choose one recipe and prepare it with verbal prompts from the home care worker

- For the next 24 hours the client will remain as comfortable as possible and will be pain free

The process of formulating these involves the writing of SMART targets in much the same way as previously described. Other methods also exist to facilitate this process. For example, in rehabilitation settings, Borcherding (2005: 38) describes the FEAST method, an acronym meaning:

Functional gain: What is the overall purpose of the intervention? In order to…
Expectation: The client will…
Action: Do what?
Specific condition: Under what conditions?
Timeline: By when?

If you would like to develop your skills in writing client goals, read the section on the website accompanying this book (www.skills4health.co.uk) and try completing the exercises in the 'Guide to successful goal setting'.

IN A NUTSHELL

This chapter has considered the importance of goal-setting in the context of the classroom and on placement. It has highlighted that:

- Goals are extremely motivating. They can help to clarify the direction in which you are heading and offer a means to measure success

- SMART targets offer a structure to write and record goals, increasing your chances of success

- The skills required to set goals in the classroom are identical to those required when setting learning objectives on placement and when developing goals for clients.

References and signposts to further reading and resources

Borcherding, S. (2005) *Documentation Manual for Writing SOAP Notes in Occupational Therapy* (2nd edition). Thorofare, NJ: Slack.

Drew, S. and Bingham, R. (2001) *The Student Skills Guide.* (2nd edition). Aldershot: Gower.

Healey, J. and Spencer, M. (2008) *Surviving Your Placement in Health and Social Care: A Student Handbook*. Maidenhead: Open University Press/McGraw-Hill.

O'Sullivan, T., Rice, J., Rogerson, S. and Saunders, C. (1996) *Successful Group Work*. London: Kogan Page.

6 Managing time effectively

AT A GLANCE

This chapter is for you if

- You feel as though you work every hour of the day but still struggle to complete everything you need to do

- Deadlines elude you

- You spend hours cleaning your room or making cups of coffee/tea or doing the ironing or washing the car before being able to get down to the task in hand

- Make list after list after list but never get to the end and always feel disappointed in yourself

- You feel that you could make more of the time you have

My friend Linda is the epitome of what it is to manage time well. We began our occupational therapy training together in the days when there were only 30 students in a year. For that first term, filled with good intentions, 29 of the group worked for 12 hours a day. But not Linda. While we all slogged away, she steadily worked from 9 to 5, taking weekends and evenings off to be with friends and care for her family. For the remaining term and beyond we all procrastinated, partied hard and pulled all-nighters while Linda would work from 9 to 5 with trips to the theatre, cinema and meals out with friends, good holidays and all the time supporting her husband and children. At the end of the course we were exhausted and grateful for our seconds and thirds, and she, modest as ever, with her glowing first.

I remember visiting her in practice five years or so after we had qualified. She was held in the highest esteem, known as one of the most efficient people there and valued by everyone. Colleagues marvelled at how she was the one person who always left work on time and always met deadlines. We laughed together and I told her that I admired her effortless organisation. On hearing this she appeared visibly shocked and told me that this was far from the case. Time management was something that she had always had to work at. The secret of her success was simple: she was clear about exactly what she needed to achieve and when she needed to achieve this by, and above all she knew how to embed work and study into her daily routines so that she used every precious moment to the full.

Being a student can sometimes feel like spinning plates. There are so many opportunities available: new and exciting skills to master, books to read, societies to join, social events to attend, friendships to make – a veritable Aladdin's cave. It is absolutely right that you want to gain the most from every moment you have. If you can master time, the rewards are great, leading to less stress and more success.

Yet the benefits of managing your time effectively are not confined to the classroom. Health and social care environments are increasingly pressurised places in which to work. As a practitioner, you will need to organise your case load, meet deadlines, undertake procedures within established routines, prioritise, respond to situations very quickly, re-order your day at a moment's notice, prepare reports – all within time constraints. Within this environment you will be required to record how you have used your time and will be held accountable for this.

Good time management is not about working every hour of the day. It is about understanding the task in hand, deciding what you hope to achieve, weighing up your priorities, recognising the conditions you need to work effectively and making the most of the time you have available. If you can develop such skills, you will work more effectively, feel more confident and increase your chances of success at university and on placement.

This chapter helps you to understand how you currently use your time and the conditions you need in order to work at your best. You will have the opportunity to explore a number of tools and techniques that you can use in the classroom and in practice so that you can be the master of time as opposed to letting time be the master of you.

STARTING POINTS

The first step to managing your time effectively is to understand how you currently use your time. Answer the following questions to uncover your present work and study patterns.

1 Read the following statements and tick which best applies to you:

Are you a lark?	**Are you an owl?**
I wake up full of ideas	I need to ease myself into the day
I feel at my best in the period leading up to lunch	My brain starts to work after lunch
I find it much easier to concentrate in the morning	I find it hard to concentrate first thing
I never stay in bed beyond 8 am	10 am is an early start for me
10 pm is a late night for me	I frequently work beyond 2 am
I feel sleepy on an evening	I feel alert on an evening

Count up your responses. Based on these, are you a lark or an owl?

2 What are your top five time wasters, i.e. those activities which take time out of your day?

Five:

Four:

Three:

Two:

Main time waster:

3 Are you time aware?

(Continued)

(Continued)

Time conscious	**In denial**
One of my most important possessions is my watch	I have never owned a watch
I use a diary/palmtop	I have a diary... somewhere
I have a wall planner above my desk	I have a poster above my desk
Other people rely on me to tell them where they need to be	I rely on other people to point me in the right direction
I love to mark things off my list when I have achieved them	I don't believe in lists. Being faced by everything I need to achieve makes me feel depressed
I am always on time or arrive early	I believe it is polite to arrive five minutes late
When travelling, I have time to buy and drink coffee before my train arrives	When travelling, I usually have to run for my train or catch the next one

Think about the factors that make up your ideal day (sleep, leisure, socialising, eating, working) and the proportion of time you would ideally spend doing these things. Divide the time up into the following areas: work activities, rest activities and play activities. Imagine that the first circle below is a 24-hour period. Shade in the proportion of time you would ideally spend on each of these types of activity, giving each one a different colour. As you review these activities reflect a moment and see if you can remember when you last did something you really enjoyed.

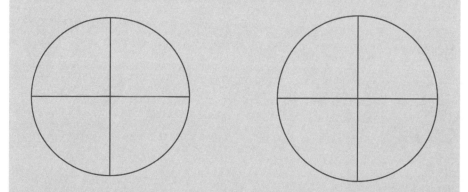

Now compare this with how you really spend your time. List all the things you do in a day and decide what proportion of your day you spend on these. It can help to group them together under the categories of work, rest and play. Shade the second circle in to represent these different categories.

Compare the two circles. What do you notice? How similar/different are they? Looking at these, do you feel that you need to achieve more of a balance between the two?

4   How to make the most of your time?

Imagine that you have the following pockets of time available. Thinking about your current work, in the first column record possible activities you could do in this time and in the second column record how you actually use the time.

Amount of time	How you might use your time	How you used your time
Ten minutes	Learn six facts for the test on Friday	Texted a friend
Fifteen minutes		
Thirty minutes		
One hour		

Summary of learning

- What do you notice about how you presently use your time?

- Can you identify areas where you could use time more productively?

- How balanced is your life at present?

- Are there any resources you could tap into that could help you manage your time more productively?

KEYS TO SUCCESS

Here are the keys to managing your time effectively:

- Be clear about what you need to achieve and the timeframes for completion
- Understand the demands of the task
- Prioritise tasks according to their importance
- Recognise the conditions you need to make the most of your time
- Understand other factors that impact on the process

Be clear about what you need to achieve and the timeframes for completion

The starting point of all time management strategies is to gain an overview of what you need to achieve and the timeframes for completion. This will help you to identify when and where you should concentrate your energies. A number of tools are available to help you do this.

For a bird's eye view

Year planners are perfect for mapping out the bigger picture. The process of recording key dates, such as hand-ins for assignments, examinations, placements as well as social events, outings and holidays, will help you to experience a sense of order and control and ensure that you avoid unnecessary clashes. The visual nature of the year planner enables you to identify key milestones at a glance and chart your progress as you move towards your ultimate goal.

For a closer look

For a more detailed portable record of your day-to-day tasks, an academic diary or a palmtop is a must. These provide the necessary space for you to map out lecture times, free periods, workshops and practicals on a weekly basis. You can make this into a working document recording details of room numbers, weekly objectives, lists of things to be completed, key telephone numbers and email addresses – a veritable survivor kit.

For a more sophisticated record

Sometimes stages of the task you hope to achieve will be dependent on other factors. This can make mapping out the timeframe for their completion more challenging as there may be a specific order in which they have to be completed. For example, you may be faced with a situation where you need to attend a particular lecture before you can start to plan your assignment or to meet as a group to plan your presentation before creating the PowerPoint slides. On these occasions you will need something more than an academic diary or palmtop. A more sophisticated tool is a Gantt chart, which essentially is a grid with a place for you to record the tasks down the far left-hand side and a timeline across the top where you can record when you will complete these tasks. Because the Gantt chart is visual, you can quickly see how different tasks are interrelated and this will enable you to decide the sequence in which they are undertaken. You can either make your own using the 'tables' function in a word-processing package or download one from the internet. An example is illustrated below.

April	1	2	3	4	5	6	7	8	9	10	11	12	13
Read text	▓	▓	▓										
Consolidate notes from lecture	▓	▓	▓	▓	▓								
Make notes from books				▓	▓	▓							
Plan						▓	▓	▓	▓				
First draft										▓	▓	▓	
Proof-read													▓

Understand the demands of the task

This ability to understand the demands of the task is one of the key factors to managing your time successfully. Indeed, students frequently fall behind time because they constantly underestimate the complexity of what they are trying to achieve. Let's take Sunita as an example. She is a second-year midwifery student. Her list of things 'to do' looks something like this:

- *Complete case study*
- *Lecture notes*
- *Plan for presentation*
- *Research for group meeting on Thursday*
- *Pick up present for Sue*
- *Reading on puerperal psychosis*

Transferring this list into an academic diary or palmtop will help her to see what she needs to achieve and the deadlines for this. However, this alone will not help her to manage her time effectively as from this list it would be difficult to understand:

(a) What is involved in each of the tasks

(b) The timeframe for each (roughly how long they will take)

(c) Her priorities. For example, by when do the case notes and the lecture notes need to be completed? Should these be done before or after the research for the group meeting on Thursday?

After making a list of the tasks, the next stage is to break these down into sub-components in order to understand what each entails. To maximise your chances of success, it can be helpful to write these as SMART targets. The more specific you are, the higher the chance of success. Based on your learning in the previous chapter you should feel quite comfortable in doing this. Here is a snapshot of Sunita's plan. Note how she lists in detail the steps she needs to meet her goal.

Goal (SMART): To read and make brief notes on the two articles on post-puerperal psychosis, as recommended by Dr Nicola West during the lecture on Friday.	When by: Thursday 25 January 2.00
Plan: Steps required (with estimated timings) 1 Book skills room 2 Collect articles from reception 3 Read: Hoffbrand S, Howard L, Crawley H, Antidepressant drug treatment for postnatal depression. Cochrane Database Syst Rev. 2001 (2) - 1 hour 4 Read: Howard LM, Hoffbrand S, Henshaw C, et al., Antidepressant prevention of postnatal depression. Cochrane Database Syst Rev. 2005 Apr 18 (2): CD004363. [abstract] - 1 hour Possible resources: Library and learning resource centre staff, Sue and Guy.	

Sunita struggles with time management and likes to plan in quite a lot of detail. She then transfers this information into her diary. This is useful because her ability to undertake the various tasks is very much dependent on other demands that are made on her time. Indeed, it is impossible to see any one task in isolation. It is necessary to put these into a much wider context, fitting these around timetabled activities, work outside university and your personal life. Here are the completed entries in Sunita's diary. Note how she capitalises activities that are fixed and not negotiable and underlines her priorities. She also uses a highlighter pen to prioritise tasks so that she can see at a glance where she needs to concentrate her efforts.

Monday: June 1	Thursday: June 4
9.00 SupaPuta IT store - **pick up cartridge** ✓ Tel. Learning centre to book study room ✓ **Print off articles** 10.00 LECTURE (print off notes) 12.00 Meet Pat to discuss Friday 2.00 Study room - don't forget to bring note book. **Notes on article one** (Hoffbrand and Howard) 3.00 Coffee with Sue 4.00 Meet Andrew at food store for weekly shop	* MUST WASH GIRLS' PE KIT 10.30 Plan seminar with Pat 12.30 SEMINAR with Dr West - present notes and feedback regarding reading Print off handouts for group on Friday Complete essay plan for assignment on 14th

Tuesday: June 2	Friday: June 5

9.00   MY TURN FOR THE SCHOOL RUN
10.30   WORKSHOP: F203 - bring
          resources
11.30   Learning centre
12.00   Salsa class with Angie
1.00   Use study room in learning
          centre - **read and make notes**
          on second article for Thursday
3.30   SAM AT SCOUTS
	9.00 <u>SEMINAR</u> (Pat and I
	          presenting)
	10.00 LECTURE
	2.00 Learning centre, look for
	          books on multiple sclerosis
	4.00 PICK UP CHILDREN FROM
	          AFTER-SCHOOL CLUB

Wednesday: June 3
 	
9.00   PLACEMENT PREPARATION
          SESSION
1.30-3.00   MANUAL HANDLING
               SESSION
3.00-3.30   **Read through notes for**
               tomorrow. Print off
               copies for group
5.00 MUM OVER FOR DINNER	

If you find that it is physically impossible to fit everything in, you will need to revisit your goals. Ask yourself, have I been realistic with my time? What could I give up? You will need to learn how to prioritise in order to work effectively.

Prioritise tasks according to their importance

Stephen Covey (2004) identified the ability to prioritise as one of the 'seven habits of highly effective people'. He devised a simple matrix to help you categorise tasks according to their importance and to help you decide which to complete first.

	Urgent	Non-urgent
Important	1. Urgent tasks with looming deadlines go in this quadrant. You will address these tasks first.	2. List tasks in this quadrant that are important but with a deadline that is slightly further away. Address these tasks next. This will help to lower anxiety so that you won't be faced with working under extreme pressure.
Not important	3. This quadrant is reserved for tasks that need to be dealt with but are not	4. Activities contained here are neither important nor pressing.

(Continued)

(Continued)

	Urgent	Non-urgent
	essential. For example, answering emails or letters. These tasks should be addressed after completing those that are important but non-urgent.	Again these are the things that it would be 'nice to do' but that are not time-limited: for example, rewriting your notes so that they look neater. Place these activities at the bottom of your priority list.

Use the matrix to help you decide where to direct your energies and decide the order in which you need to tackle things. Try experimenting with activities or projects you are undertaking at the moment. This is quite a skill but practice makes perfect.

Recognise the conditions you need to make the most of your time

The above steps offer a basic toolkit of skills to manage your time effectively. However, the very personal concept of time means that you need to place these in a far broader context and spend time understanding how your goals for study fit within a much bigger picture of who you are, your personal values, priorities, work patterns, and the factors that enable you to work at your best. The exercises in the introductory section of this chapter hopefully began this process of reflection and increased self-awareness. The remainder of this section helps you to recognise the bigger picture and explore further techniques that will help you to make the most of your time.

Identify where you work best

The image of the poor student in a freezing garret is far removed from the reality or ideal. However, the environment can have an enormous impact on how effectively you work. For a few moments, imagine that you have the opportunity to design your ideal work space. Begin by deciding ten criteria this space must meet. For example, does it need to be warm, cool, quiet? Should there be music? Do you need a view or a desk to work on? What kind of a chair (straight backed, comfy)? What about lighting (desk lamp or natural light)? Do you work best when your environment is uncluttered or do you need your work files within arms' length? Draw up a checklist placing these in order of importance.

Now look at the environment where you currently work and use the checklist to see how closely it matches your ideal criteria. If it falls short, are there other environments you could access or could you make changes to the environment? For example, if you spend a lot of time working in the learning centre but you find it hard to concentrate when there are lots of people around, could you aim to work at times when it is a little quieter?

As well as considering your optimum conditions for study you also need to identify 'time-wasters' (you should have named these in the introductory exercise) – for example, television, telephone or email. Once you have decided what these are, make sure that you remove them or minimise their impact.

Recognise your creative time and your down time

Recognise when you work most effectively and divide tasks accordingly. For example, if you are a morning person, make sure that you use this time to complete more complex assignments. You can then use the remainder of the day or 'down time' for tasks that require less concentration. You may find that there are significant gaps on your timetable between lectures. Plan ahead and decide how you can best use this time. For instance, even short pockets of time between lectures can be used productively to review notes, make lists, learn key facts or locate references for books.

Discover activities that are restorative

Not all that we do is physically or psychologically costly. Indeed, many activities can be extremely restorative. These are easy to identify: when you take part in them you find that you are completely focused and absorbed, to the degree that you can temporarily put any work concerns or worries to one side. On completion, you feel relaxed, refreshed and raring to tackle the next challenge. Restorative activities are individual to you but may include some of the following: cycling, running, walking, having a soak in the bath, telephoning a friend, cooking, reading, singing and dancing.

When you have made your list, make a note of how long you ideally need for the activity and write this into your timetable. It is essential that you consciously schedule these times, otherwise you will find yourself unable to completely engage in the activity and the restorative component will be replaced by feelings of guilt which will undo any of the potential benefits.

Multi-tasking

To make the very most of your time you need to learn the art of multi-tasking so that every second counts. Multi-tasking or activity-combining works on the premise that during the day there are certain activities or routines you will inevitably need to engage in: travel, shopping for food, cooking, cleaning, phone calls. In order to optimise your time, seek ways to embed other activities into these routines. For example, is it possible to use time travelling to university to read a journal article or could you combine eating a meal with catching up with friends and family.

Tap into your support mechanisms: delegate and communicate

Enlist the support of family and friends. They can contribute in all kinds of ways helping out with tasks around the house – washing, tidying and shopping – so that you can devote your time to study. Make links with other students and form informal support networks, perhaps teaming up with like-minded people who can act as 'study buddies'. There is more about this in Chapter 8 on accessing support.

Learn how to compromise

There will be times where you need to make sacrifices in the short term in order to meet your long-term ambitions. These may involve a slight adjustment of standards or a decision to participate in a particular activity less frequently. A few examples are provided in the table below. The key is to hold on to the bigger picture and to see these as only a temporary measure.

I gain satisfaction from...	For the duration of my course I am willing to...
Socialising with friends three evenings a week	Socialise with my friends one evening a week
Having an immaculate house	Have a tidy house
Keeping fit by going to the gym every day	Keep fit by walking up to university and swimming once a week

Sometimes things will happen that are beyond your control. As a result, you may be unable to complete a piece of work. You will not be the first person this has happened to, nor the last, and universities have strategies and procedures to help at these times. Extenuating circumstances forms and extensions exist for this very reason, but you need to plan ahead and keep your tutors informed so they are aware of the situation and can support you.

Understand other factors that impact on the process

Identify procrastination

It is human nature to put off things that we find difficult or boring. There will always be pleasurable activities that we would rather engage in, particularly when deadlines are looming. The first stage of overcoming procrastination is to identify when you are putting things off. Poker players often have unconscious habits called 'tells' that other players know to look out for as a sign that they are bluffing. What is your procrastination 'tell'?

Here are examples of other 'tells' you might be familiar with:

- Tidy house, tidy desk, tidy car, tidy garage, tins of food/packets/books/CDs arranged in alphabetical order
- Polished floors
- Clean children, clean pets
- Empty coffee cups
- Empty packets of biscuits

Tell-tale thoughts include:

- If I eat this/do this/complete this... I will be able to work better
- I cannot work unless...
- Today is a write-off. I will make up for this tomorrow...
- I will be able to write these notes/this assignment at home
- This will be the perfect essay
- For an activity to be meaningful, I must be able to work for at least an hour on this...

Procrastination can be a reflection of how interesting you find a task in comparison with all the other things you like to do. However, it can also be a symptom of a deeper problem. Use the table overleaf to see if you can identify why you procrastinate and find possible ways to overcome this.

Skills in practice

Your experiences at university should prepare you well for managing time in practice. The remainder of this chapter provides you with the opportunity to see how these techniques may be applied to placement. You will have the opportunity to look at some of the subtle differences and consider possible strategies to help you overcome these.

Problem	Symptom	Solution
Fear of failure	Feeling low, feelings of being unable to cope	• Recording successes
Feeling overwhelmed	Not knowing where to start, jumping from one task to another	• Working for a fixed amount of time on a piece of work • Breaking down time into manageable chunks • Deciding tasks you can achieve in 5 minutes, 10 minutes, 30 minutes, 1 hour • Making lists
Boredom	Avoiding sitting down to do something, using mobile phone, going on to Facebook	• Varying the task • Making tasks appealing • Building in rewards • Establishing rituals for working
Perfectionism	Over-preparation, fear of committing pen to paper on an assignment	• Overcoming the blank page • Challenging negative thoughts with phrases such as 'I am here to learn'

Be clear about what you need to achieve and the timeframes for completion

Let's begin with the example of Peter. He is on his first placement which is a busy in-patient ward on the acute mental health unit. He meets with his placement educator. The conversation runs something like this

Right Peter, a few things to do this week. Mrs J's coming in today to begin an informal admission. I'd like you to be responsible for the initial assessment here please. I'd like to bring Mr X's family in on Wednesday for a meeting. Can you arrange this? There's the report for the MDT about Mr X for Tuesday – how are you coming on with that? It would be good if you could present this – the meeting is between 2–5 on Tuesday. We're a bit short-staffed during the latter half of the week. I've put it to the team that you will be around to help with the lunches from Wednesday to Friday. I hope that's OK. Things are moving on full steam ahead with the community-based anxiety management group. Colette is coming over on Friday morning. I would like it if you could arrange to meet with her and sort out some of the details. In the afternoon on Friday there is the case conference for Mr M. That's 4–5. It's the only time the consultant could make. Friday might be a bit tight because your university tutor is coming over then. I suggested that you met with her at 12.00 and then I will join you at one. How is your assignment coming along for that? Did you manage to fix up a visit with the psychologist yet? I thought this week might be a possibility given that it's not too busy.

The first thing that Peter has to do is to be clear about what he needs to achieve and the timeframes for completion. As Peter has been listening to his educator he has been making a list of things to do and dates to do these by. He does not enter these straight into his diary in case they become amalgamated with everything else he has in there, but he does bring his diary along so he can refer to other things he is involved with during that week and spot any problems and clashes quite quickly.

Task	Timing
Mrs J admission – initial assessment	Monday (today) 10.00–11.00
Write report for Mr X Present report for Mr X	Tuesday 2–5
Mr X's family for meeting Do I need to be there? Lunches	Wednesday am 12–1
Lunches	Thursday 12–1
Meet with Colette am Case conference Mr M University tutor Lunches	Friday am Friday 4–5 12–2 12–1
Additional	
Visit with psychologist	

Even before the conversation has ended, he can see a clash with Friday and can check this out immediately. He also seeks clarification as to whether he needs to physically be at the meeting on Wednesday for Mr X, as he has previously arranged a visit to a local resource centre at that time.

Understand the demands of task

Just as before, the next step is to undertake a task analysis so that he can identify what exactly is required. Peter has been on the placement for some time so he can also break down the tasks into smaller parts and anticipate what he may need to do next.

Goal	Sub-components	Estimated time to complete	Priority level
To admit Mrs J	Prepare paperwork Ask Sue to inform me when she arrives See Mrs J Write up paperwork	3 hours	
Write report for Mr X	Gain overview of admission from notes Plan report Write report Ask educator to read this	3 hours	
Present report for Mr X	Check where room is, obtain copies of report Present at the meeting Follow-up notes and record recommendations	20 minutes 3 hours	
Contact Mr X's family for meeting	Speak to ward to sort out where meeting should take place and who needs to be involved Find telephone number in notes Contact family Let ward know the details	1 hour	
Meeting with Colette	Telephone Colette to clarify whether I need to do anything for Friday Read previous notes of meetings about the project	1 hour	
University tutor	Arrange a room for the meeting Complete self-assessment form	1 hour	
Lunches	Speak with staff involved as to role in this	1 hour for lunches	
Visit psychologist	Identify time slot to do this, telephone and arrange Book in visit	30 minutes to arrange	

Peter then quickly transfers this information into his diary so that he can see at a glance how this fits into the rest of his week and book further appointments around this.

Prioritise tasks according to their importance

You may have noticed that Peter included an additional column indicating level of priority. In a busy health and social care environment, the ability to prioritise tasks is a key skill. With so many conflicting demands and pressures on your time, prioritisation is not easy. Individual hospitals and care environments will all have their own systems to support you in the process. For example, in some settings, notes have different coloured stickers to indicate levels of urgency. In some roles you will need to make split-second decisions. For paramedics and emergency nursing this may be particularly true. However, across all professions you will need to adopt a flexible attitude. Things can change at a moment's notice and you must be prepared to weigh up new demands that are made on you, make a decision as to their importance and re-prioritise. Nonetheless, the principles suggested by Covey (2004) are still the same regarding this process.

	Due soon	Not due soon
Important		
Not important		

Using the above grid, give each of Peter's tasks a priority rating. If you would like to find out how he prioritised these tasks, look on the website that accompanies this book where he also offers a short rationale explaining how he made these decisions (see www.skills4health.co.uk)

Breaking down tasks into smaller pieces and placing these in order of priority will help you to set clear, identifiable and manageable goals and enable you to see when things need to be completed. Some students find it helpful to use this as the basis of a 'to do' list, which they complete on a daily basis. The advantage of having a list is that they can quickly see what needs to be accomplished and tick things off as they do this, which immediately gives a sense of achievement.

Where tasks are pretty much on a level in terms of the order in which they need to be completed, you may wish to think about your own learning style. Here students share their experiences and offer ways to approach this:

I start with the easiest task first. This helps me to get started and once I can see that I have achieved this my motivation levels increase and I feel that I can approach other things on my list.

I start with things that I can achieve quite quickly, then I do things that I enjoy and finally approach things that are more challenging.

I like to get the most boring or difficult task out of the way first. Even though this can be really hard, once I have done this I know that everything else is easy.

Recognise the conditions you need to make the most of your time

All you need to do now is to translate the skills developed at university on to placement. This includes thinking about what you know about where and how you work best so that you play to your strengths in this new environment. Going back to the example of Peter, he recognised that to work effectively he needed to find a quiet space at the end of the day to record his reflections and create an action plan of things he wanted to achieve during the following day. By the time he returned home he was just too tired to do this, so he chose to go to the library for half an hour at the end of each day where he had the momentum to feel that he was still at work but without all the distractions of a busy and noisy ward. Students I have worked with have recognised when they work most effectively and where possible have tried to schedule complex home visits or report writing at these times. Other students have sought out opportunities for leisure activities to gain some form of balance and relaxation or have taken the decision to focus on work for university on specific days.

Understand other factors that impact on the process

The real challenge on placement is recognising the bigger picture. Getting to grips with time management at university will help you to recognise and understand how to make the best use of your time and will provide you with a good foundation on which to build. However, one of the first things that will strike you on placement will be the vast number of factors that eat into your time and the various fixed routines that you will need to work around. This is particularly the case if you are working on a ward or in an in-patient setting where you will need to navigate around:

- Hand-over
- Medication
- Set meal times
- Bathing and dressing routines
- MDT meetings

Working in a very acute setting or in a community setting will carry its own set of challenges, particularly if you are in a role where you are unsure as to what any day may bring.

The secret here is to get to grips with the culture and complexities of the setting. Spend time recognising and gaining a feel for the different routines of this new environment. Even if you are a paramedic or working in emergency medicine where you are unaware of what you are doing on a moment-to-moment basis, you will still be able to gain a sense of the rhythm of the day. Within in-patient environments, spot the un-movables (breakfast, lunch, dinner, baths, drugs trolley and hairdresser) and find ways of working with these.

Here students share some of the challenges they have faced and the coping mechanisms they have employed.

The environment

The first thing that struck me was the noise level and constant ringing of the telephone. It was so difficult to concentrate and a million miles removed from the library at college. What a nightmare! The idea of writing up notes or compiling reports was impossible. The only way that I could overcome this was to arrive early. We had a system of flexi-time and I found that just arriving one hour earlier meant that I could complete all the paperwork I needed to. I guess in this way I was finding where the 'dead time' was and understanding when I worked best. After this placement I am going to start to practise writing notes and reports in the classroom. It's something I need to master. (Chloe, year two learning disabilities)

Shift patterns

Shift patterns have been a killer and a real shock to the system. Your body clock goes haywire and in the beginning I felt physically ill. It was awful. The hardest thing is having to work with very different routines at different times. I've found that difficult, although it is getting easier. A few things have helped. For example, one colleague told me to have breakfast at breakfast time even if it was the end of the shift. Someone else told me to keep a regular routine on days off so that it is less of a shock to the system. (Peter, general nursing)

Distractions within distractions

The main difficulty I've faced has been the distractions within distractions. I've learned how to spot my danger points. For example, I know that if I don't write up my notes immediately, they just don't happen. So I make myself physically stay there until they are completed. (David, year one physiotherapy)

Managing competing demands

I've had to master the art of living in the present with one eye on the future. Let me explain. When I started, I was swamped with demands on my time. Sometimes people would ask 'would you undertake an assessment next week?' and in health terms, next week seems a million miles away. But of course by that time I had lots more other things to do too! Now I try to keep an awareness of things that are coming up in the future in the back of my mind and always answer with this in mind. I've also had to learn how to say no. This was really difficult at first but I ended up being completely swamped. My secret weapon is my diary. When someone asks me to do anything I refer to this and say something along the lines of 'I'm really sorry, but this week is incredibly busy...' etc., etc. Somehow this makes it less personal. It's my secret tool of negotiation. (Chantel, year three social work)

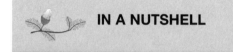

IN A NUTSHELL

Learning how to use your time effectively is one of the key self-management skills required by all health and social care practitioners. This chapter has considered:

- Ways to understand your current work patterns and the demands placed on your time

- How you can manage your expectations

- A range of techniques you can use to help you plan your day

- How to experiment with a range of tools to help you to manage your time

- The importance of learning how to know and understand the flow and the routines of the place where you work

The secret now is to find your own rhythm and a way of organising your time in such a way that works for you.

References and signposts to further reading and resources

Boniwell, I. (2005) 'Beyond time management: how the latest research on time perspectives and perceived time use can assist clients with time related concerns,' *International Journal of Evidence-based Coaching and Mentoring*, 3 (2): 61–74.

Clegg, B. (1999) *Instant Time Management*. London: Kogan Page.

Covey, S. (2004) *The Seven Habits of Highly Effective People*. London: Simon & Schuster.

Dement, W. and Vaughan, C. (1999) *The Promise of Sleep: The Scientific Connection between Health, Happiness and a Good Night's Sleep*. New York: Macmillan.

Honore, C. (2004) *In Praise of Slow: How a Worldwide Movement is Challenging the Cult of Speed*. London: Orion.

7 Managing anxiety

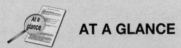 **AT A GLANCE**

You will find this chapter useful if

- Anxious thoughts and feelings affect your work

- You frequently find yourself stuck in a vicious cycle of worry and anxiety

- Worrying about work affects your sleep pattern

- Tutors and friends have suggested that you worry unnecessarily

Studying at university can be one of the most exciting times of your life: new friends, new experiences and new challenges. However, such opportunities will also present their own pressures and demands which can result in feelings of anxiety. Sometimes these will relate to specific events with regard to your course, such as exams, assignment hand-in dates and oral presentations. At other times, such feelings may arise as a result of difficult or challenging situations on placement, for example, coping with the death of a client or undertaking a complex procedure. Further sources of stress may include issues beyond university: financial worries, relationships or balancing work with other commitments.

Anxiety is a normal reaction to these situations. Problems arise when the level of anxiety is out of proportion to the actual threat posed or when these feelings continue long after the event has passed, affecting your performance and impacting on your health. The first part of this chapter looks at ways to manage your anxiety, focusing on how to recognise your response to stress and identify the triggers so that you can take positive steps to address the cause and manage these feelings. This range of simple strategies offers a 'toolbox' of skills that you can use in the classroom, on placement and beyond. The final part of the chapter focuses on a worked case study to illustrate how to apply these skills on placement.

Stress in context: the science behind the feelings

It is easy to think of stress in purely negative terms and as something that should be avoided at all costs. However, while the stress response may feel unpleasant, it is in fact a self-preservation mechanism, preparing your body for action in the face of a perceived danger. While exams and assessments are not life-threatening, we may perceive them as anxiety-provoking. Technically, this is not a problem, as in the height-ened state of arousal you are in the best position mentally and physically to respond to the challenge and perform at your optimum. However, if the level of anxiety is too great, the immediate effect is that your ability to concentrate is impaired and it is highly likely that you will have difficulties in remembering and recalling information. This can impact negatively on performance, particularly if you are taking an exam. The implications for clinical practice are more serious as many procedures you will perform will demand your full attention. Failure to recall information or to focus can compromise your ability to do this safely and may impact on the level of care you can offer.

At its most severe, anxiety experienced over a prolonged period of time can lead to a phenomenon known as 'burnout', where the body, which has been in a constant state of physical preparedness, is literally exhausted. The term describes a range of physical and psychological symptoms that impact on health and well-being and requires professional help.

It is therefore essential to develop and master effective skills to manage anxiety. The good news is that, as you will discover from reading this chapter, there are a vast number of tried-and-tested approaches and techniques that enable you to do this.

STARTING POINTS

Use the following quiz to help you recognise your response to stress. Tick the boxes below of the symptoms you have experienced in stressful situations.

Body (physical symptoms)

I experience a tight band around my chest

I feel my heart pounding and have palpitations

I am prone to bad headaches

I notice that my breathing becomes shallow and fast

I have pain in my neck and shoulders

I develop eczema or other skin conditions

I often have indigestion or an upset stomach

I have difficulty in sleeping

Head symptoms (cognitive)

Forgetfulness

Mind going blank

Negative thoughts

Loss of concentration

Poor judgement

Inability to make decisions

Inability to think or focus

Heart symptoms (emotional)

Feeling anxious

Feeling angry or irritable

(Continued)

(Continued)

Feeling low in mood/depressed	
Feeling helpless	
Low self-esteem	
Mood swings	
Tearfulness	
Loss of confidence	
Feeling a failure	
Feelings of panic	

Wine, chocolates (behavioural)	
Avoid situations	
Lose interest in sex	
Lock myself away from family and friends	
Pace up and down	
Become clumsy	
Eat more	
Drink more	
Smoke more	

Now count up your responses.

If you ticked responses in the 'body' section, you respond to stress in a very physical way. This is probably very frustrating at times as it can *prevent* you from working and lead to a negative cycle where being unable to work makes you feel more anxious, and so on. If you experience stress over a long period of time you will be prone to a number of physical complaints, including high blood pressure and ulcers. When exploring strategies to help you cope with anxiety, you may find techniques focusing on muscle relaxation and breathing particularly helpful.

If you ticked mainly heads, negative thoughts can make it difficult to concentrate and result in feelings of helplessness and hopelessness. You may find that when facing a difficult situation that your mind goes blank. This can be problematic when undertaking examinations. When it comes to developing anxiety management strategies, you may find techniques focusing on visualisation or reshaping your thinking particularly useful.

If you ticked mainly hearts, the quiz suggests that you have a strong emotional reaction to stress. This can lead to feelings of low confidence and low self-esteem which can make you feel more anxious and helpless. Again, strategies that focus on reshaping your thinking and ways to express these feelings can be advantageous.

If you ticked statements in the wine and chocolate section, you tend to have a very behavioural response to stress. These responses can be automatic and occur before, during and after the event. This is not unusual and most people will be able to identify times when they have reached for a glass of wine at the end of a hard day. These coping mechanisms may work in the short term. However, the problem arises if you find yourself depending on these to alleviate or blot out feelings.

KEYS TO SUCCESS

The key to successfully managing your anxiety lies in your ability to:

- Recognise your response to stress
- Identify your personal triggers
- Use a range of tools and techniques to manage your anxiety

Recognise your response to stress

The exercise you have just completed is useful as a starting point when beginning to understand your stress response. Stress has a habit of creeping up on you when you least expect it. By the time you have identified that you are feeling anxious you can be engaged in an unhelpful coping mechanism or in the middle of a full-blown panic attack. For example, how often have you been munching your way through a slab of chocolate or smoking a cigarette or eating your way down a packet of biscuits before you have made the connection that you are in fact feeling worried? The thoughts that precede these feelings can happen so quickly that they are difficult to identify. Yet the sooner you can recognise that you are feeling anxious the better, as you can then take steps to address these emotions before they escalate out of control.

Identify your personal triggers

The next stage to managing your anxiety is to identify situations you find stressful. Stress is a highly individualised response to a perceived threat which means that a situation which to one person is anxiety-provoking to another is an exciting challenge. Use the following exercise to identify your anxiety triggers.

Imagine that your top three stressful situations at university lurk behind a door. Take a few moments to sketch out what these situations look like, finding an image or a metaphor to represent them. For example, money concerns can be portrayed by a pound sign. Give the situation a stress rating and in the final column below unpick what you actually fear. For example, is it embarrassment, feelings of being out of control, physical pain, emotional pain or something else?

Situation	Level of stress (on a scale of 1 (low)–5 (high))	Your fears
1.		
2.		
3.		

Use a range of tools and techniques to manage your anxiety

Once you have identified your stress response and the situations that may trigger this, the final step is to look at possible tools and techniques to help you break the cycle of anxiety. Broadly, these fall into two areas.

1 Techniques to enable you to relieve the physical and psychological symptoms of stress.

2 Strategies to help you change your response to the situation.

Top tips to manage anxiety

The next time you are feeling anxious try these simple anxiety management techniques. Those at the beginning of the list focus on ways to help you relieve the physical and psychological symptoms of stress either during or after the situation. The ones described in the latter part are techniques to help you change your response to the situation.

Breathe

Anxiety results in an increased breathing rate and an imbalance between oxygen and carbon dioxide in the blood. This in turn can lead to hyperventilation. To counter-act this, breathe more deeply from the diaphragm (the muscle underneath the ribcage). Breathe in through your nose and out through your mouth. This helps to slow your breathing down. There are many techniques you can use. However, the following is one of the easiest.

> Breathe in deeply for four counts, hold for one second and then breathe out deeply for five, lowering your shoulders as you do.

Progressive relaxation

This relaxation technique works on the principle of tensing and relaxing different muscle groups. This is a shortened form of Jacobsen's progressive relaxation and focuses on the upper body only. You should not use this if you have a musculoskeletal condition such as arthritis or any back or shoulder problems. Another method of relax-ation is found on the website (www.skills4health.co.uk).

Sit in a chair and make yourself comfortable. Focus on your breathing. Breathe deeply and slowly. Breathe in deeply for four counts. Hold for one second and then breathe out deeply for five lowering your shoulders as you do.

Now focus on your hands. Make a tight fist. Hold for 10 seconds. Then relax. Repeat. Then move your focus to your shoulders. Are you aware of any tension here? Gently pull them back. Hold for 10 seconds. Relax. Now push your shoulders forward. Again stop. Hold for ten seconds then relax.

Close your eyes. Breathe in deeply through your nose, feeling your tummy rise. Hold for four. Then release. Now breathe normally for 15 seconds.

Focus on your stomach. Pull this in as far as possible. Tense. Then relax. Now push your tummy out as far as you can. Hold. Relax.

Sit for a moment. Enjoy the feeling.

Visualisation

If you see stress as a series of horrible, unknown feelings, then it can become larger and more amorphous than it really is – something to be feared in itself. One way of managing these feelings is to make it visible. Try this simple visualisation.

What does your stress look like? What colour is this? What does it smell like? What does it taste like? How does it feel: slimy? Icy to touch? Hot and sticky? Try drawing this.

Now find an image to counteract this. For example, if you see anxiety as a gloomy dark cloud descending over you, then imagine that you have a bottle of sunshine or a machine that creates bright light to counteract it. When you start to feel anxious, just visualise yourself using this secret antidote to banish it away.

Meditation

Many people find meditation extremely helpful. A number of techniques exist. One of the simplest is to think of a place which you associate with positive memories. Picture it in your mind and as you do, imagine each detail – the colours, sounds and scents. Let the image fill your mind. Close your eyes and as you do focus completely on this place, breathing slowly and rhythmically. If you find meditation helpful, why not explore the possibility of attending a yoga class or taking up T'ai Chi?

Find a way to express yourself

It is possible to liken the experience of being stressed to a pressure cooker. Unless you release some of the steam the cooker will explode. Find an outlet for your emotional tension. Cry, shout, run, paint, write about your experiences, sing. Above all, find a way to express yourself so that these feelings are no longer trapped inside.

Access your support mechanisms

Friends and family can all provide support and act as a buffer to minimise the effects of stress. Talking about the situation can create an outlet for some of the feelings you have been bottling up as well as offering a different perspective on events. Sharing your fears with someone you trust can help to break down the isolation you experience and you may even learn some of the techniques others have used in managing or overcoming similar pressured situations.

Reshape your thinking

If your thinking goes something along these lines: I can't do it, I'm a failure, I am hopeless, there isn't any point. Is there any wonder that you feel dreadful? Cognitive behavioural psychology looks at the relationship between thoughts, feelings and behaviour. It suggests that we can develop unhelpful thinking patterns which can cause anxiety. For example, over-exaggeration of the consequences of an event (catastrophising) or setting ourselves impossible targets we are unable to meet (over-perfectionism). Many excellent resources exist that describe ways to challenge and reverse these patterns, replacing negative, automatic thoughts with more realistic alternatives.

Rehearse

Sometimes you may know in advance that you have to face a particular situation and it can be useful to visualise exactly what you will say. Even better, enlist the support of a friend to role-play the situation with you. This way, you can gain a sense of the types of things you may need to say and plan ahead so that you feel more confident and prepared.

Change the situation... take action... problem solve

Many of the experiences we perceive as being stressful are situations where we feel out of control. One way of lessening the stressful component is to take positive action and to take steps to change the situation. For example, you may find it difficult to assert yourself in a group. Recognising this, you decide to speak to other group members or look at ways of contributing to the decisions made. There are various ways to use skills in problem solving to affect positive change. Chapter 15 provides some additional ideas.

Find other interests outside your course

Do not invest all your time and energy in your course. Try to build in some work/life balance. Find something that you really enjoy doing that is not work-related. For example, you can become a volunteer or join a theatre group or take up a sport. Spending time away from the situation causing anxiety can offer you a different perspective on things and ensures that if things do not go to plan it does not take on mammoth proportions.

After the event

Turn your experiences into learning opportunities. It would be unrealistic to think that you will never make a mistake, forget something or upset someone. The secret is to transform these into learning opportunities. Chapter 9 on reflective practice offers a number of suggestions in terms of how you might do this.

Know when to seek help

If you feel that stress is having a negative impact on your health and is making you ill, then seek outside help. Many universities have their own confidential, onsite counselling service where you can talk through your experiences with qualified professionals. If you do not have access to such a resource, then your GP will be able to help. The next section on accessing support will help you to recognise the range of support you can tap into.

Skills in practice

Figures released by the Health and Safety Executive showed that in 2007/8 442,000 people in the UK experienced some form of work-related stress at a level that was making them ill (Health and Safety Executive, 2008). People working in health and social care are particularly at risk as a result of the increasing pressure on resources and the challenges of working with individuals and families with highly complex needs. The stress management techniques outlined in this chapter can be transferred directly into practice, enabling you to cope more effectively with some of these pressures as they arise. You may also find some of these techniques helpful when developing anxiety management clients and carers. The remainder of this chapter focuses on a detailed case study to illustrate how to apply these skills on placement.

Recognise your responses to stress

Nigel is in the second year of his social work degree at university. He gained very high marks during his first year and his aim now is to achieve a first-class degree. He enjoyed his first placement, although his organisational skills let him down and he struggled to manage his high levels of anxiety which impinged on his overall performance. His educator suggested that he should look at possible stress management techniques prior to his next placement.

Identify your personal triggers

Three weeks before he is due to start, Nigel is informed that his next placement will be in older people's services. The first step he takes is to list the situations he is concerned about in terms of the placement. This is based, in part, on his previous experiences and also in relation to this new specialism. For each situation he seeks to understand the source of the anxiety and awards an anxiety rating to help him to prioritise and channel his energies.

Situation	Fear factor	Anxiety rating
Meeting my educator	What happens if they don't like me? I could fail my placement and this would impact on my ultimate dream of gaining a first. This leads to me feeling out of control.	Very high
Unable to manage workload	People will think that I am incompetent or lazy. I feel embarrassed to admit that I cannot do this. This let me down in the past. What happens if it lets me down again?	High
Working with a challenging carer	On my last placement I felt very defensive. Fear of not knowing how to respond or what to say, what I'm allowed to say. In these situations my mind goes blank. How will I cope in this setting, where I know I will be working with a number of carers?	Medium

Even at this point Nigel can take some steps to address the issues identified. For example, he discusses possible time management strategies with his tutor, buys a diary and a wall planner, and reads the chapter in this book. He also decides to include this as one of his learning objectives for the placement as he is fully aware that this is an area he must address to be an effective practitioner.

Nigel has also spent time *identifying his response to stress*. From the questionnaire we discussed at the beginning of the chapter, he has recognised that he experiences a number of 'head symptoms'. He is frequently plagued by negative thoughts, to the extent where his mind goes blank. When reading the results of the questionnaire he notes that strategies focusing on addressing unhelpful thinking patterns and reframing situations can be useful. He uses the ideas outlined in this chapter, looking at *tools and techniques to manage anxiety* and puts together a short action plan.

Progress: three weeks into the placement

The placement began well. The work Nigel put in to brushing up on his time management skills prior to placement paid off and although he is busy, he is coping and his educator has already suggested that he is making good progress towards meeting his learning objectives in relation to this area. He also found the reshaping of his thinking and breathing techniques helpful in terms of the first day. Spending time understanding his concerns and rationalising his fears with simple cognitive techniques meant that when he met his educator for the first time he felt relaxed and confident. This was a far cry from his first placement where he was so nervous he felt ill and stammered over his words.

He regularly keeps his anxiety management plan up to date as the occasional difficult situation arises. For instance, the dynamics of the team means that meetings are fraught and can be a source of conflict. Whereas at one time he would have tried to think of a way to avoid these meetings, to the point where the fear associated with attending the session would have escalated out of all proportion, he now looks forward to exploring techniques to manage these feelings.

Use a range of tools and techniques to manage your anxiety

However, four weeks into the placement something unexpected happens. A client Nigel has been working with very closely dies. Nigel is the last person to have seen him alive and he cannot get the thought out of his head that he 'missed something' and is to blame in some way. These feelings stay with him, leading him to experience extreme anxiety. His educator is very preoccupied with supporting the person's family and Nigel feels that he 'shouldn't bother' her. The death of this person affects him profoundly. While on the surface he is going through the motions, underneath he is struggling, as the following extract from his diary (written three weeks after the event) reveals.

I feel such a failure in this place. I really don't know whether I am cut out for this role. I keep replaying that last meeting with Ernie through my head. The most difficult part is not sleeping, which means I am exhausted all the time. The only way I can blot things out and get some sleep on a night is to drink excessively. The mornings at work are particularly bad. I feel physically sick, irritable and annoyed. I just feel so unmotivated. What's the point anyway? I seem to be existing on junk food and I'm losing weight. My blood sugar must be all over the place since I am finding it hard to concentrate. I feel incredibly anxious all the time and keep double-checking what I am doing, just in case I have missed something. My girlfriend keeps asking me what is the matter but I fear that if I tell her she will realise what a bad person I am and want to leave me. I'm just not sure what to do.

Highlight the areas of concern and imagine that you are Nigel's placement educator. Based on your reading of this chapter, what strategies could Nigel put into place to cope with these feelings? How might he have approached this differently?

Conclusion

Happily, Nigel does confide in his girlfriend, who is in the final year of her nursing diploma. The situation reminds her of how she felt following the death of her first client and she offers him support. Together they revisit his action plan. At present there are two situations that cause him particular anxiety:

- Undertaking assessments on his own

- Presenting the findings of the home visit to case conferences

When Nigel unpicks these, he finds that the main concerns all relate to issues about responsibility and to the fear that he has missed something. Revisiting the broad anxiety management techniques, he knows that he can:

(a) Change his response to the situation.

(b) Relieve the physical and psychological symptoms of stress during or following the situation.

In this instance it seems reasonable for him to do both. Using the technique of problem solving (see Chapter 14), he decides that he will:

- Request additional support during the next assessment he undertakes in order to build confidence (changing his response to the situation)

- Speak to his placement educator during supervision about the death of the client (relieving the psychological symptoms of stress following the situation)

- Use simple breathing techniques to control his anxiety levels once in the case conference (relieving the physical symptoms of stress in this situation)

This short case study illustrates the value of recognising and taking steps to manage anxiety. Hopefully it has highlighted that anxiety management is an ongoing process requiring you to constantly revisit and adjust your response to situations, drawing on a range of different techniques. Nigel's response to the death of a client is a profound reaction but is not uncommon. When you work in any field of health and social care practice you will encounter situations that are very difficult and outside your normal experience. This is why the development of strategies to manage your anxiety is so important. Hold on to this example as you begin to read the next chapter, which looks at how to access support.

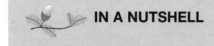 **IN A NUTSHELL**

The chapter has considered some of the situations you may find anxiety-provoking during your time at university and beyond. It has explored some of the underlying biological reasons which explain why you experience the symptoms of stress and has suggested a number of tools, rules and techniques which can help you to take control of your anxiety. In reading this chapter you should now:

- Understand the stress response

- Identify the things that make you feel stressed in the university environment and on placement

- Recognise when you are experiencing the symptoms of stress

- Understand your personal response to these stressful situations

- Be able to use a series of simple anxiety management techniques

- Have a toolbox of resources to use during your course and in your career as a practitioner both for yourself and with your clients

 References and signposts to further reading and resources

Burns, D. (2000) *The Feeling Good Handbook.* New York: Plume.
Craig, C. and Mountain, G.A. (2007) *Lifestyle Matters: An Occupational Approach to Healthy Ageing.* Milton Keynes: Speechmark.

(Continued)

(Continued)

Davis, M., McKay, M. and Eshelman, E.R. (2000) *The Relaxation and Stress Reduction Workbook*. Oakland, CA: New Harbinger Publications.

Goleman, D.P. (1995) *Emotional Intelligence: Why It Can Matter More than IQ for Character, Health and Lifelong Achievement*. New York: Bantam Books.

Health and Safety Executive (2008) *Statistics: Stress-related and Psychological Disorders*. Available at: www.hse.gov.uk/statistics/causdis/stress/ (last accessed 01/01/09).

Kelman, E.G. and Straker, K.C. (2000) *Study Without Stress*. London: Sage.

Loftus, L. (1998) 'Student nurses' lived experience of the sudden death of their patients', *Journal of Advanced Nursing*, 27: 641–8.

Wilkinson, G. (1997) *Understanding Stress*. London: British Medical Association.

8 Accessing support

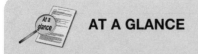

AT A GLANCE

This chapter is for you if

- You believe that seeking help is a sign of weakness

- You think that supervision is a song contest that takes place in Europe

- You know what you need but you struggle to ask for this

- You are unsure of the name of your personal tutor

One of the great things about being a health and social care professional is that you are very much part of a wider team. Collectively, you form a remarkable resource, sharing skills and drawing on each other for support when required. This support will take a number of forms. It may, for example, be about developing a skill or sharing up-to-date knowledge, such as the evidence base for a particular treatment or intervention. Support can also be more personal in nature, for example, when coping with a difficult situation, or managing feelings following an incident at work or in the community. The foundations of this process begin at university.

Within university, many students find that informal support networks with friends are sufficient to get them through their studies and beyond. However, other students require more help to brush up on their skills or cope with unexpected problems as they arise. On placement, this support is more structured and you will be required to meet regularly with your placement educator, but it is up to you to take responsibility and seek out further opportunities for personal and professional development within each setting.

This chapter looks at the range of support mechanisms available and considers how to gain the most from these. It offers advice in terms of how to recognise when you need help and barriers you may face when accessing this. Above all, it demonstrates that if you are able to tap into the resources available, then your journey from student to practitioner will be made all the more easier.

STARTING POINTS: ARE YOU RESOURCE-READY?

1 How many sources of support within your university can you name? (Award yourself one point for each.)

2 Where would you go if …

    (a) You were concerned that you were not on the right course

    (b) You were worried about your finances

(c) You were struggling with an assignment

(d) You were worried about placement

(e) You had problems with your housing

(f) You needed careers advice

(g) You were having problems structuring your assignment

(h) Relationship problems were affecting your work

(i) You thought that you might have dyslexia

(j) You felt very low in mood

You can find the answers to this on pages 92–3. Give yourself a point for each correct answer.

Results

0–3   Hmm, you either have a perfect life or you find it difficult to know where to find help. It might be that you already have a good informal support network in place, but it is always worth knowing where to go if future problems should arise.

4–6   You are aware of some of the support networks you can tap into. This chapter will show you areas you may not have considered, just to make sure all your bases are covered.

7–8   You are definitely resource-ready. You have a broad understanding of the networks that can support your study. This chapter will show you how to access these and gain the most from these sources and resources.

9–10   You are more than resource-ready: you are positively bullet-proofed. This is excellent news. It is still worth reading on to see if there are any additional sources of support you have not yet seen on placement.

KEYS TO SUCCESS

In order to successfully access and gain the most from the support mechanisms available you need to:

- Recognise your needs and identify when you should seek help

- Find out about the range of support mechanisms available and how to access these

- Be clear about what you want to gain from the support

- Be prepared

- Identify what stops you from accessing help

Recognise your needs and identify when you should seek help

At university, there is an expectation that you will take responsibility for your learning. You are an adult learner and must walk the fine line between managing yourself and knowing when to seek help. If you are experiencing problems with your work or personal life, then the onus is on you to identify and access support. The most difficult aspect of this is recognising that there is a problem and deciding at what point you should seek help.

Which of the following students should access formal support?

- June has just failed her first assignment

- Cathy has gained the same marks for the last three assignments. She would ideally like a 2:1 but she is unable to move above 50%, which puts her in the 2:2 banding

- Richard is having problems sleeping because he is worrying about work

- Raj constantly feels overwhelmed to the point where he is finding it hard to read or concentrate

- Financial worries are affecting Phil's ability to study

- Fran was diagnosed with dyslexia before starting her course

- Fahten has just broken up with her boyfriend of six years

- Darren's grandfather died a few days ago. He was extremely close to him

Each of these students could warrant seeking some form of help. In the case of Darren and Fahten, it might be something as simple as informing their personal tutor so that they are aware of the situation in case the shock of this impacts on them at a later point. Timing is the key. The earlier you let someone know that things are not going well, the sooner support can be put in place.

Generally, it is worth seeking support if:

- You find that you are struggling to keep up academically

- Your studies are having a negative impact on how you feel about yourself

- Your work is affecting other areas of your life

- Other areas of your life are affecting your work

- Friends and family have commented that you are not yourself and are worried about you

Find out about the range of support mechanisms available and how to access these

The biggest hurdle many students face is knowing where to go for help. Indeed, the main challenge you have is to decipher what is available and what each resource has to offer. Here is a quick guide to the 'top ten' sources of support you may be able to tap into:

1 Your peers/friends inside university

This is great for informal academic and emotional support. The advantage of seeking support from your friends is that you are experiencing the same pressures and they will have a really good idea about how you feel.

2 Family and friends from outside university

Not only do they know you well, but they can offer a healthy 'outside' perspective on the situation.

3 Your personal tutor

Your personal tutor can be the anchor point and main contact between you and the university. She/he is there to offer help in personal and professional issues and will signpost you to other resources as required. During the first few weeks of university life you will have the opportunity to meet your personal tutor, where they will clarify their role. After this, the onus in on you to make contact. Do not feel that you should only see your personal tutor when there are problems. They are also responsible for writing your reference and so it is worth arranging regular appointments to see them and to inform them of your progress.

4 Module tutor

They will be able to offer advice and feedback about any work or assignments you are undertaking as part of the module. When you start to work on your dissertation you will be allocated a research tutor who will work closely with you and guide you through the research process.

5 Year tutor

The year tutor has an overview of issues such as timetabling and placement. If you are having doubts about whether you are on the right course your first port of call will be your personal tutor, but then you might need to speak to the year tutor, who will offer you a broader overview of the course and will be able to advise you of your options.

6   Librarian/learning resource centre staff

University libraries offer a range of resources. Many run study skills support sessions or offer individual help around specific academic skills.

7   Student support officer

Universities are increasingly employing student support officers who have a predominantly pastoral role. These offer a confidential service and can advise you about extenuating circumstances forms and extensions for assignments. They offer support outside the wider teaching team.

8   Student Academic Services/Guidance Service

Your university may have a slightly different name for this resource but generally most institutions have a department dedicated to welfare issues facing students. Services include careers advice, disability services (who can arrange learning contracts for students with disabilities, including dyslexia), financial support and housing.

9   Students' Union

The Students' Union is not only there to organise parties. It plays a major role in dealing with issues impacting on student welfare. From housing to disability rights, it can provide advice as well as legal representation.

10   Chaplain/counsellor

Most higher education institutions have excellent counselling services. These can offer you the opportunity to talk through your difficulties and provide you with strategies to manage your feelings, signposting you to additional services if required. Many students at university access counselling for a whole host of reasons, including anxiety resulting from their course, depression, stress, and for support with pre-existing mental health problems.

Activity

Based on the above, go back to our characters (page 86). Which source of support would you direct each person to and why?

Be clear about what you want to gain from the support

You need to spend time thinking about what it is you hope to gain from seeking help. For example, is the aim of seeing your tutor to clarify a question, to look at a specific piece of work or to develop broader skills that you will take with you to your next assignment? Similarly, are you seeking emotional support in relation to this one event or are you hoping to develop new coping mechanisms that will help you in approaching future issues? It can be helpful to clarify your expectations at an early point. This does not mean that they will be set in stone, but the process of goal-setting can offer a focus and help you to identify an end point in the process. From the perspective of the person offering support, this can also help to clarify their thinking and help in the management of resources.

Be prepared

Once you have identified the resource you are going to tap into you need to ensure that you gain the most from this. Many tutors complain that students fail to make the best use of tutorial time because they simply turn up unprepared. Here are some of the ways to annoy your tutor:

Mildly frustrating...

- Not saying thank you

- Students who turn up late and then expect you to stay late because they have not been able to fit everything in

Frustrating...

- Lack of organisation, jumbled notes in a carrier bag, notes on the back of the hand

- Students who refuse to listen and who find a reason why every solution will not work

Very frustrating...

- The student who has no ownership and sits expecting their tutor to magically sort the problem out

- The student who does not listen or is not open to solutions

- The person who tries to play one tutor off against another

The motto here is 'Be prepared'. It is not sufficient just to turn up. You need to plan ahead. The following pointers can be useful:

- *Make an appointment.* Note the time and place and make sure that you are punctual. You need to demonstrate that you understand that time is precious and that you are treating the meeting seriously. If you are unable to keep your appointment, then let the tutor know in plenty of time.

- *Be clear about the purpose of the meeting.* If it is about something specific, it can be helpful to let your tutor know in advance so that they can be prepared.

- *Begin the meeting with an overview of the topics you would like to discuss.* You could then decide how you will prioritise these depending on the time you have.

- *Listen carefully to what your tutor says.* It can be helpful to keep a record and document your meetings, recording important points as you go along. An example of a record-sheet is included below. This will act as a reminder and can be used as evidence of your personal development planning. It is also good practice for the tutorials you will have on placement.

Date of meeting	Name of tutor
Purpose	Priorities
Issues discussed	
Outcomes	Action points
Date and time of next meeting	Place of next meeting

Remember that the tutorial relationship is a two-way process. Try not to assume a passive role and expect your tutor to 'solve' your problems. Be prepared to enter into joint problem-solving and explore all the options available.

- *Be clear about what you want to happen to the information.* If it is confidential and you would rather other tutors did not know, you can say so. If your tutor is extremely concerned about you, they may feel that it is in your best interests to speak to a third party, but they will negotiate this with you before anything happens.

- *Summarise what has been said.* At the end of the meeting, summarise what has been said and develop an action plan of steps you are going to take.

- *Bring your diary with you.* If you require another appointment, book this in.

- *Finally, remember to thank your tutor for their time.* Record the points discussed and make a note of the discussion at the earliest possible moment, while it is still fresh in your mind.

Identify what stops you from accessing help

The final step to successfully gaining support is to recognise the barriers that prevent you from doing this. Spend a few minutes answering the following questions:

What would stop you from…

(a) Accessing key skills support in the learning centre or library

(b) Seeing a counsellor if you were feeling depressed

(c) Arranging to speak to your personal tutor about concerns over work

(d) Speaking to a student support officer if your dyslexia was impacting on your ability to keep up with the work

Reflect on your responses. What are the main reasons why you don't access support?

- Do they relate to worries? *(What if this means I can't carry on with my course? What if my tutor thinks any less of me? What if there just isn't a solution?)*

- Are they about your attitude? *(Asking for help is a sign of weakness. I should be able to cope with this.)*

- Do the barriers relate to practicalities? *(I am unsure of where to go. I am confused about how you go about that.)*

- Are there other factors? *(A personality clash with the tutor or with other students.)*

For a moment, list all the consequences of not seeking support and gently start to challenge the factors that prevent you. Here is an account by one student.

Going to university was a big thing for me. I was the first person in my family to go and I had to give up a great deal – balancing my family and home life. While I was doing my Access course, I was diagnosed with dyslexia. When I arrived at university I worried about this. What if having dyslexia made it difficult for me to qualify as a social worker? What could the potential consequences be? To make matters worse I started to struggle with the work. I felt so worried. I could not sleep or work. One day I was particularly upset and confided this in a friend. She suggested that I went to the student disability officer. I was really worried but I didn't need to be. They were incredible. They gave me a learning contract and arranged for me to have a laptop. Tutors made sure that I had the notes prior to lectures. My marks went up two full classifications within the year. I will qualify in September and my tutors have predicted that I will achieve a 2:1 degree. My advice to anyone who is teetering on the brink of seeking help is 'go for it'. It has been a complete turning point for me and my only regret is that I didn't seek help earlier.

Are you resource-ready? Answers

(a) **You were concerned that you were not on the right course**

Any of the following: personal tutor, year tutor, course leader, careers adviser (often within student and academic services).

(b) **You were worried about your finances**

Student and academic services focus on welfare. You could also try going to the Students' Union or to your bank.

(c) **You were struggling with an assignment**

Definitely your personal tutor or the tutor for that particular module.

(d) **You were worried about placement**

A member of the university practice placement team. It is also worth speaking to other students and listening to their experiences.

(e) **You had problems with your housing**

Again student and academic services. Many universities also have departments that specifically deal with housing.

(f) **You needed careers advice**

A careers adviser.

(g) **You were having problems structuring your assignment**

Your personal tutor would be a good starting point. You could also discuss this with the module tutor, who would have a clearer understanding about the content of the module. Finally, many library and learning resource centres also have drop-in support for study skills.

(h) **Relationship problems were affecting your work**

Your personal tutor or a university counsellor. Anything you discuss with the counselling service will be treated with the utmost confidence.

(i) **You thought that you might have dyslexia**

Your personal tutor will be able to signpost you to the necessary services. Most universities have a student disability officer and will be able to arrange for you to have an assessment of needs. If you have dyslexia, then the university will be able to put a learning contract in place to support your learning. This may include giving you more time to complete assignments, certain allowances for examinations and assessments, and providing equipment to help you study.

> (j) **You felt very low in mood**
>
> Your personal tutor, university counsellor (often found within student and academic services) or your GP.

Skills in practice

The prospect of going on placement can feel pretty daunting even to the most confident of students. It is completely accepted that you will require guidance and this will form a key element of your learning. The remainder of this chapter looks at how to gain the most from the support mechanisms available in practice, focusing on supervision and the role of your placement educator. It ends by taking a broader look at what happens beyond university and what preceptorship can offer (for more details about preceptorship see Chapter 19).

Recognise your needs and identify when you should seek help

On placement you will immediately notice that support mechanisms are more clearly designated, more formal and focused on professionalism than those at university. Your educator is there to offer support and guidance, but she/he also has a role in assessing your competence and will decide whether you pass or fail the placement. Your relationship will have set boundaries and there will be expectations on both sides about your respective roles. Meetings will take place on a regular basis and follow a tight agenda. The relationship offers you an excellent taste of what will happen once you are qualified and gives you a good grounding in how to gain the most from this.

Having said this, your placement educator will be checking to see that you have a good level of insight and self-awareness, and that you are able to identify situations when you need to draw on their knowledge and expertise.

Reasons why you might access support on placement

Reassurance. To check that you are following a correct protocol or procedure, to discuss a particular course of action you feel you should take, to check that you acted in an appropriate manner in a difficult situation.

Learning. To make sure you have understood something correctly, such as a piece of evidence, a treatment approach, something you have read or studied at university, to learn an unfamiliar procedure or to find out how to use a piece of equipment.

Guidance (when the personal is impacting on the professional, or vice versa). You may encounter a number of very difficult situations for the first time on placement. For example, a person dying, a client who has been abused, a child with a terminal illness, someone with particularly horrific injuries following a road traffic accident, a person with a mental illness who is being made to comply with a form of treatment against their will. Aspects of the job you believed to be fine may suddenly present as an issue and affect you professionally and personally. Alternatively, you may be coping with issues in your personal life that are impacting on your ability to perform your role. You need to make your placement educator aware of this, particularly if it could impact on the clients who are in your care. The role of your educator might then be to guide you to support or to help you to look at ways to manage the situation.

Guidance (if you have a disability that could impact on your performance). You may be concerned that you have a disability or long-term health problem that could impact on your ability to succeed on placement. These may range from learning difficulties such as dyslexia or dyspraxia to health problems, including mental health difficulties, physical conditions such as diabetes, epilepsy or ME. Under the Disability Discrimination Act, employers and education providers have a responsibility to put into place reasonable adjustments to enable you to carry out your role effectively. The choice of whether or not to disclose this to your placement educator is up to you. However, if you fail to disclose this information, your educator cannot take the necessary steps to support you. If, as a result of not disclosing, you go on to fail the placement, then it would be very difficult to argue that the necessary mechanisms were not in place.

Your placement link tutor or disability support officer can advise you when and how to disclose. Remember that it is not necessary to go into every detail and you can request that the information remains with your placement educator as opposed to being shared more widely. If you do disclose, it can be helpful to:

- Be clear about how you think it could impact on your placement experience
- Highlight coping strategies you use (e.g. if you have dyslexia, one of the strategies might be to keep a list of key words in a pocket diary that you can use when you write up your notes)
- Outline how your educator can best support you
- Discuss how you manage your disability at university and on other placements

Find out about the range of support mechanisms available and how to access these

We have already identified your placement educator as a key person in supporting your personal and professional development. However, there are other support mechanisms you may choose to draw on.

Other students on placement

You may be fortunate enough to be joined by other students either from your university or other institutions. You can share your experiences, offer ideas about how to cope with particular issues and use each other as a sounding block. Having a peer to talk things through with can be invaluable. If the student is from another university, it can be good to exchange experiences and look at different ways of doing things.

Band five/basic grade practitioners

Placement educators are usually senior members of staff with a great deal of experience under their belts. However, most departments also have more recently qualified staff. These practitioners are possibly able to identify more closely with how it feels to be a student. They are probably getting to grips with particular skills and procedures and are able to share useful ways of doing things. In some areas, students are able to attend the band five/basic grade practitioners' support group.

Care for the Carers

A number of organisations seek to provide support for those working in health and social care practice. Care for the Carers is an example of one such organisation. These are probably more common in mental health settings and in palliative care, but can be helpful if you are struggling to cope with some of the feelings or facing quite challenging situations.

Journal clubs

If the type of support you require relates to getting to grips with the clinical aspects of the placement – the evidence underpinning particular interventions or key concepts you are encountering – then it would be worth investigating if there is a journal club. These tend to be informal meetings where recent papers are debated and discussed. It can be a good way to get to grips with the bigger picture in relation to your placement as well as developing skills in reading and debating information. It also offers you the chance to get to know team members in a less formal situation.

Your university link tutor

Invaluable as the link between university and placement, the university link tutor or liaison tutor acts as a bridge between the two.

University resources

Do not forget that just because you are on placement does not mean that you cannot tap into all the resources you use at university!

These are just a few examples of the support mechanisms available to you. Remember that if you are discussing issues with anyone other than the team involved in your client's care that you must maintain complete confidentiality. It would be unethical to divulge any details or to refer to someone in such a way that they can be identified by others.

Be clear about what you want to gain from the support

It will take you time to get to grips with the different types of support mechanism available on placement and the parameters surrounding these varied resources. You may find yourself requiring different types of support as your placement progresses. Supervision is a regular, formal meeting with your placement educator. It offers you the opportunity to discuss your work, receive feedback on your performance and explore particular issues that have arisen. To gain the most from these meetings you will need to focus and think very carefully about what you hope to gain from the session. For example:

Clinical: questions relating to procedures or approaches you are using.
Organisational: discussion regarding how you are managing your case load – how you are prioritising your work.
Your professional development: exploration of your strengths and areas for development, and the progress you are making in terms of meeting your placement objectives.

Be prepared

Be proactive, not pushy. Once again, the key to gaining the most from support offered on placement is to be organised. You need to spend time thinking ahead and either mentally draw up an agenda or write out a plan. This is especially the case for supervision, where you will have a relatively short amount of time to reflect on your learning, review your objectives, demonstrate that you are working towards your assessment and discuss any issues that have arisen. A summary of areas for discussion could include the following elements:

Strengths: ways you have addressed issues identified during earlier supervision sessions.
Challenges: areas you have found personally and professionally challenging. How you have turned this experience into learning. Examples of strategies and coping

mechanisms used and discussion around further possible steps and approaches you could take in the future.

Specific skills: skills you have developed which could contribute towards a skills passport or your assessment.

Issues: areas that you have not addressed as yet where further guidance is needed or where impending challenges are to be faced over the coming weeks.

At the beginning of the meeting negotiate the priorities for discussion and then work through these methodically, keeping an eye on the time. Most importantly, listen to your educator's feedback, and make written notes of key points and tasks for completion. At all times work in partnership with your educator, drawing on their wealth of experience and specialist knowledge. Use this as an opportunity to gain support, build confidence and identify areas for development, setting your objectives for the following week either in the meeting or directly afterwards.

At the end of the meeting remember to thank your educator and arrange the time of the next supervision session. At the earliest convenient moment reflect on the experience and include your observations in your personal and professional development portfolio. Joan Healey and Margaret Spencer (2008) provide a clear diagram of this process in their book (details are provided in the References and signposts to further reading and resources section at the end of this chapter).

Identify what stops you from accessing help

There are no excuses here. At the very least you will have regular supervision. This is not like being in university when the decision to see or not to see your personal tutor is up to you.

Your university will explain in its handbook how regularly supervision should take place. It is not an optional activity but a requirement set down as part of the government's clinical governance framework. Many professional bodies also specify the number of hours of supervision students undertaking their qualification should receive and build this into course documents. If you are not receiving supervision, you should contact your university tutors.

Your main barriers then will revolve around your relationship with your educator and around your organisational skills. You need to identify these and work through them at the earliest possible moment. If there are issues that cannot be resolved through discussion, contact your link tutor.

Support beyond university

Supervision will continue to be a mechanism on which you can draw once you have completed your course and begin paid employment. However, it is worth highlighting the additional support framework of preceptorship. Preceptorship is a process of support to enable you to make the transition from graduate to practitioner. It recognises that starting a new role can be challenging and you may need support to allow you to negotiate this period successfully. It comprises a number of ingredients (Nursing and Midwifery Council, 2006):

- **An experienced colleague** (your preceptor) to guide you through the early months of your practice.

- **A framework offering a graded introduction** to the various elements of your job, with opportunities for work-shadowing and with increasing responsibilities as time progresses.

- **Regular meetings with your preceptor** to discuss learning goals, monitor progress and identify areas for further professional development.

- **Protected time for learning** during your first year of qualified practice.

- **A file or portfolio** where you will be required to evidence skills and competencies.

During the first year after you start paid work, you will work closely with your preceptor, who will support you in identifying, completing and evidencing a series of learning goals to reflect your increasing confidence and competence in fulfilling the different aspects of your new professional role. Learning goals will vary from demonstrating a knowledge of and the ability to follow procedures relating to health and safety and progress through to skills relating to self-motivation and professional development, communication, teamwork and your ability to make and implement decisions.

Preceptorship offers an excellent mechanism to enable you to make the transition from student to practitioner. If you have understood how to access and gain the most from the support mechanisms at university and on placement, then you will be ideally placed to make the most of this and to seize the opportunity to flourish.

IN A NUTSHELL

Recognising when you need support and actively tapping into available resources demonstrates that you are able to take responsibility for managing yourself and your learning. This chapter has highlighted that:

- A range of support mechanisms exist for your benefit both at university and on placement

- You need to actively explore and identify the support mechanisms available. It is best to do this before you are at the point when you need to access these.

- Exploring issues in a supportive atmosphere can help you to gain greater self-awareness

- In order to get the most from the support mechanisms you access plan ahead. Have a clear picture about what you want to gain and set a clear agenda to keep the meeting focused

References and signposts to further reading and resources

Butterworth, T., Faugier, J. and Burnard, P. (1998) *Clinical Supervision and Mentorship in Nursing* (2nd edition). Cheltenham: Stanley Thornes.

Healey, J. and Spencer, M. (2008) *Surviving Your Placement in Health and Social Care: A Student Handbook*. Maidenhead: Open University Press McGraw-Hill.

Morrison, T. (2005) *Staff Supervision in Social Care: Making a Real Difference for Staff and Service Users*. Brighton: Pavilion.

Nursing and Midwifery Council (2006) Circular 21/2006. Available at: www.nmc-uk.org/aDisplayDocument.aspx?DocumentID=2088 (last accessed 23/03/09).

Van Ooijen, E. (2003) *Clinical Supervision Made Easy*. Edinburgh: Churchill Livingstone.

Part III Building and developing skills

9 Reflective practice: turning experience into learning

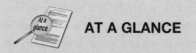

AT A GLANCE

This chapter is for you if

- You believe that reflection is something that only happens when you look in the mirror

- You make the same mistakes again and again

- You find it difficult to use feedback

- You are frequently overwhelmed by an emotional response to a situation and find yourself getting 'stuck' and unable to move on

- Your heart sinks when your tutor asks you to reflect on an event or incident

This chapter looks at ways of turning experience into learning. For one moment, consider the question 'Where does learning happen?' Circle the correct answer.

(a) In the classroom

(b) In the library

(c) During placement

(d) At exam time

(e) In the pub

(f)   All of the above

(g) None of the above

Award yourself a point if you circled (f) – 'all of the above'. Traditionally, learning has been associated with a formal process occurring in the classroom and on placement. Images of rows of students sitting in a lecture theatre or of groups working together on a clinical problem may spring to mind. A great deal of learning does happen in these formal situations but this is not quite the whole picture.

Reflective practice is a way of thinking about a situation in order to turn it into learning. It enables you to transform everyday experiences on placement, in the classroom, at home, in the pub, into learning opportunities. It is a process that does not depend on a tutor, but allows you to make links between theory and practice. It means that learning begins from day one of your course and extends far beyond your graduation. Through this you can gain rich personal insights, recognising strengths and acknowledging and finding a way to overcome limitations. As your career progresses you will use reflection to grapple with complex clinical situations and it will feed into something called personal and professional development planning, enabling you to make the transition from novice to expert practitioner.

This chapter helps you to get to grips with what is meant by the term 'reflection' and shows you some of the different ways of doing this. It looks at the kinds of situation you might use to reflect on and ways to record your learning in the classroom and on placement.

STARTING POINTS

Try this quiz to see how reflective you are. Simply circle the statements that apply to you:

1   You receive a poor mark for an assignment. Do you...

(a) Look at where you went wrong, seek advice and talk to your tutor about how to improve future performances?

(b) Feel overwhelmed by emotion and think 'I'm a failure, I'll never be able to do this, I might as well give up'?

(c) Feel quite angry and dismiss the mark arguing 'It was good enough before coming to university – clearly they haven't a clue'?

2   You are facilitating a group. The session goes particularly well. Do you...

(a) Spend time thinking about the group and try to identify what made it so successful, drawing up ideas for ways to facilitate future sessions?
(b) Think 'What a complete fluke. More luck than judgement'?
(c) Take it in your stride: 'Of course it went well. After all, it was your group'?

3   What items do you associate with reflection?

(a) A journal and a diary.
(b) A notebook and a mirror.
(c) A hairbrush and a mirror.

4   Which statement do you most closely identify with?

(a) Before I tackle something new I tend to think back to previous experiences and draw on my learning from these.
(b) I worry about trying new things, particularly if I have not done anything like this before.
(c) I tend to jump into situations. I enjoy the thrill of seeing what happens.

5   Circle the statement you agree with most.

(a) Reflection is a skill that needs to be developed.
(b) We all reflect naturally.
(c) Reflection is a form of navel-gazing.

If you answered mainly (a), congratulations! You recognise that reflection is an active process that enables you to transform experience into learning. This chapter offers you a few ideas of how to structure your thinking in order to gain the most from the reflective process and to transfer this learning into placement.

If you answered mainly (b), you may mistakenly assume that reflection is quite a passive process and something that you are already doing. However, your answers suggest that at times you are too emotionally close to a situation which makes it difficult for you to revisit experiences to gain the depth of learning reflection offers. This chapter will enable you to develop a range of strategies to overcome this hurdle and to find ways to systematically think about these experiences and document your reflections.

If you answered mainly (c), your confidence does you credit but make sure that it does not act as a barrier to your learning and prevent you from gaining insight to areas where you need to develop. If you constantly find yourself thinking 'I'm all right, it is the rest of the world that is wrong', this is a sure sign that this chapter is essential reading.

Before you begin: Five things you may not know about reflective practice

1 Reflection has its roots in education (Dewey, 1933).

2 The importance of critical reflection in health and social care has been recognised and a range of authors, including Boud et al. (1985), Benner (1984) and Moon (1999), have argued that reflection can improve practice.

3 The United Kingdom Central Council for Nursing, Midwifery and Health Visiting (UKCC, 1986) adopted reflection as one of the key skills required by nurses. Reflection is also named as an essential competence in the Health Professions Council's *Standards of Proficiency* (2003).

4 Many pre- and post-registration courses have included reflective practice as an integral component of their programmes (Ghaye and Lillyman, 1977: 7).

5 Donald Schön (1983) is a 'daddy of reflectors' in the field and suggested that there are two types of reflection: *reflecting in action* (thinking on your feet) and *reflecting on action* (looking back on events).

Unpicking reflection

Here are some ways that reflection has been defined:

Reflection is a process of reviewing an experience of practice in order to describe, analyze, evaluate, and so inform learning about practice. (Reid, 1993: 305)

A generic term for those intellectual and effective activities in which individuals engage to explore their experiences in order to lead to a new understanding and appreciation. (Boud et al., 1985: 19)

When we are engaging in reflection about ourselves, we try to look at something from lots of different angles and ask ourselves what happened, what went on and why. From asking ourselves those questions we can gain new insight into ourselves and our practice and identify ways in which we can develop to our full potential both personally and professionally. (Healey and Spencer, 2008: 22).

If we take the essence of these definitions, we can safely say that reflection:

- Is active – it is something that you consciously choose to do

- Is a process you engage in to understand/make sense of what is happening

- Can generate new knowledge or insight

- Results in an action

You may be thinking, 'Hang on, I spend a lot of time going over situations in my mind'. While we all reflect to some degree, reflection in the context of this chapter is about a far more systematic process involving critical thinking, recording of ideas and taking steps to change. Here are examples of things your tutors might ask you to reflect on:

- Your work – evaluation of feedback and how this has been used

- Placement

- Your experience of being in a group

In the realm of academia you might be asked to reflect on:

- *Something you have read.* Here your tutor will be looking at your response to a book or article. For example, did this reading change your thinking? How did it relate to your experience? Did it sit well with your understanding or challenge your ideas?

- *On your experience of learning.* Here you need to focus on what you have learned about the process. For instance, how did you undertake the task? How did it feel? What helped or hindered you? How would you do things differently the next time? What will you do the same?

Clearly, reflection is a valuable skill to develop. Here is a short narrative by a social work student describing the value of reflection. Note how it is divided into three sections: description, evaluation/analysis and action planning.

Background/description

When I started university we attended a number of sessions about reflective practice. To be honest, I was pretty sceptical at the time. I couldn't see how it would help me be a better social worker. I went along, though, and grasped the basics. At the end of the semester, when we received our marks, it turned out that I'd done very poorly in one of the assignments. I was completely gutted. Although my other marks weren't great, I felt angry. The tutor was wrong! The work was a clear pass and I was convinced of this. I emailed the module leader who said he was happy to see me but before doing so he asked me to read through the assignment and use this as the basis of a piece of reflective writing.

I did. I read through my assignment imagining I was the tutor. It was a dreadful piece of writing, which came as a complete shock. If I was honest, I felt that the final mark had been pretty generous. I contacted the tutor again and explained that I was happy with the mark. However, rather than leave it at that he suggested I followed a simple reflective process and make notes about how I approached the assignment, how I planned this, who I had turned to for support.

Evaluation/analysis

As I began to look in more detail at the process I realised that I had never felt happy about the question and, as a result, I had put off seeking help and knuckling down to the work. The result was that I had left it all until the last minute and it had been pretty rushed. There were other things happening in my personal life at the time.

I started to see this pattern in other pieces of work I had tackled. I realised that mistakenly I had seen asking for help/clarification as a sign of weakness. This, combined with all the other demands on my time, meant that procrastination was not an option.

Action planning

My tutor helped me to devise a simple action plan. For the next assignment I was to speak to the module leader straight away to clarify my understanding and draw up a study schedule with milestones of what I needed to complete and when this needed to be completed by.

You probably want to know the result. I have just received the mark for this piece of work. My best yet, 64%. Magic.

🔑 KEYS TO SUCCESS

Successful reflection depends on your ability to:

- Identify a learning experience/critical incident

- Find a way to structure/think about this experience

- Find a way to record/articulate the experience/thinking

- Develop an active/next step component

Identify a learning experience/critical incident

The starting point for reflection is identifying a learning experience. Can you think of a moment or an event in your time at school or college that acted as a turning point? It might be something that challenged the way you thought about something or acted as a 'light bulb' moment when things clicked into place. Here are some examples offered by students:

My light bulb moment came when my tutor told me that my writing was good. I had gained a poor mark simply because I hadn't answered the question. She said it was the equivalent of making a victoria sandwich cake when she had asked for flapjack.

My turning point was a round of applause following a verbal presentation to the rest of the group. For the first time in my life, I believed I could actually succeed at this.

The most profound learning experience of the semester came when Frank, a person with schizophrenia, came to talk about living with hearing voices. It completely turned my thinking upside down.

In 'reflective practice-speak', these would be termed as 'critical incidents'. A critical incident is the starting point for learning, the catalyst for the reflective process. It can be something that excites you, challenges you or makes you feel uncomfortable, it might be an instance where something has gone particularly well or particularly badly. Basically, it is anything that promotes learning. At university, a critical incident might include:

- getting a high mark for a piece of work

- failing an assignment

- being part of a group that is working well

- being part of a group that is not working well

- reading a book/journal paper that challenges your thinking

- watching a documentary/film that challenges your thinking

Find a way to structure/think about this experience

Once you have identified your learning experience, you need to gain the depth of analysis. The crux of reflection lies in finding a way to structure your experience. Authors have offered a range of models to help you frame your thinking. It can be useful to think of these in terms of reflective shapes: loops and lines. Some models, such as those proposed by Gibbs (1988), see reflection as a circular process. Others take a more linear approach, focusing on a series of questions or prompts, probably best represented by a flow chart. This is just a brief outline and it is worth looking at the various models in more detail. The list of references and resources at the end of the chapter will point you in the right direction. The following table offers you an overview of other reflective structures you may be interested in.

Key player	Shape or representation of the model (circle, list, other)	Strengths	Limitations
Johns (2004)	List Series of cue questions to stimulate thinking	Clear questions Very structured way of reflecting	A bit formulaic Can feel constraining
Gibbs (1988)	Circle Focuses on a reflective cycle to guide thinking: description – feelings – evaluation – analysis – conclusion – action plan	Less constraining than other models	Can be difficult to pin down what you are meant to include in the different stages
Atkins and Murphy (1993)	Also a circle Questions scattered at key points of the cycle	Nice fluid structure, including enough questions to ensure that you are clear in your thinking	Suggests that reflection begins with 'an awareness of uncomfortable feelings' Does not directly take into account that an achievement

(Continued)

(Continued)

Key player	Shape or representation of the model (circle, list, other)	Strengths	Limitations
			may be the starting point
Schön (1983)	Circle within a circle Describes two kinds of reflection: reflecting in action (thinking on your feet) and reflecting on action (looking back on a situation)	Acknowledges that reflection can be instantaneous and can result in action at the time	Can be difficult to know exactly how to reflect in action – hard to capture these automatic processes It is also challenging to gain distance when you are emotionally in the middle of the situation
Bolton (2005, 2006)	A painting. Bolton sees reflection as a creative process. Making the subconscious conscious	Very creative, leads to depth of learning and authentic change	May struggle to fit reflections into something more structured

Evaluation

There are strengths and limitations to all these approaches. The main advantage of using a model is that it helps you to kick-start the reflective process to achieve the depths of thinking required to gain real insight. Being able to refer to a model also shows your tutor that you are aware that there is a body of literature relating to reflective practice which you have applied to your own learning.

The downside of using such a structured approach is that it can become quite repetitive and for some students can be too constraining, boring or formulaic. Experimenting with different models can help to keep the process fresh and exciting. Increasingly, students and practitioners are tapping into more creative ways of engaging with reflective process, using:

- Photography

- Drawing

- Cartoons

- Creative writing

The biggest challenge is to find a reflective process that suits you. Here are two exercises for you to try. The first is based on the model developed by Atkins and Murphy (1993) and consists of a series of questions. The second exercise is based on a more creative approach advocated by Gillie Bolton (2006). Rate how useful they are in helping you to:

- Step back from the situation

- See a different perspective

- Gain new insights

- Change how you feel or think about something

- Make changes

Use a star system to score

0 stars	hopeless
1 star	helpful
2 stars	very helpful
3 stars	extremely helpful

Exercise 1: Atkins and Murphy (1993)

Think of an incident, something that has happened at university or college that challenged you, or where you were suddenly aware of uncomfortable feelings or thoughts.

Use the space below to describe the situation, including thoughts and feelings, significant moments, key features.

Spend time analysing these feelings. Can you identify why you should have felt this way? Can you account for how you felt or think of times when this has happened to you before? How does this link to your existing knowledge? What do you think might have been going on?

Thinking more broadly, can you recall anything you have read that could account for why you felt as you did? (Theories of motivation, transference, links to self-esteem, anger, group dynamics.)

Does this help to explain the experience? Can you think of alternative ways of thinking or behaving based on this understanding?

What have you learnt from this experience? How can you draw on this in the future? Use the space below to identify any actions you need to take to help you in future situations.

Exercise 2: Creative writing (adapted from Bolton, 2006)

Think about the same critical incident. Imagine that you have two pairs of spectacles for each person in that situation. The first set of glasses lets you see the situation exactly as it was, from your perspective. Imagine that you have put on these glasses and, using an additional sheet of paper, describe the event exactly as you saw it.

The second pair of glasses allows you to see the situation from the point of view of another person. When you put these glasses on you see the situation exactly as they saw it and experienced it. Using the same sheet of paper, describe the situation from their perspective. If you were the only person there, imagine that these glasses belong to a complete stranger who is looking on from a distance.

Read the two accounts. What do you notice? Are they similar or very different? What do they tell you? Do they help you to think differently about the situation or offer any new insights? Based on your reading of these, how might you approach similar in the future? What would you do differently?

Finally, compare the two methods of reflection (Atkins and Murphy, and Bolton). Which do you prefer and why?

Find a way to record/articulate the experience/thinking

The next step to successful reflection is to find a way to record/articulate your experience. Students frequently ask whether they can just talk through their reflections. This might be part of the reflective process but to gain a deeper level of understanding it is helpful to record these in a more systematic way. Written reflections have the added advantage of:

- Providing a concrete record of the journey travelled

- Demonstrating the depth of learning experienced

Within reflective practice there is a real dichotomy. On the one hand, reflection is a very personal and incredibly private process. On the other hand, it is often read and marked by tutors, and judged, along with other pieces of academic work, against a set of assessment criteria.

This public vs private face of reflection creates serious tensions. If you only ever engage in the process for others, there is a danger that it becomes a tick-box exercise and, as a result, your reflections will never achieve the depth that is required for true personal development. For this reason, it is preferable to keep the two separate. On the one hand, keep a private journal 'for your eyes only'. Here you can be as creative and as expressive as you want, recording your experience in a style and way that works for you. This freedom will enable you to engage in the rich learning that leads to change.

You can then take the essence of these reflections and present a more 'public' record, where you are mindful of the language you use and where you choose what is appropriate given the nature of the academic task you have been given. When you do this, you will need to make a number of decisions including:

- What will you choose to share with your tutor/peers?

- What assessment criteria are you being marked against? Your ability to learn from a situation that hasn't gone well? Identification of an area for personal development, e.g. forward planning, organisation, communication? Recognition of personal strengths? Ability to look outside the situation and see other factors that were affecting the outcomes of the event?

- How will you structure your reflective writing?

Structuring your writing: what does this look like in practice?

This final point about structuring your writing is important. In completing the two reflective exercises, you have already had a taste of this. Most models of reflection contain the following ingredients.

1 They begin with a description of the experience and any thoughts or emotions you experienced. Price and Maier (2007) describe this stage as recapping or replaying events.

2 Then there is some form of evaluation. This involves stepping back and taking a more objective look at events so that you can make judgements about what went well and what did not go so well.

3   This is followed by analysis, where you process the experience and try to understand what was happening. This involves drawing on previous experiences or wider theories to inform this understanding.

4   Finally, there is the drawing of these strands together, where you identify your learning and make a number of decisions about how this experience will change how you approach similar situations in the future.

The problem is that many students lose marks because they make the mistake of ending the reflective process at the point of description. However, the reflective process is a bit like an orange. The description represents the outer skin with all its bumps and craters. If you delve a little under the surface and break through the skin, you begin to reach the juicy parts. The deeper you dig the juicier they become. This is the evaluation part. You need to keep digging until you finally arrive at the pips. These represent action planning, which, when planted, lead to future growth.

If you are not very confident, use one of the reflective models to guide your thinking. At some point within your reflection you need to draw on and make reference to the literature, demonstrating to others that you are able to make links between experience and theory. Neither is occurring in a vacuum. Here are a few tips from students.

Think carefully about the language you use. Although reflection is very personal, if you are writing this for a tutor it will be read by others and you may wish to censor particular words or phrases (definitely no slang or swearing).

Make sure that you preserve confidentiality: anonymise any details. This is good practice for when you are reflecting on placement.

Be honest. I thought I would lose marks if I showed that I had made a mistake. However, some of my best marks have been achieved when I have highlighted areas requiring further development and I have been praised for my level of insight.

Do not worry about writing in the first person. It is perfectly acceptable to use the word 'I'. After all, reflection is about you and your learning.

The website supporting this book (www.skills4health.co.uk) contains examples of reflective writing produced by students. Read these to gain a feel for how you can present your reflections.

Develop an active/next step component

There is a well-known saying where a person walks down the road and falls in a hole. The next day the same person walks down the same road and falls down the same hole. On the third day the person walks down a different road.

For reflection to mean anything, it must result in some kind of action or change. Reflection without action is navel-gazing. It is the equivalent of the person walking down the road and falling down the hole. To prevent this from happening, you need to ask yourself:

How will this change how I do things in the future?

If your learning has been a positive experience or achievement, your focus will be on ways of ensuring that your future work contains those ingredients, considering how you can continue to build on these strengths. If your critical incident has been around a more negative experience, you will need to decide how you will change your approach to similar situations in the future. This might be in relation to:

- Planning
- Setting realistic objectives
- Clarifying what is expected
- Identifying sources of support you could draw on
- Your attitude
- The assumptions you made about a person or situation
- Seeking support to develop a skill

You could summarise these action points in the following way:

As a result of x
I will...
by when...
with support from...

Revisit Chapter 5 on setting and achieving goals and consider ways to embed the process of reflection into the wider skill of action planning.

Skills in practice

The emphasis placed on reflection during your undergraduate career says something about the key role it will play in practice. This part of the chapter looks at how to translate the skills of successful reflection on to placement.

Five reasons why you should reflect

1. Because your professional body tells you to (Health Professions Council, 2003).
2. Because it can help you to recognise personal values and beliefs and gain greater self-awareness, which can then inform your practice.
3. It helps you to identify areas for development.
4. It means that you can turn experience into learning so that learning becomes a lifelong process.
5. Reflection enables you to identify and evidence your learning and can be used in your portfolio of personal and professional development.

The keys for successful reflection on placement are identical to those in the classroom.

Identify a learning experience/critical incident

In practice, whether on placement or as a qualified professional, you will discover a far wider range of 'critical incidents' from which to learn. This is to be expected. You are venturing into new territory and the learning curve will be steep. However, unlike university, where your tutor directs you to specific areas of your work to reflect on, you will need to be more disciplined and take the initiative in identifying your own critical incidents.

Critical incidents in practice frequently begin with a feeling: discomfort, surprise, disappointment, confusion, puzzlement, or an 'ah, ha!' moment. Learn to tune in to these feelings since, by and large, they relate to events that lead to learning.

Here are examples of critical incidents described by students on placement:

A difference of opinion between myself and my educator

A comment made by the consultant about a client

A treatment session/intervention/procedure that went particularly well

A treatment session/intervention/procedure that went particularly badly

A disastrous home visit where I forgot the address of where we were going

A comment by a client about the way I made them feel

Find a way to structure/think about this experience

Once you have identified a critical incident, the next step is to find a way to think about the experience. The reflective models you have used at college or university can all be transferred directly into practice situations. Placement presents additional opportunities that you may want to take advantage of:

- Joint reflection with colleagues or other members of the multidisciplinary team can offer an added dimension to the reflective process, although this depends on your setting and how open your team are. It would be difficult to reflect honestly in an environment where there is a dominant blame culture.

- Supervision meetings with your placement educator. A reflective log or record can offer you the opportunity to consider your reflections, discuss your progress with your educator, and provide a talking point on which to focus, where you can explore areas for further professional development.

Here, a student shares her experience of the first method of joint reflection within practice.

I was fortunate to go on a mental health placement where team reflection was a feature of the setting. At first I was incredibly self-conscious and shared very little, but the drama therapist was wonderful in terms of putting people at their ease. She used a range of techniques, including storytelling and photography to help everyone to reflect. The process was extraordinary. It was really interesting to hear all the varied perspectives people brought and the different ways of looking at the same situation. It offered powerful insights into both the dynamics of the team and the clients we were working with. The process was incredibly supportive. Sadly, one of the clients committed suicide and we came together to talk about the experience. This was very sensitively done. I learned a great deal about myself on the placement. When I qualify, this is something I would really like to introduce into the setting where I will work.

All that is left to do is to systematically capture and record these reflections in some kind of written log or journal.

Find a way to record/articulate the experience/thinking

Your tutor at university may have spoken to you about something called personal and professional development planning. Basically, this is a process where you:

- Demonstrate how your reflections on experiences have fed into your learning

- How this understanding has enabled you to identify future areas for development within your professional practice

- How you have then met these

It is common practice to record these results in a portfolio. This is a quick resumé of who you are, a summary of your experience and evidence that you have engaged in a continuous process of professional development, where you have identified gaps in your learning and taken steps to address these. This is the portfolio you take with you when you go for an interview for a job and the basis of the profile you write to maintain your registration once you have qualified.

It therefore makes sense for you to record your reflections in such a way that they can slot directly into your portfolio. This will help to keep you motivated (what could be a better motivation than these contributing to your dream job?) and ensure that your reflections are focused. Your portfolio will help you to link reflection with action planning and thereby ensure that you are not spending too much time navel-gazing!

Again, your reflections on placement will contain a 'public part' and a 'private part', and the same rules apply around confidentiality. Most students say that they prefer to use a separate part of their portfolio or journal to record their very personal thoughts and reflections around placement, and then select which they will share with their tutor, educator or colleagues.

Chapter 19 discusses continuous professional development (CPD) and looks at ways you can organise your portfolio. The remainder of this chapter looks at how you can pull together the final steps to successful reflection on placement. It starts by looking at a possible template where you can record your reflections, and at how to use this to develop an *active/next step component* (when using this don't forget to anonymise clients/staff or services you describe.)

Develop an active/next step component

In order to provide a clear structure and a plan of how you will take your learning forward, it can be useful to record your reflections in an ordered and structured way. The action plan you develop will then form the basis of future learning experiences.

A template for recording reflection on placement

Date:

Name the critical incident:

Give the critical incident a title – something snappy that will remind you when you look back what this was about. For example, 'The day I learned not to...' or 'first assessment'.

Description:

Describe what happened. It can be helpful to use one or more of the following to enable you to do this: visualisation, drawing the situation, transforming the different stages into a cartoon strip.

Exploration, evaluation and analysis:

This section is where you critically examine the event. From your reading, you have at your fingertips a range of reflective tools. Identify the model of reflection and use this to critically explore the experience. Ensure that you identify theories or bodies of existing knowledge you have drawn on during the process to explain what has happened.

Summary of learning:

What has this experience taught you? What do you know now that you didn't know before you started to reflect?

> **Action planning (looking towards the future):**
>
> Next time I encounter a similar situation I will… (this can also be positive: I will remember that…).
>
> **Resources that can help me to do this include:**
>
> You could include training opportunities, courses, people, mentorship, reading.

Reflecting on reflection

Hopefully, this chapter has offered you a number of simple techniques to help transform experience into learning and to help you feel more confident about the process of reflection. This calls for patience as you take time to develop an approach that works for you.

Whatever you do, keep going. Experiment and find out what helps you to reflect. For example, you could make reflection part of what you do on a daily basis, building it into the rhythm of your day. Write it in a way that is personal to you: a lovely journal that says 'write in me'; online in a document that says 'for your eyes only'; a sketch book or photograph album where you can stick bits, draw, write.

As you reflect, note what you find helpful. Do you find it easier to set aside a 'chunk' of time to reflect in or is it much easier to build in an odd 15 minutes here and an odd 15 minutes there as you carry out your day-to-day activities? Is it useful to have a reflective partner, someone you trust implicitly, whom you feel able to share your reflections with and to talk through the process with, or are you definitely a 'lone reflector', someone who needs their own space?

As well as identifying what helps you to reflect, you should also recognise the barriers to reflection. Be honest. At times, you will need to 'probe' a little. Here are some of the things students have described as being barriers to reflection.

Finding it difficult to admit that I have made a mistake

Being overwhelmed by feelings

Being too close to a situation

Fear of being criticised

Problems moving beyond deeply-held views or preconceptions

Feeling defensive

Not feeling supported

Worrying about how to write these down

Pay attention to the barriers and use these as critical incidents in order to gain a depth of reflection and to turn experience into real learning.

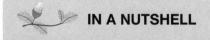

IN A NUTSHELL

Reflection is an ongoing process and a key to transforming everyday experiences into learning opportunities. This chapter has provided a brief overview of the process and has highlighted some of the techniques you may use. The key, however, is to experiment and find a reflective process that works for you. After working through this chapter you should be able to:

- Describe why you need to develop reflective practice as a core skill

- Name and use at least one model of reflection

- Move from reflective writing that focuses only on description to writing that is more *critical* or *evaluative*

- Develop an action plan based on your reflections

References and signposts to further reading and resources

Atkins, S. and Murphy, K. (1993) 'Reflection: a review of the literature', *Journal of Advanced Nursing*, 18: 1188–92.

Atkins, S. and Murphy, K. (1994) 'Reflective practice', *Nursing Standard*, 8 (39): 49–56.

Benner, P. (1984) *From Novice to Expert*. Reading, MA: Addison-Wesley.

Bolton, G. (2005) *Reflective Practice: Writing and Professional Development* (2nd edition). London: Sage.

Bolton, G. (2006) 'Narrative writing: reflective enquiry into professional practice', *Education Action Research Journal*, 14 (2): 203–18.

Boud, D., Keogh, R. and Walker, D. (1985) 'Promoting reflection in learning: a model', in D. Boud, R. Keogh and D. Walker (eds), *Reflection: Turning Experience into Learning*. London: Kogan Page.

Dewey, J. (1933) *How We Think: A Restatement of the Relation of Effective Thinking to the Educative Process*. Chicago: Henrey Regnery Co.

Ghaye, T. and Lillyman, S. (eds) (1997) *Learning Journals and Critical Incidents: Reflective Practice for Healthcare Professionals*. Dinton, Wiltshire: Quay Books.

Ghaye, T. and Lillyman, S. (2000) *Effective Clinical Supervision: The Role of Reflection*. Dinton, Wiltshire: Quay Books.

Gibbs, G. (1988) *Learning by Doing: A Guide to Teaching and Learning Methods*. Oxford: Oxford Polytechnic Press.

Healey, J. and Spencer, M. (2008) *Surviving Your Placement in Health and Social Care: A Student Handbook*. Maidenhead: Open University Press McGraw-Hill.

Health Professions Council (2003) *Standards of Proficiency*. London: HPC.

Jasper, M. (2003) *Beginning Reflective Practice*. Cheltenham: Nelson Thornes.

Johns, C. (2004) *Becoming a Reflective Practitioner* (2nd edition). Oxford: Blackwell.

Johns, C. (2006) *Engaging in Reflection in Practice: A Narrative Approach*. Oxford: Blackwell.

Moon, J. (1999) *Reflection in Learning and Professional Development: Theory and Practice*. London: Kogan Page.

NHSME (1993) *A Vision for the Future – The Nursing, Midwifery and Health Visitors' Contribution to Health Care*. London: Department of Health.

Nursing and Midwifery Council (2004) Standards of Proficiency for Pre-registration Midwifery Education. London: NMC.

Price, G. and Maier, P. (2007) *Effective Study Skills: Unlock Your Potential*. Harlow: Pearson.

Reid, B. (1933) 'But we're doing it already. Exploring a response to the concept of reflective practice in order to improve its facilitation', *Nurse Education Today*, 13: 305–19.

Schön, D. (1983) *The Reflective Practitioner*. New York: Basic Books.

UKCC (1986) *Project 2000: A New Preparation for Practice*. London: United Kingdom Central Council for Nursing, Midwifery and Health Visiting.

10 Researching information

AT A GLANCE

This chapter is for you if

- You have developed huge biceps from carrying lots of books to and from university

- Most of the books you have taken out of the library remain in a pile on the floor propping your door open

- You frequently feel overwhelmed by the amount of information you have gathered

- The only source of information you use is the internet

- You think that a database is how you get to meet people

- You only use the library to 'hang out' with your friends

- You constantly feel that you are one book/one click/one article away from the perfect answer

It would be easy to assume that the process of researching information is something that you do/engage in either:

(a) When studying at university, or

(b) If you decide to become an academic.

When we hear the word 'research', we often automatically think of Research with a capital R and imagine some distant process. However, this is far from the case. Every time you see a client you will engage in some kind of process of accessing a range of information in order to find out who the person is and what has brought them into contact with your service so that you can determine the most appropriate treatment. The skills you will use in deciding what type of information you require, where this is located, how you find it and decisions in terms of its reliability will be exactly the same as the skills you use when researching information for an assignment.

The ability to research information and make clear judgements about what you read is a skill required throughout your working life. As a health or social care practitioner, you will need to be able to keep up to date with all the latest developments in practice in order to ensure that the approach you adopt and the interventions you use are underpinned by sound clinical evidence, and that this evidence is reliable. Indeed, evidence-based practice:

> requires that decisions about health care are based on the best available, current, valid and relevant evidence. These decisions should be made by those receiving care, informed by the tacit and explicit knowledge of those providing care, within the context of available resources. (Dawes et al., 2005: 1186)

Up to this point in your academic career you may be used to being given a set of references by a tutor or being directed to a particular textbook. At university this will be different in a number of ways. First, you will be expected to work far more independently. You will need to seek out the information and will not be able to rely completely on a set of references on a reading list. Secondly, you will need to access and use a number of different sources of information, including textbooks, journal articles, electronic resources, clinical guidelines, national statistics, policy documents, protocols, dissertations and unpublished materials. Finally, you will need to make judgements about the reliability of these in a way that you might not previously have needed to do. With the advent of the internet and electronic databases, information has never been so readily accessible, so rich, convenient and easy to find. The downside is that with so many possibilities it is easy to feel overwhelmed to the degree that you can feel 'paralysed' by the amount of information and the number of decisions you may need to make.

The aim of this chapter is not to provide minute details about specific search strategies and descriptions of how to use complex information systems. It is highly probable that with the pace of change that this information would be out of date as soon as the book is published. Rather, it looks at the broad range of resources that are available to you and at the strengths and limitations of different types of information you may wish to use both in university and in practice.

STARTING POINTS

Try the following quiz to find out whether you are research-ready. Award yourself one point for each correct answer.

1   Read the following statements and decide which are fact and which are fiction. You will find the answers on page 134.

Statement	Fact	Fiction
Textbooks are the only reliable source of information		
Journal articles present current research and can signpost you to further reading		
All electronic resources are bad		
You should read all books on the reading list		
You should only read books on the reading list		
To gain the highest marks for assignments you need to include as many books as you can		
It is better to use a range of sources		
References and bibliographies are one and the same		
There is only one way to reference		

2   Name five services your learning centre offers.
3   Describe the process of finding a book where you already know the title.
4   Name an information adviser or a librarian in your learning centre.
5   What are your library/learning centre opening times?
6   Name the summer opening times of your library/learning centre (for a bonus mark).
7   Give the reference numbers for books covering your subject area.

8   What is your library card number? (deduct one mark for sadness)
9   How many different sources of information can you think of? (Clue: journals, newspapers, books...)
10 Describe an occasion where you have used these.

If you have scored:

30 plus You are positively sizzling. This is a sure sign that you are research-ready.
20–29   You are hot. You might find the section on putting your research skills into practice helpful.
10–19   You are warm. This chapter will offer you plenty of ideas to build your confidence in the research process.
0–9   You are feeling cold. This chapter will help you kick-start the research process.

 KEYS TO SUCCESS

There is a dizzying array of resources that you can use. The secret of successfully researching information is being able to:

- Identify the resources available

- Decide what type of information you are looking for

- Find out where material is located and how to access it

- Be selective

The key to this process hinges on the ability to be selective, to filter out irrelevant information and to seek help if you are unsure.

Identify the resources available

Many students fail to take full advantage of the wide range of resources offered by their university library or learning centre. For the most part, this is because they are not aware of the full extent of what is available. During the first few weeks of the semester, universities offer short induction sessions which can provide an excellent overview. The downside is that these sessions usually take place in the first few weeks, when the library is at its most busy and crowded with the greatest amount of pressure on staff. It is definitely worth following these visits up, either looking out for organised tours or speaking to a librarian or tutor. There are many time pressures that can prevent you from doing this, but view it as an investment in terms of time. The number of hours it will save will be invaluable.

For some students the reasons for not accessing the learning centre are more complex and relate more to lack of confidence. The problem is that it is easy to approach the learning centre with the unrealistic expectation that you will be able to go there once and know all there is to know about where to find the information. This may well have been the case for a small college or school library, but the university learning centre is huge by comparison. If you are unable to find a book or article, it is easy to feel overwhelmed or embarrassed and put the responsibility back on to yourself with statements such as 'I should be able to do this', 'I should know how to find x'. This can lead to feelings of inadequacy, embarrassment and anxiety, the result of which is a general reluctance to return to the library where these feelings originated.

If this scenario relates to you, it is important to take action. Your university library is a rich and vital resource and will play a key role in helping you throughout your university career. It can offer a wide variety of resources and services, including:

- Printed materials such as textbooks, journal articles, policy documents, newspapers

- Electronic resources such as databases, e-journals, e-books

- Audio-visual material such as films, videos, documentaries, DVDs, photographs

- Computers and scanners, photocopiers and printers

- Assistive technology (such as page readers) for students with disabilities

- Study rooms for group work

- Study skills support (including sessions about referencing and using databases)

If the thought of even going into a library fills you with dread, the following action plan offers a gentle step-by-step approach:

Stage 1: Find a friend. New things are always easier to do if you are not alone.
Stage 2: Orientation. The aim of this visit is to spend time in the library and gain a feel for the space. The easiest way to do this is to take your own book with you, find a desk and plan to spend 20 minutes reading at a table. From time to time, look around, see where people go, how they use the areas. Repeat this process until you feel confident.
Stage 3: Set yourself a task. For example, you could use the 24-hour self-service book drop, book a study room or borrow a video.

Getting to grips with the range of resources available in the learning centre will take time. The secret is to go with the flow and ask for support when you need it. Friends, library staff and tutors will be happy to help. Once you feel confident in finding your way around the learning centre, the next stage is to hone your skills in locating and finding information.

Decide what type of information you are looking for

The first step is to decide what type of information you need. For example, if you are asked to consider how multiple sclerosis impacts on a person's relationships with close family members there would be very little point in looking at the demographic data which tells you the incidence of the disease, or at a research paper which explores the most up-to-date medication. Textbooks may provide some insights into the signs and symptoms of multiple sclerosis, but the rich information will be found in autobiographies and accounts written on personal websites.

On the other hand, if you were asked to answer a question about the most appropriate treatment approach for people with multiple sclerosis, an autobiography might illustrate the impact of the particular approach taken, but you could not make sweeping generalisations relating to the wider population based on this. Rather, you would need to look at research papers in journals using different interventions across groups and countries. The table on the following page will help you to navigate the information maze.

Once you have decided on the type of information you require, the next stage is to locate this information.

Find out where material is located and how to access it

Finding and accessing materials is a bit like finding a CD in a music store. You can arrive at the store with the title of the CD and the artist, in which case you can go straight to the relevant section. On the other hand, you may arrive at the music store having heard a piece of music but without the name of the CD or artist. You can take a guess as to the type of music you have heard and spend time undertaking a hand-search in the section for that music genre, or you can ask the salesperson to do a search on the computer using any key words you can remember, either in the title of the CD or in one of the tracks. Once the computer has matched your key words to the artist, you can go straight to the appropriate section and claim your disk.

Just like the music store, reference books are arranged according to subject area and each book is given a separate reference number which you can usually find on its spine. To find this reference you can look this number up in the library catalogue or library index. Many of these catalogues are now computerised.

Worked example

Imagine that you have moved from a CD store to the library at your university. Consider the following scenarios:

Claire has just started her occupational therapy degree. Her tutor has provided a reading list which includes reference numbers. The shelves correspond to numbers. When she goes to the library, she simply looks for the number to locate the text.

Source of information	This is good for...	It is less good in terms of...
Textbook	Gaining an overview of a subject area. Textbooks provide established knowledge, pulling together ideas from a range of sources.	Very current information: ideas can quickly date Providing personal perspectives.
Journals	Providing current knowledge and ideas within articles of a manageable size with useful references to further reading, e.g. *Nursing Times*, *British Journal of Occupational Therapy*.	Very general information. Journals tend to focus on a very specific area of research or topic. This makes it difficult to make links with other subject areas. Journals do not always offer an overview of the literature base.
Policy documents	Providing information about the wider policy context of the area you are looking at.	Looking at anything other than policy.
Newspapers	Presenting a popular, reader-friendly view of medicine. Newspapers often report on the latest research.	Providing a balanced and realistic view. Newspapers tend to focus on headline-hitting items which are not always accurate and may carry a specific slant.
Novels and autobiographies	Offering clear insights into how it feels to experience a particular illness or condition, or how family members may be affected by this. Giving a very personal view.	Offering information that can be generalised, although some may be transferable to certain similar situations.
DVD, video, documentaries, MP3	Providing three-dimensional audio-visual accounts. These media offer information that does not depend on the written word. As such, it can provide very current accounts, making links to political, economic, contexts. Offering an engaging and useful starting point for research.	Providing unbiased accounts. Many of these sources offer an 'angle' and can be sensationalist.
Internet	Offering a wide variety of information and rich sources, including online journals, electronic collections, e-books, library catalogues, websites of professional organisations, carers' groups and service users, specialist interest groups, government departments, email lists, blogs and wikis.	Information that is of a consistent quality. Much information is unregulated and unsolicited and care needs to be taken in checking the reliability of the source.

Neil, who is a first-year paramedic, has been given a reading list for his assignment. It contains the following books:

Cooper, J. (2001) *Emergency Practice for Paramedic Education*. Edinburgh: Craig Publishing.
Lintott, J. (2000) *The Evolving Context of Paramedic Practice*. Oxford: Carol Books.
Woolley, P. (2007) *Basic Life Support for Health Professionals*. Cambridge: Mayne Books.

Neil's university library has an electronic catalogue system which contains reference information about all the books in the library. This computerised catalogue is common in most libraries and is known as OPAC (the open public access catalogue). All that Neil has to do is to type in the name of the author or the title of the book and the reference number of the book appears onscreen with details of how many copies are in the library and the number that are in stock or out on loan. Once he has the reference number, all he has to do is to look under the reference number on the library shelves.

June also has an assignment to write but this time her midwifery tutor has not provided a reading list. Rather, June has to go to the catalogue and find relevant information that she might use. This is still not a problem as she knows the general themes she needs to research and performs something called a *key word search*, where she types in a key word which then brings up lists of books which cover that particular theme and their reference numbers. Under this facility she can also find relevant audio-visual material held by the library and again the catalogue brings up the relevant reference numbers which she then uses to locate the information. When she started her course, she was frightened of the computer system and would spend hours and hours scanning the shelves manually looking for books which might be of interest. This system saves a great deal of time. The only downside is that it is difficult for June to know from looking at the title just how relevant and useful the book will be.

More advanced searching

So far, so good. However, there is another level of searching you may not be familiar with. For one moment, imagine that June decides that the question set by her tutor requires a more systematic, up-to-date review of the evidence of how best to manage a breech birth. She is aware that this information can be found within the midwifery journals and she therefore performs a hand-search, scanning the index of each journal, looking for key words that can take her to relevant articles. However, this is extremely time-consuming. A fellow student suggests that she looks on a database.

The university catalogue system will allow you to identify the references of all the textbooks, audio-visual material and associated materials it holds. In addition to this, your library will also subscribe to a wide range of journals that can be accessed electronically. These articles will offer a wealth of up-to-date information that will be vital to your studies. Because they are electronic they can be easily downloaded.

Basically, a database is a way of holding information so that it can be easily accessed. The databases you are interested in are those that hold information about health-related journal articles. Information is held and cross-referenced under a range of categories, including:

- Author name

- Journal name

- Theme and topic

- Article title

- Date of the article, its volume and page numbers

Simple steps to mastering a database search

The first thing to do is to *find out where the database is held*. Some libraries still have these on CD ROMS or computer disks, or you will be able to access these directly from your library or university's intranet page.

The second thing you need to decide is *which database you will use*. There are many databases, which are constantly being added to, so there is little point in listing them here. Basically, different databases will focus on different areas of practice. For example, if we take five databases at random. Consider for a moment their different coverage. Note particularly the years, the subjects and the national/international focus.

Name of database	Coverage	Areas
MEDLINE	1966–	4,600 biomedical journals. Medicine, nursing, midwifery, dentistry, healthcare systems. International
CINAHL (Cumulative Index to Nursing and Allied Health Literature)	1982–	1,200 journals in nursing, midwifery, allied health. International
BNI (British Nursing Index)	1985–	220 journals. Nursing, midwifery and community healthcare. UK
AMED (Allied and Complementary Medicine Database)	1985–	600 journals. Complementary medicine, palliative care, occupational therapy, physiotherapy, podiatry, speech and language therapy. UK
ASSIA (Applied Social Sciences Index and Abstracts)	1987–	650 journals. Health, social services, psychology, sociology, economics, race relations and education. USA and UK

(Adapted from Maslin-Prothero, 2005: 59–60)

Define your search terms

Once you have chosen and accessed your database or databases I'm afraid that you have to make even more decisions. The first thing you need to do is type in your search terms, based on the subject/topic you are looking at. Everything hangs on you getting this part right. If you do not take care at this point, then you could end up with something that is not appropriate. The best way to describe this is to take an example from shopping. Imagine that you ask a friend to fetch you some beans. In your mind you have a tin of beans in tomato juice but he/she brings you back a bunch of runner beans, a tin of broad beans, a tin of butter beans... need I say more?

This will take time to master. Do not worry. At first it will involve trial and error. There is a real knack to it. On the one hand, you need to make sure that your search term is as wide as possible and covers all the possible ways you can describe the subject. On the other hand, you want to ensure that you specify clear boundaries. Confused? Let's take student stress as an example.

Imagine that you have been asked to identify the main *causes* of *stress* for *undergraduate students* studying on *health and social care courses*.

Immediately, you circle the words: causes, stress, students, health and social care.

Now how are you going to define the search terms? Let's look at the variations for each one in turn:

Student could also be learner, mature learner, freshman, undergraduate.
Stress could also be anxiety, concern, burn-out, pressure, fear, worry.
Health and social care could literally list each of the courses in turn: physiotherapy, occupational therapy, nursing, midwifery, operating department practice.

Luckily, lots of the databases have in-built help and a handy tool called a thesaurus which allows you to type in your word and then offers you suggestions for alternatives. So, feeling happy with your choice of terms, you type these in and the database indicates there are 4,500 entries that match your search. Clearly, you need to narrow this down further. Under the search tool or advanced search tool, you can set specific parameters and tell the database to only include articles that were published:

- Within a specific timeframe
- In a particular language
- In relation to age
- In relation to gender
- In a particular country
- According to a type of research

Boolean operators: to boldly go...

There is an additional tool that can help you to extend or narrow down your search even further by linking search terms. These Boolean operators comprise the words 'and' or 'not'.

When you use the term 'not', this lets you narrow down your search term. For example, 'nursing, not therapy' would exclude all articles that are not specific to nursing.

Surprisingly, 'and' also helps you to undertake a more specific search. For example, 'nursing and stress' would provide you only with references where both key words feature.

The term 'or', on the other hand, widens the search. For example, 'nursing or therapy' would include articles relating to both.

Choose the articles you would like to look at

Nearly there. The computer will then list possible articles that you might like to use. You can highlight your selection and there is often the choice of being able to look at the abstract, which gives you a gist of what it is about before finally taking the plunge to access the full article.

If your university subscribes to the particular journal, you should be able to download this electronically. Job finished. If not, you may need to order the journal via the learning centre, which will offer this service.

Be selective

To read or not to read, that is the question

Mastering skills in searching for and researching information means that you will have the maximum number of choices available in terms of what you choose to read or choose not to read. The problem with research is that potentially you can reach a point of information overload (or bunny-in-the-headlights syndrome) and not know which way to turn. You can end up with lots of information that is unusable. Clearly, you need to make some decisions and quite quickly. Some of these will be based on sound academic reasons, others on more personal preferences, such as the readability of the text or how easy it is to access. The following can act as a guide.

Are you seeking to gain an overview of the subject area or to look at something very specific?

Key textbooks offer a general overview and a summary of established learning in the field and would be a good place to start. Journal articles tend to be more focused and will look at a very specific area or aspect of research.

Is it readable?

There is little point in taking out lots of huge tomes which make you feel ill at the thought of reading them. It is far better to choose books that you want to spend time with.

Is it accessible or easy to access?

Sometimes you will need to be pragmatic. The ideal might be to spend half a day at the learning centre reading reference books, but if you are juggling a family and a part-time job you may need to take a few books out on loan and access the remainder of your information electronically.

How much time do you have?

What can you feasibly read in the time given? A textbook to gain an overview? A few journal articles? Decide what is reasonable in the time you have.

Is the information current?

When was it published? Has it been superseded by other information? There is nothing wrong with reading earlier articles so long as you complement these with more up-to-date research. This way, you can show how ideas have changed.

Is the information relevant and trustworthy?

This can be a difficult call and you probably will not know for sure how relevant the text is until you read it. However, use the following clues to help you decide. Is the book on the reading list? Do the index and contents page make reference to your subject area? Where was the text published? Does the abstract/introduction/summary/conclusion seem to relate to the topic? In terms of trustworthiness, you will discover that there is a hierarchy relating to this, with reviewed textbooks and peer-reviewed articles considered as the most reliable. There is more on this subject in Chapter 11 on reading for information.

Students often make the mistake that they rule out particular sources of information because of sweeping generalisations. For example, 'Do not use x source of information'. What tutors should say is 'Do not use this source of information without thinking this through and reading it critically'. In fact, if you are writing a discursive assignment, it can be an advantage as you can highlight its unreliability and demonstrate that you are able to justify why this is so.

Decide on the order in which you are going to read the information

Finally, decide on the order in which you will read the information. The secret here is to move from the general to the specific. Gain an overview of the area and then focus in on the details. If you are finding the reading hard-going, then begin with texts that are easier to read so that you feel a little more confident in your understanding before tackling the more difficult ones.

Answers to 'research-ready' quiz on page 124

Textbooks are the only reliable source of information

Fiction: Textbooks are reliable but there are other sources that are more up to date, e.g. peer-reviewed journal articles.

Journal articles present current research and can signpost you to further reading

Fact: The reference list at the end of a journal article can provide an invaluable source of useful literature related to the subject area and is an excellent starting point for further reading.

All electronic resources are bad

Fiction: There are a number of excellent electronic resources and there are an increasing number of journals that are only held in an electronic format. It is true that the internet contains unsolicited information. However, knowing this means that you can critique this source in your assignments. Technically, there is no such thing as a 'bad' source of information; the only problems arise if you treat information indiscriminately and do not test its reliability.

You should read all books on the reading list

Fiction: It would be nice to read all the books but given that you will be working to a tight timeframe, this is completely impractical. When you start to read the same things or find themes are repeated, it is probably time to stop reading.

You should only read books on the reading list

Fiction: The reading list is there to guide you and certainly should not limit your reading. Imagine that the reading list is a starting point.

To gain the highest marks for assignments you need to include as many books as you can

Fiction: The secret here is quality not quantity.

It is better to use a range of sources

Fact: Different texts have different strengths and limitations. For example, a textbook will contain a more established body of information which can be slightly dated, whereas a journal article will focus on a narrower area but represents more up-to-date information. Combining sources therefore gives you the best of both worlds.

References and bibliographies are one and the same

Fiction: Your reference lists contains texts that you have referred to directly in your work and your bibliography captures your wider reading.

There is only one way to reference

Fiction: There are many ways to reference, from the Harvard referencing system to footnotes. Your tutor will direct you to the format your references need to take.

Skills in practice

On placement, your understanding of evidence-based medicine will click into place. You will see how reading and research about the most up-to-date interventions feed directly into client care. On the one hand, you will be required to find information about a particular condition, for example, up-to-date research relating to a type of medication or treatment intervention. On the other hand, you will engage in a process of locating and accessing a range of information every time you receive a referral for a client. Seeing the direct relevance of this process can feel incredibly motivating. In spite of the very different context, the keys required to successfully researching information in practice are identical to those used in the classroom. The remainder of the chapter looks at the range of resources available on placement and ways to apply your skills to the placement setting in which you are working.

Identify the resources available

List all the resources and sources of information you imagine will be available on placement in the space below.

Reflect on the answers you have just provided for one second. Were you surprised by how many you listed? One of the first things that will strike you about placement is the range and variety of resources there. These will be particularly good if you are on placement in a teaching hospital. Medical libraries offer similar services to universities and the medical librarians will be on hand to offer support and training in finding and critiquing the literature. You will probably have access to electronic journals and online literature services, and your university may have an agreement with the Health or Social Care Trust that allows you to use loan facilities and take books out. The following mind map represents just some of the resources you may wish to tap into. Add to this with your own ideas.

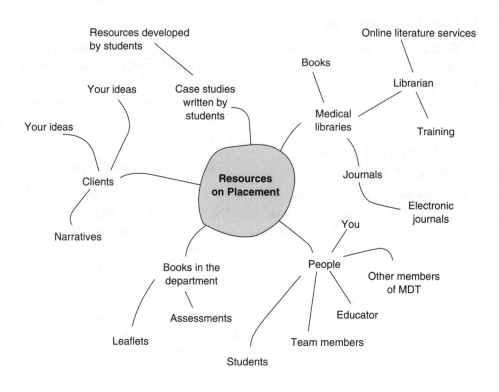

Decide what type of information you are looking for

The mind map includes resources you would expect to see, for example the learning centre and library, but you will also note that it has embraced a range of additional sources from clients through to carers and the results of assessments and medical tests. This is because every time you receive a referral you will engage in a research process. Being a health and social care professional is a bit like being a detective. You are presented with an array of information from a range of different sources and perspectives and your role is to piece this together in much the same way that you would a jigsaw puzzle. Your ultimate aim is not to solve a crime but to find a solution or approach that will meet the needs of the client. At times you will therefore need to make judgements about the reliability and importance of information, disregard some of the views or opinions you are presented with and identify further avenues or sources of evidence you might explore to complete the picture. Once you are clear about the range of resources available, the next stage in the process is to decide what type of information you are looking for. Use the table below to guide your thinking.

Type of information	Where you might find this
Medical facts: results of tests	Medical notes, consultant, radiographer
Cognitive functioning	Results of formal assessments (e.g. the mini-mental status examination or the Rivermead). You may also see references to levels of cognitive functioning in home visit reports, and notes made by staff on the ward
Mood and emotional well-being	From the client and/or their carer: results of formal assessments, i.e. Beck's depression inventory, Geriatric Depression Scale, observations made in notes by staff
Perceptions, views, opinions	The client, their family
The impact of the condition	The client and their family
Possible contra-indications for particular interventions	Medical records, previous admissions to hospital, drug cards/summaries
The person's home situation	The client, family members; if services are already in place, relevant members of the MDT (social worker, occupational therapist, home carer, district nurse)
Factors leading up to request for services	Letter from referring agent, client and family
Current level of functioning	The client, observations by family members, observations by staff (if the person is in hospital)

Clearly, the most important source of information is the client. You need to understand their perspective, views, priorities and goals. There may be times when these are difficult to ascertain. For example, if you are working with a person with complex communication needs who does not communicate verbally, or if you are working with children who may also have difficulty in articulating their experiences.

Moreover, there may be other information you require. Again, it is important to be clear about the type of information you are looking for in order to decide where to find it. Remember that you are bound by confidentiality, and if you wish to consult with a relative, then you must seek the client's permission first.

Find out where material is located and how to access it

Once you have identified the sources you need to consult, your next challenge is to find out how to access these sources. Here are a few starting points offered by students.

The first thing I do when I start a placement is to find out where the notes are kept. Our department notes are different from those kept on the ward and I always check out both. I like to begin the placement by reading through these and familiarising myself with patients I will be working with.

Make yourself a list of key team members and their contact numbers and keep this in your diary. If possible (and the placement allows) arrange a visit to these areas. This way you are clear about who plays what role and where/how to find them.

Note to self: check with the patient when it is convenient to see them and if anything has already been arranged. Not just medical things either. I remember dashing from one appointment to see a person to carry out a social work assessment and when I arrived on the ward she was with the hairdresser!

I start with the medical notes. I tend to focus on the notes concerning the present admission. Usually there is a quick summary, including previous medical history (PMH). If I'm not sure about something, I will read further back as necessary. If I'm looking for something very specific, I will go to this section of the notes. When I've been on placements with electronic records this is always much easier.

I always ask permission to speak to a family member and the person will usually let me know who, where and when. Staff on the ward are also very helpful in terms of who visits on what days. Information about next-of-kin can be found in the notes.

I use the referral to direct me to relevant personnel. There are usually details on here about other services the person is receiving.

Be selective

With such an array of information you will need to make clear decisions as to where you will concentrate your energies. Your focus will be determined by the *relevance* and *reliability* of the information, its *currency* and the *order* in which you will read this.

Currency

Although it may be useful to look at information relating to previous admissions, in the main, you will be looking for up-to-date information. One of the challenges of working in an acute setting is that things can change very quickly. For example, if a person has a condition which fluctuates, the results of an assessment undertaken just three weeks ago may give you a false and inaccurate impression. You therefore need to constantly check when the information was recorded and whether any changes have occurred.

Relevance and reliability

This is where your detective skills go into overdrive. It is not that anyone will deliberately set out to mislead you, but everyone will have their own agenda and perspective. Where inconsistencies arise, you will need to dig deeper, gathering information from a range of additional sources, undertaking further assessments and looking for clues in the notes in terms of other staff's perceptions and observations. Chapter 11 on reading for information provides more details.

Order

You will need to think about the order in which you carry out your research and reading. This is not as straightforward as it sounds – there are pros and cons no matter which way you do this. Reading sets of medical records and listening to the opinions of others will colour your view of the situation and present you with a perspective of the person that will influence how you relate to them. But this can help to direct your questions and provide you with a wider context in which to work. Then again, it could present you with a particular bias which will act as a filter and prevent you from getting to the real issues. In the same breath, you will need to be aware of any potential risks....

You will need to weigh up all these factors when deciding the order in which to undertake your research.

IN A NUTSHELL

Research can be challenging, exciting, illuminating and frustrating. Yet this ability to engage in the research process at university and on placement is a key skill that will underpin much of your practice. This chapter has briefly explored the skills and processes of undertaking this process, providing you with an overview. The trick now is to take these ideas and put them into practice. Above all, the chapter has highlighted that:

- High-quality research will underpin all that you do, whether in the classroom or on placement

- The secret to mastering the research process is to be clear what you are looking for, where to look and who to ask

- Time invested in familiarising yourself with the learning centre and library will save you time in the long run and make the research process less painful

- Be selective in terms of what you read. You don't have to read everything!

- If in doubt, ask!

References and signposts to further reading and resources

Chelten, S. (2000) *The Essential Guide to the Internet for Health Professionals*. London: Routledge.

Crombie, I. (2006) *Pocket Guide to Critical Appraisal*. London: BMJ Books.

Dawes, M., Summerskill, W., Glasziou, P., Cartabellotta, A., Martin, J., Hopayian, K., Porzsolt, F., Burls, A. and Osborne, J. (2005) 'Sicily statement on evidence-based practice', *BMC Medical Education*, 5 (1): 1186–93.

(Continued)

(Continued)

Evans, D. (2002) 'Database searches for qualitative research', *Journal of the Medical Library Association*, 90: 290–3.

Fink, A. (2005) *Conducting Research Literature Reviews*. Thousand Oaks, CA: Sage.

Giustini, D. (2005) 'How Google is changing medicine', *British Medical Journal*, 331: 1487–8.

Maslin-Prothero, S. (2005) *Baillieres Study Skills for Nurses and Midwives* (3rd edition). Edinburgh: Elsevier.

Polit, D.F. and Beck, C. (2005) *Essentials of Nursing Research*. Baltimore, MD: Lippincott, Williams and Wilkins.

Tang, H. and Hwee Kwoon Ng, J. (2006) 'Googling for a diagnosis – use of Google as a diagnostic aid: internet-based study', *British Medical Journal*, 333: 1143–5.

11 Reading for information

JARGON-BUSTING

Glossary: A mini-dictionary containing specialist terminology or unfamiliar words.

Reflective reading: A more thoughtful and considered reading process, where you think about and question the text.

Scanning: An approach to reading where, rather than reading every word, you look for key words relating to specific information.

Skimming: An approach to reading where, rather than reading every word, you skim through the text to gain the gist of what it says.

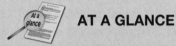 ## AT A GLANCE

This chapter is for you if

- You find that it takes you a long time to read even a short piece of information

- You find that as you read your mind drifts

- You struggle to understand what something is saying

- You get lost in the 'detail' of the text

- You feel compelled to read every single word of a book, article or set of notes

- You often feel overwhelmed by the amount of information you have to read

- You spend a great deal of time reading but find it impossible to remember what you have read

Reading is a dangerous occupation. It can change how you see things and how you feel. It can challenge you to think and to behave differently and equip you with new information and skills, which, if you choose to act on them, can change the lives of others. Reading is a core skill that is fundamental to your development as a student and as a clinician. Case notes, reports, notes, journal articles, textbooks are all presented in written form and your success as a student and practitioner will be dependent on your ability to comprehend what is written, make judgements about the reliability of the source and extract relevant information.

However, in this digital society, where information is readily available in multi-media form, we can easily lose the art of reading. In my own experience as a tutor, even when I provide the information my students require to pass their course, many do not engage with the text and uncover the treasure it holds.

The problem is that in order to read well you must engage with and interact with the information. Reading an academic text or a set of clinical notes requires very different skills from those you use when reading for pleasure. It is not enough to passively let the information wash over you. You need to direct your focus, locate where the information is contained so that you can read as widely and as quickly on the subject as possible. You must interrogate the text, make judgements about how trustworthy it is and integrate the information into what you already know and understand. This approach requires lots of discipline and accuracy. However, if you can develop these skills, you will be able to assimilate information more easily and use your time more effectively.

STARTING POINTS

So what type of things are you reading at the present? Are you aware of how you use different techniques depending on what you read? Are you reading enough? To find the answer to all these questions and more, try the following quizzes to gain a snapshot of your reading profile.

1   Read the following list of texts. Circle all those you have read over the last three weeks.

Category A – Novels, autobiographies, magazines, comics, letters, emails from friends, entries on Facebook, newspapers, jokes.

Category B – Manual, bus/train/academic timetable, knitting pattern, flat-pack instructions, instructions for a game, telephone directory, television listings, bank statements, recipes.

Category C – Reference book, anatomy textbook, piece of legislation, book review, journal article, demographic data, academic papers, policy documents, medical dictionary.

If you answered mainly A, this is a good start. It is clear from your responses that you enjoy reading and that this is a pleasurable activity. As you go through university you will realise that the reading you do for assignments is very different. Rather than savouring every word and focusing on enjoying the actual process, you will tend to read with a purpose in mind, the aim being to extract information quite quickly.

If you answered mainly B, you are certainly not a stranger to reading for information. The good news is that you will be used to looking for key words, using an index and contents page, skimming the text and picking out relevant information. These texts are all examples of factual information so although you are engaging with what you read, there is not a need to think too closely about what you are reading and questioning how reliable it is. This is something you will begin to develop at university.

If you answered mainly C, you have either been studying on a course, are a born academic, or have too much time on your hands. These are the kinds of text that you will be using at university. For the slightly more factual sources (anatomy textbook and medical dictionary), you will be looking for specific information that you will largely take at face value. However, for the other types of reading you will need to engage with the text, read this with a critical eye and ask: how reliable is this information? What is good/poor about this line of argument? Oh, and remember that it is nice to read books for pleasure too.

2   Book worm or book squirm: How do you score on the reading thermometer?

The more you read, the easier it will be to concentrate and the more confident you will feel when finding your way around unfamiliar texts. Record on the following line how many different texts you have read over the last week (include everything you read) and check out whether you are a book worm or a book squirm.

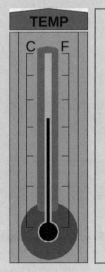

5 +
Clear
bookworm

2–5
Definite
bookworm
tendencies

0–1
Book squirm

(Continued)

(Continued)

3   Reading: true or false?

Many myths about reading exist. Decide which of the following statements are true and which are false. Answers can be found on page 150.

Statement	True	False
If you read every word, you will remember more information		
How you read depends on the reason why you are reading and the type of information you are reading		
Pictures can help you to remember information		
At university, it is important to read all the books on the reading list		
When reading, it is important to recognise the source of information and to determine its reliability		
Different texts have different ways of setting out information		

4   Finally, make a list of everything you have read. Jot down any 'techniques' you use when reading (e.g. looking for key words, skimming the text) and note anything you notice about your motivation for reading and your ability to recall information.

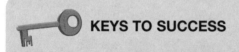 **KEYS TO SUCCESS**

Five keys can help to unlock your potential and enable you to gain the most from your reading. These are:

- Be clear about the purpose of your reading
- Be aware of the range of techniques you can use to get the most out of information
- Understand how information is organised within a text
- Make reading an active process
- Make reading a critical process

Be clear about the purpose of your reading

It is a common myth that we read all texts in the same way. This is not the case. The way you read depends on the nature of the information and the purpose of your reading. Take, for instance, the difference between reading a novel and reading a bus timetable or a manual. When reading for pleasure you will be soaking up each word, savouring the moment and reading the book sequentially from beginning to end. Compare this with how you read a manual. Here you are looking for specific information, scanning the text using clues (titles, indexes, contents), dipping in and out of particular chapters (possibly with a wrench, screwdriver or spanner in your hand). Clearly, the two are very different.

When you are at university you will rarely read a book from beginning to end. You will not have the time to do this. Imagine trying to get through 18 books on the reading list – you would be either completely overwhelmed or totally bored, given that you could not possibly digest and remember everything. Reading in an unfocused way also makes you very passive. Going through the motions, reading the words, is not the same as understanding what you read or reading critically.

Before you read any text, therefore, you need to be clear about exactly why you are reading. Is it to:

- Gain an overview of the subject area?

- Weigh up the information?

- Answer a specific question as part of an assignment?

Be aware of the range of techniques you can use to get the most out of information

Happily, a range of simple techniques exist to help you gain exactly what you hope to from your reading. Here is a summary of the main ones you can try.

Gaining an overview: receptive reading

Purpose: To orientate you to the main themes of the subject area.
When: At the beginning of a module when you need to grasp the main issues.
How: Find a basic text and read at a steady pace. Do not worry about remembering everything or getting bogged down in questioning.
Where: Anywhere. This is the type of reading you can do while travelling on a train or bus or eating lunch.
Concentration rating: Low

Weighing up the information: reflective reading

Purpose: To critically examine a text and make decisions in relation to the arguments it contains.
When: Once you are familiar with the core concepts of a subject and want to position yourself in relation to the arguments in the literature.

How: Read the text with a series of questions in mind. For example, 'Do I agree with this? How does this relate to other concepts? Does this make sense in light of what I already know? What is the evidence? How trustworthy is this?

Where: Somewhere you can concentrate. When reading reflectively you need to take frequent breaks and make sure that you have a pen and a notebook at hand so you can jot down your thinking.

Concentration rating: High

Focused reading: reading with a question in mind

Purpose: To ruthlessly extract information from a text.

When: Usually for a specific purpose, for example when researching an essay question or preparing for a presentation or assignment.

How: Use the contents page and index to direct your reading. Scan pages for key names or words, skipping over irrelevant material (no matter how interesting). Use the technique of skimming to gain the gist of what is being said before deciding whether you should read this in more detail.

Where: This technique requires you to focus, focus, focus. A quiet environment is essential.

Concentration rating: Very high

Understand how information is organised within a text

When reading reflectively or with a question in mind you can save yourself a great deal of time and energy if you understand how information is organised within a text. Different types of reading material are set out in different ways but all texts contain certain short-cuts or signposts which can help you to locate information quickly. You are probably already familiar with many of these. Try the following two-minute quiz to test your understanding. Simply draw lines between the term and its definition (answers can be found at the end).

1. Introduction

    (a)   Contains the topic sentence, a clear indicator of what the paragraph is about. Read this to decide if you want to read the paragraph.

2. Index

    (b)   A mini-dictionary of all the unfamiliar words. Useful if there is lots of unfamiliar terminology.

3. Chapter heading

    (c)   Sums up or condenses the main points of what you have read.

4. Conclusion

    (d)   An alphabetical listing of subject matter found at the back of the book. Good if you know the subject area you want to look at. Saves you reading the whole book.

5. First lines	(e)	Found at the beginning of a book or a chapter. Provides an overview of what it contains. Can help you to decide whether you need to read any further.
6. Glossary	(f)	A list of chapters at the beginning of a text.
7. Contents page	(g)	Presents information in a grid format. Can help you to see information quite quickly.
8. Table	(h)	A title. Handy to indicate what the chapter is about.

Answers to the quiz: 1e, 2d, 3h, 4c, 5a, 6b, 7f, 8g

Focusing in: reading a journal article

You may be familiar with many of the features of textbooks. However, during your course, you will increasingly refer to a range of different types of reading material with additional signposts. A key resource will be the professional journal.

Most professional bodies publish a regular journal. These journals contain current, up-to-date information and research relating to the profession. The advantage of journal articles is that they are peer-reviewed. This means that before they are published, they have undergone rigorous examination by a range of highly regarded professionals who are experts in the field. Often, information contained in the most recent articles is more up to date than that contained in textbooks as the time taken between writing a textbook and the date of publication can be considerable. It is therefore useful to spend a few moments considering how information is organised within these. Each journal will be slightly different but generally speaking most will contain the following features.

The abstract (short written piece either above or below the title)
This provides a summary of the entire article. A quick read of this will help you decide whether the article is relevant or not.

The introduction
This sets the scene and places the article in context. It will probably define key terms and if it is a research article, it will define the research question. Reading the introduction will provide an instant picture of what the article is about.

Literature review
This looks at the breadth of literature relating to the themes in the article. It may demonstrate holes in previous studies. If you are looking for a wider body of knowledge relating to a topic, then the literature review may indicate articles to explore further.

Method
If the article focuses on research, the method describes how the study was carried out, who participated and which approach the study adopted. This can help you to decide how rigorous or trustworthy the article is.

Findings

Again, in the research article the findings summarise the results of the study and what happened. This may be arranged according to sub-themes.

Discussion

The discussion talks about the findings in relation to the wider literature. The author will probably highlight the limitations of the study at this point.

Conclusion

This summarises what has been said, extracting 'the essence' of what it was about.

References

The references contain the body of literature that the author has used. These provide a really useful starting point for future research and avenues you might explore if you wish to extend your reading.

Make reading an active process

We touched on this briefly at an earlier point in the chapter and the importance of reading with a specific question or purpose in mind. Here are two other methods that can help you to actively engage with the text. The first can be used when making notes and is called the SQ3R technique. It consists of a number of simple steps (adapted from Price and Maier, 2007).

Survey the text

Skim the text to identify whether it is relevant and to help you decide where to focus your energies. Use what you know of the layout to guide you.

For journal articles, use the abstract, introduction and conclusion to direct your reading.

For books, use indexes, contents pages, chapter titles, tables and charts.

Question

Ask yourself 'Why am I reading this? What specifically do I hope to find out? Develop a question to give your reading a focus.

Read

Spend time reading the information. There is no need to make notes at this point.

Recall

Close the text or put the journal article to one side and summarise your reading, making a note of the main points. Write this in your own words.

Review

Revisit the text, checking this against your notes, ensuring that you have understood the ideas and have answered your question.

Compare this with a second method: goal-focused reading (adapted from Cottrell, 2008). Once again, it follows a series of stages:

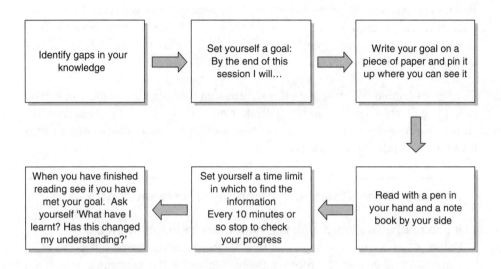

Make reading a critical process

The final step takes you from master to grandmaster in the reading stakes. By now you should feel comfortable in understanding how you might approach a range of different texts and ways to navigate around these so that you can focus your efforts and extract what you need from them. The final stage in the process is to subject the text to rigorous questioning so that you can make sound judgements about the reliability of what you read.

There are a number of tools and techniques you can draw on to help you read more critically. Imagine these on a continuum. At one end you will find the heavyweight critical appraisal tools which can help you to critique research articles. At the other end are checklists with questions as prompts. At this point it would be useful to review Chapter 10 on researching information and revisit the ideas, looking at the currency and relevance of information. However, for a quick overview, use the following abbreviated checklist. As you read decide whether the information is:

Relevant: Is the information relevant to the area you are studying? Does it relate to a specific population or nationality, and can what is written be easily generalised to your current area of study or practice? (For example, an American edition of a text may contain subtle differences that would not translate easily to a UK health or social care context.)
Reasoned: Is the argument well reasoned? Do the conclusions reflect the line of reasoning?
Reliable: Is the source reliable? Is the author established in the field? Is she/he well respected? Is there a hidden agenda behind the work? Some form of bias?

Reviewed: Has the information been through a process of rigorous review and testing (as in a peer-reviewed journal, as opposed to some internet sites which are unsolicited)?
Researched: Are the arguments made by the author supported by evidence?
Referenced: Are sources of evidence referred to appropriately referenced?
Recent: When was the information published? Are the ideas still current or out of date?
Readable: Is the work well written and engaging? Is it easy to follow? Is key terminology explained?

The key to gaining the most from this information is to interact with the text. The techniques described in this chapter will take time to develop, but once mastered will ensure that you are well placed to become a critical reader who is able to gain breadth and depth of understanding.

Answers to the 'Reading: true or false?' quiz on page 144

If you read every word, you will remember more information
False: You can remember just as much information by gaining the gist of something as you will be more actively involved in the process.

How you read depends on the reason why you are reading and the type of information you are reading

True: This chapter provides lots of examples of this. The way you read a novel will be very different from how you read a manual.

Pictures can help you to remember information

True: Pictures can act as a prompt in visual memory and help to illustrate the content of what you are reading.

At university, it is important to read all the books on the reading list

False: Perhaps in an ideal world where you have hours of time to do this. However, in reality, the reading list should 'guide your reading'. Also there is a danger that if you read absolutely everything you will reach information overload.

When reading, it is important to recognise the source of information and to determine its reliability

True: You need to make clear decisions as to whether you are able to trust what you read and this may help you to decide whether to read it or not.

Different texts have different ways of setting out information

True: This is particularly true of books and journals which are set out in a very specific way. This chapter provides examples of ways to read a journal article.

Skills in practice

All the reading techniques described in this chapter will be invaluable in practice. Once on placement, you will need to read quickly and accurately, extracting key information relating to clients. Failure to do so can have huge implications. Imagine reading a case file in preparation to undertake a cooking assessment and failing to register that the person is allergic to a particular type of food. The remainder of this chapter looks at how you can translate the steps to successful reading into placement settings. It describes how to find your way around clinical notes and ways to understand some of the abbreviations you may encounter, before looking at how to test the reliability of what you read.

Be clear about the purpose of your reading

On placement you will read predominantly in order to obtain information. This might relate to a client's:

- Past medical history: previous admissions, diagnoses and interventions

- Details of the presenting problem

- Background information relating to home circumstances, social networks and services

- Medical information: pre-existing conditions, allergies, contra-indications to particular treatments, lists of current medication

- Results of assessments or tests

- Current behaviour and mood, recent incidents that could impact on treatment

The interesting thing is that two professionals can read exactly the same set of client notes for completely different reasons/purposes. Here is an illustration from practice.

Rozena is in the second year of a mental health nursing degree course. She is currently on placement and has been asked by her placement educator to see a client for the first time. Her educator has suggested that she should read through the case notes to gain some background information.

Paul is in the first year of his physiotherapy course. He has been asked to see the same client but with a view to focusing on her mobility needs. He has met the client before and has already spent some time with her.

Activity

List some of the questions Paul and Rozena may wish to consider in order to get the most from their reading.

Rozena and Paul will be reading with very different purposes in mind. Rozena has been asked to gain an overview of the client's history. She will probably need to look through most of the case notes for information about the person's:

- Past medical history: previous admissions, diagnoses and interventions the client has received. This may inform the current treatment approach adopted.

- Presenting problem: she will need to understand the circumstances that led to the person being referred to the service.

- Background information: who does the client live with? Does she have any dependents, or are there others involved who look after her needs? This may highlight possible support networks which can be drawn on in the future. Does the client work or is she unemployed or retired?

- Other services they receive: again, this will provide valuable information regarding potential resources Rozena can tap into.

- Medical information: for example, it might be important to know about medical conditions such as diabetes, epilepsy or heart conditions. Equally, Rozena will need to find out any current medication the person is taking and potential side effects or food that these may react with.

- Current behaviour and mood on the ward.

Compare this to Paul's focus. Paul, or his placement educator, has probably already undertaken this background reading. Paul is reading the notes with a very specific question in mind. He will probably focus on nursing notes recorded over the last few days, seeking out references about how the client has managed transfers between bed and chair and any comments made in terms of how she is mobilising around the ward. He will probably also want to review any medication as he will need to know if the tablets have any side-effects in terms of lowering blood-pressure, causing dizziness or impacting on perception. All these may have a potential effect on mobility.

This illustration highlights the importance of being clear about the purpose of your reading before you even pick up a set of client notes.

Be aware of the range of techniques you can use to get the most out of information

Once you are clear about what you are looking for, you can use the same reading techniques previously described. Skimming and scanning are particularly helpful. If we return to the example of Paul, this is what he reads in the notes.

Settled morning. **Atenolol** *administered as per b/d. No diurnal variation present. Struggled when* **mobilising** *between bed and chair. Stated that she felt* **dizzy** *and* **light-headed***. Supported to lay down. Good appetite. Three cups of tea, four biscuits. Nurse spoke with Mrs A as BNO now for three days. Some concerns regarding this. C/o feeling bloated. Would not accept enema* *but agreed to begin treatment on lactulose o.d.* **Independently walked** *between ward and kitchen area. Did rely on tables to* **support mobilisation***. Asked whether she could have a* **frame***. Explained that she had been referred to* **physiotherapist** *who is planning to see her this p.m.*

Paul will use the technique of scanning, looking for key words. These are highlighted in bold. Some words will relate to physiotherapy terminology: mobilising, frame, movement, mobilisation, walking. Others will relate to factors impacting on mobility: dizzy, lightheaded, Atenolol. He will focus in on sections of the notes that make reference to this. He will probably also skim the text in order to gain a gist of what is being said before deciding whether it is worth reading in more detail. In selecting the appropriate technique and reading with a question in mind, he will save himself valuable time and energy. The additional challenge he must face is how to read the abbreviations. We will return to this at the end of the chapter.

Understand how information is organised within a text

The next step to successfully reading information on placement is to have a basic understanding of where information is located. Just as books and journal articles are organised in a particular way, clinical notes also have a set format. Understanding this will enable you to go directly to the relevant section. Different settings will have their own system. Here are some you may encounter:

- Many notes are arranged so that the most recent information is at the front of the case file and not at the back.

- Some sets of notes will have sections at the back of the medical notes that relate to specific professions, such as physiotherapy, radiography, occupational therapy, social work and speech and language therapy. These may be colour-coded so that occupational therapy notes are often on green paper and physiotherapy notes on blue.

- With the advent of the single assessment process, some hospitals have moved towards a system whereby every member of the multidisciplinary team records their entries in the medical notes in chronological order.

The key, then, is to find out as much as you can about how this information is organised and the most efficient way to access it. If you can do this at an early point, you will save yourself a great deal of time and energy.

Make reading an active process

When you are on placement or in clinical practice, most of your reading will relate directly to client care. It is likely, therefore, that you will approach written information with a purpose in mind and engage with the material in order to actively seek specific information. Many students find it helpful to use written questions to act as a prompt to guide their reading and to read with a pen or pencil in one hand and a note book in the other so that they can record information as they go along.

Make reading a critical process

Reading on placement is just as much a critical process as reading in the classroom and you still need to ask questions regarding the reliability of this information, particularly when it contradicts what you already know about an individual. The chapter on researching information highlighted this. Let's look at examples of this. Consider the following: an older person has been admitted to the ward following a fire in the warden-controlled flat where she lives. The warden has provided the following account:

When I arrived at the flat Mrs Andrews was extremely confused. The kitchen was filled with smoke and she was insisting that it was not her fault. I have had grave concerns regarding her safety for some time. She is a danger to herself and others and could in the future burn the entire complex down. She is very confused and it is difficult to speak to her. I believe that she is a real risk and danger to others who live there. She needs to be re-housed somewhere else. Otherwise I cannot be held responsible for the horror of what might happen next. I have a long waiting list of other people who would like to be in that flat and I believe that someone else should be given a chance as she really is too poorly to be there.

What is your response? Would you take these concerns at face value? If not, why not? Could there be a hidden agenda?

In much the same way that you would check the reliability of a piece of literature, you would also seek to substantiate the facts using other sources of information. In this case, the first person to speak with would be Mrs Andrews. You might also consult with staff observing Mrs Andrews on the ward, and look at the results of assessments, such as the mini-mental state examination, and at reports from emergency services who will have checked for electrical malfunction. This is an extreme example but illustrates the importance of always seeing the 'fuller picture' before jumping to conclusions after reading one piece of isolated information. More is said about this in Chapter 14 on thinking as a skill.

Finally: Making sense of abbreviations

Using abbreviations is not good practice and is not to be recommended. However, reading medical notes can sometimes feel like reading a secret code. You will quickly see that there is an entirely different level of reading, which includes medical language and abbreviations. The following are just a few of the abbreviations recognised by the Royal College of General Practitioners (www.rcgp.org.uk).

(a) BP	(i) 0	(q) c/o or co
(b) +/–	(j) +++	(r) MI
(c) CNS	(k) FH	(s) Ix
(d) COAD	(l) HNPU	(t) BOR
(e) b/d	(m) BNO	(u) Ca
(f) CXR	(n) FROM	(v) od
(g) D&V	(o) COPD	
(h) DNA	(p) Hx	

See if you can match the abbreviation with its full medical term. The answers can be found on page 156.

1	Not present: no abnormality	12	Chest x-ray
2	Uncertain	13	Diarrhoea and vomiting
3	Present in excess	14	Did not attend
4	Bowels not opened	15	Family history
5	Bowels opened regularly	16	Full range of movement
6	Blood pressure	17	Has not passed urine
7	Cancer	18	History
8	Central nervous system	19	Investigations
9	Complains of	20	Myocardial infarction
10	Chronic obstructive airways disease	21	Twice a day
11	Chronic obstructive pulmonary disease	22	Once a day

IN A NUTSHELL

This chapter has described a range of simple techniques to help you gain the most from your reading. The website that accompanies this book (www.skills4health.co.uk) offers a number of additional tips, including how to improve your reading speed. Remember the key to successful reading hinges on the following pointers:

- Always read with a purpose or question in mind
- Spend time finding your way around the text so that you understand how the information is organised
- Make use of shortcuts
- Be active
- Get critical

References and signposts to further reading and resources

Buzan, T. (2006) *Speed Reading: Accelerate Your Speed and Understanding for Success* (3rd edition). Harlow: BBC Active.

Cook, L.K. and Mayer, R.E. (1988) 'Teaching readers about the structure of a scientific text', *Journal of Educational Psychology*, 80: 448–56.

Cottrell, S. (2008) *The Study Skills Handbook* (3rd edition). Basingstoke: Palgrave Macmillan.

Greenhalgh, T. and Taylor, R. (2001) How To Read a Paper: The Basics of Evidence-based Medicine. London: BMJ Books.

Price, G. and Maier, P. (2007) *Effective Study Skills*. Harlow: Pearson.

Riegelman, R.K. and Hirsch, R.P. (1996) Studying a Study and Testing a Test: How To Read the Health and Science Literature. Boston: Little Brown.

Royal College of General Practitioners: www.rcgp.org.uk (accessed 08/06/09).

Wade, S.E. and Reynolds, R.E. (1989) 'Developing a metacognitive awareness', *Journal of Reading*, 33(1): 6–14.

Answers to abbreviation quiz on page 155: 1i, 2b, 3j, 4m, 5t, 6a, 7u, 8c, 9q, 10d, 11o, 12f, 13g, 14h, 15k, 16n, 17l, 18p, 19s, 20r, 21e, 22v.

12 Recording ideas and information

JARGON-BUSTING

Care record: A collection of material relating to a client's care provision.

Flow charts: A way of presenting information sequentially.

Linear notes: Notes presented using bullet points or numbered lists.

Mind map: A technique which represents information in words and pictures.

Professional standards: A set of agreed practices set down by a professional body.

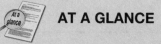 ## AT A GLANCE

This chapter is for you if

- You tend to write down everything you hear or read

- Your notes comprise photocopies where every other line is highlighted with a marker pen

- You start off with good intentions but soon feel overwhelmed by the detail and amount of information, become bored and give up

- You tend to copy out chunks of text and rarely write things in your own words

- On clinical placement you find it difficult to know what to record and how to write it

- You struggle to use or organise your notes

It would be impossible and probably quite undesirable to remember everything that you heard, observed or read. To begin with, you would need a brain the size of an elephant. Then there is the question of what you would do with the information and how you would decide what is important so that you could relay this to others.

Making notes is a way of processing information and filtering out what is unnecessary in order to present relevant facts and figures in a useful and usable format. While the notes you make represent a record of your reading, listening and observations, they also reflect a broader process of active engagement with information, an ability to make links, prioritise and order this into a coherent picture for your reference or to communicate to others. Effective note-making requires you to select information based on its relevance to the subject or situation and to record this in a format that reflects the purpose of the notes.

In clinical practice, notes take on an extra dimension. Here they act as a means of communicating key observations and information to a wider audience. The notes you record in relation to a patient constitute a legal record and if a treatment or intervention is disputed, they can form your defence in a court of law.

This chapter looks at note-making as a vehicle for processing information and organising your thinking. It begins by exploring the principles of taking and making notes from your reading and in the classroom, and considers a range of different methods you can use. It then takes these principles and looks at how they are applied within a clinical context, first, with reference to ways of extracting information from case notes and, secondly, in terms of recording your intervention.

STARTING POINTS

Try this exercise to decide whether you are a note-making novice or know-all. Tick the sentences that relate to you:

1. When it comes to note-making, I believe that more is better and that most is best.
2. I begin with good intentions, tend to record lots of detail, feel overwhelmed and give up.
3. When I start making notes, I have a series of fixed questions in my head.
4. I write down everything my lecturer says. After all, they are the experts.
5. As soon as the lecture is over I close my file and then do not look at the information again until it is time to write the essay or prepare for an exam.
6. 'Just in case' is my motto.
7. My filing system is a carrier bag.

8.   I studied a range of ways to make notes so that I can use what works best for me.
9.   I make notes from every book on the reading list.

Filtering information

If you ticked statements 1, 4, 6 or 9, oh dear! The chances are you have huge biceps from carrying your bulging files around with you. You need to remember that notes are just, well, notes. They are a condensed version of what you have heard or read. If you record too much information, you risk losing the main thrust of the argument among the detail.

Making vast quantities of notes can indicate that you find it difficult to make choices about what is relevant or irrelevant, or it can be an indication that you have not understood what you have read and are trying to hedge your bets by writing everything down. Try focusing your reading with a question in mind and when you do make notes write these in your own words. This will help you to check that you have understood what you have read.

Structuring information

If you ticked statements 2, 4 or 6, it sounds as though you know the theory of note-making but find this hard to put into practice. You may have set yourself unrealistic goals, be trying to study for too long, or you may be reading without a specific question in mind. The secret here is not to put yourself under too much pressure. Simply record the name of the book and its reference and write a brief summary of the overall theme, ideas, topic area that it covers. As you gain more of a sense of the topic you will be able to revisit the literature in order to direct your reading and note-making.

Organising information

If you ticked statements 5 or 7, you have made a classic mistake, believing that making the notes is the end of the story. Yet there is little point in taking detailed notes if you cannot find them again. A few moments invested at the end of a lecture re-reading your notes to make sure you understand them before filing them away will save you time in the long run. Better still, write a short summary to consolidate your thinking. This chapter offers ideas on ways of organising your notes so that you can move beyond the carrier bag and gain some kind of order.

Finally, if you ticked statements 3 or 8, you are definitely thinking along the right lines. Reading with a question in mind enables you to focus your thinking and actively engage in the note-making process. As you try different ways of recording information, you will find the method that works for you.

KEYS TO SUCCESS

The key to successful note-making is based around the following steps:

- Be clear about what you need to record
- Record information in a way that reflects the purpose it will serve
- Record information clearly and legibly so that it can be understood
- Record this information in a timely fashion
- Organise and file your information so that it can be easily accessed

A good set of notes should be like a conversation: a two-way process, memorable, easy to understand, not laboured, and with lots of opportunity to make connections. it should be something you want to return to again and again.

Be clear about what you need to record

The first stage of the note-making process is to decide what information to record. The quantity and detail of the information you note down will depend on the purpose of the lecture or workshop, the topic area and your familiarity with the subject matter.

Before you begin to take notes, ask yourself the following questions. Is the purpose of your note-taking to:

(a) Gain an overview of the subject area?

(b) Consolidate your thinking?

(c) To answer a specific question, for instance in response to assignment or essay question?

(d) For the purposes of revision?

(e) A combination of the above?

Jot down the answers to the following questions on a sheet of paper:

(a) What do I understand about the subject area?

(b) What do I need to clarify?

(c) What do I need to find out?

Then keep this sheet of paper close to you as you read or listen for information. Every few minutes, glance at the sheet and ask yourself whether you are still focused and answering the question. This will help you to keep on track. If you are less familiar with the information you need to record, the SQ3R technique described in Chapter 11 can be useful.

Making notes from lectures or in class

You may be reading this chapter thinking 'That's all well and good for making notes from books when you can see the information in front of you, but that doesn't help me when I'm trying to make notes in class'. Making notes from lectures requires a different set of skills. The following can help you to decide what to record.

Before the lecture

Many tutors make their lecture slides accessible online beforehand. Print these off as handouts (three on a page). This will leave you with the space to record supplementary information and allow you to focus on the content of what you hear instead of frantically scribbling down what is on the slides.

Make a glossary of words or phrases that you are unfamiliar with and take these into the lecture for reference. There is nothing worse than trying to get to grips with new information when you are unfamiliar with some of the technical terms associated with the subject area.

Finally, spend time noting the 'shape of the lecture' and the areas it covers. This will help you to mentally prepare, and will help you to decide the main themes around which to structure your notes.

During the lecture

Listen for the verbal signposts and use these to direct your note-taking. Lecturers should tell you what they are going to tell you at the beginning of the lecture, tell you again in the main body of the presentation, and then tell you what they have told you in the summary at the end.

Learn to 'read' lecture slides. Key points can be identified from the titles of slides or acetates, with supporting detail included in the bullet points.

Make a note of the key points the lecturer emphasises. Again, listen out for clues: 'So, to recap…', 'Let me emphasise…', 'Of central importance…'. Such phrases indicate that the information is noteworthy.

Record information in a way that reflects the purpose it will serve

Once you have decided what you need to record you need to decide how to record it, taking into account the nature of the information and the audience for whom it is intended. A common misconception is that all notes look the same and that one format suits all situations. This is far from the case. The way you record information depends on:

- *Your personal preferences and learning style*. Are you someone who remembers things by visualising information? Do you find it easier to remember ordered facts or do patterns and pictures help you to recall information and make sense of key ideas? Do you prefer to type your notes directly on to a computer or write them in longhand?

- *The type of information you are recording*. For instance, are you recording a process (flow chart), anatomical features (diagrams), or strengths and limitations of an approach (category chart)?

- *How you obtain the information*. Some methods of note-making are better suited to recording information through listening to ideas, as in a lecture or in class, while other methods sit well with recording information from reading.

- *The reason why you are taking notes*. Will your notes be used for the purpose of revision (notes on small cards offer a portable record) or to provide an overview of the subject area (mind maps can help you make connections between ideas)?

- *Past experience*. Do you prefer to type your notes directly on to a computer or write them out in longhand?

Types of note/note-taking techniques

Notes tend to be described by the shape they adopt.

Linear notes

Linear notes are highly structured using main headings and bulleted or numbered lists. You may already be familiar with this format of recording information.

1   Heading

   (a)   Main idea

      (i)   Supporting detail
      (ii) Supporting detail

   (b)   Main idea

      (i)   Supporting detail

For example:

Strengths and limitations

(a) Advantages

      (i)   Provides a good structure: clear and easy to read
      (ii) Easy to use: helps you to find information at a glance

(b) *Drawbacks*

(i) Can be quite rigid
(ii) Not useful if you need to make connections between ideas or link information

Mind maps

Mind maps, on the other hand, offer a much freer visual structure for presenting ideas and concepts (Buzan, 2006). The great strength of this form of note-taking is that it offers you a way of recording an overview of a topic or subject areas and a way to make links between the different pieces of information. Using a mind map is an incredibly creative process and can help to free up your thinking, making learning fun. Because information can be represented in written, pictoral and symbolic forms, you will draw on different parts of your brain and this can help you to revisit information and see it from different perspectives.

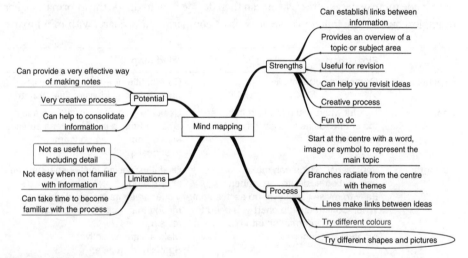

Flow charts

Sometimes it can be important to remember the *sequence* as well as the *content* of information, for example when looking at a clinical process or stages of thinking or reasoning. If this is the case, then a flow chart can be extremely useful.

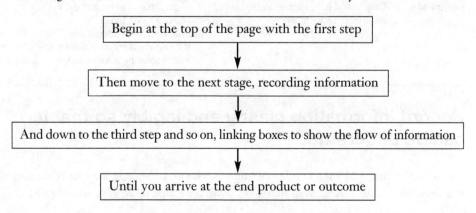

Recording information in this way reinforces the sequence, making it easier to recall.

A less conventional way to record information that has a certain shape or flow is to create a cartoon strip.

Diagrams

A picture can speak a thousand words, particularly if you are studying anatomy and physiology where it is also necessary to understand and recall the location and relationship between structures. Diagrams give a three-dimensional quality to information and can help you to remember complex details.

Category charts

Category charts are helpful if you need to compare different types of information, for instance when looking for similarities or differences in approaches to treatment or models of practice. These are also useful when planning comparative assignments. It is often easier to construct a category chart once you are familiar with the topic area and have made more general notes, as you can then decide how to divide the information. For example, consider the following category chart comparing flow charts with mind maps.

	Flow chart	Mind map
Organisation	Organised sequentially.	Central title or image in centre of page, links and ideas radiate from this.
Use	Helpful when you need to remember the sequence as well as the content of information.	Useful to gain an overview of a subject area and make links between subject areas. Focus is on conceptual relationships.
Strengths	Very visual, which can make information easier to remember. Easy to revise (just cover up each stage). When constructing a chart you need to break down information into manageable 'chunks'.	Useful for seeing relationship between information. Visual presentation of information means that it can be helpful when revising. Makes learning active. Spatially attractive. Helps you to make links between different subject or topic areas. A range of software is available to enable you to create mind maps on the computer.
Limitations	Only useful for information that is organised sequentially.	More difficult to record detail. More difficult to use when you are unfamiliar with a topic area. If it is necessary to include more information than expected, this can become messy.

Record information clearly and legibly so that it can be understood

You would be amazed by the number of students who make copious notes and then find that they are unable to read what they have written because of illegible handwriting or impossible abbreviations. If you use abbreviations, write yourself a small key somewhere in your notes and if your handwriting is illegible, then type your notes into your computer. Although this is time-consuming, it is better to create a shorter set of word-processed notes that you can read instead of reams of handwritten notes that you struggle to understand. The other useful tip here is to always write your notes in your own words. This will make sure that you are clear about what you have read or heard. You can also add your own spontaneous thoughts and links if you become familiar with engaging with information like this.

Record this information in a timely fashion

This relates particularly to the notes you make during lectures. Following the session, spend a few minutes reading through your notes, checking that you understand what you have written and adding any additional comments you may have forgotten. If you do this quickly, while the information is fresh in your mind, you will have a clearer memory of what you heard and create a more accurate and comprehensive set of notes.

Organise and file your information so that it can be easily accessed

Completing and reviewing a set of notes based on a topic area is not the end of the story. The most beautifully written notes are of little use if you are then unable to access these. When thinking about ways of organising your notes you need to consider two factors:

1   Before you even begin to put pen to paper you need to think where you will record the notes.

2   Once you have completed your notes, you need to spend time considering how you will organise and store these.

Where to record notes

This will largely depend on the purpose of the notes and the systems you have in place.

For essays or general assignments, it is probably helpful to record your notes on A4 sheets of file paper which you can then organise in a lever arch file. The advantage of this is that it is relatively easy to integrate additional information, such as handouts from lectures, workshops and your own reading. This degree of flexibility ensures that you can organise your notes in a logical order, making them easier to use. Separate the different topic areas using dividers and store different modules or different subject areas in different folders. A key or contents page at the beginning of the folder can make the process of locating information easier.

If, on the other hand, you are making notes for revision or exams, it is a good idea to record these on small cards. Write the question or area of study on one side and the answer or the information relating to this area on the other. The advantage of recording notes in this way is that they are easy to carry with you and you can use any 'pockets' of time to memorise the information contained on them.

If you record notes directly on to your computer, you need to spend time deciding how you will name and organise these files. It is good practice to also print off your notes and have a hard copy. This way all is not lost if your computer is stolen or breaks down.

The secret is to find a system that works for you. Here are some techniques shared by students:

Write the date, subject and page number at the top of each page. This way if your notes become separated, then it is easy to put them back in order.

To avoid carrying a heavy file to university (which could get lost), I store notes relating to the subject area I am studying for that day in a cardboard file. Once I have completed the module I store it in a larger folder.

I like to use sheets of different coloured paper for different topics. That way I can see at a quick glance what the topic is without opening the file.

I create a summary sheet for each lecture. I keep this at the beginning of the file as it helps me to find information more quickly.

When making notes from textbooks, always keep a record of where information came from. If you use quotations, be sure to record these exactly as they are written, the book, author and page number where they can be found.

Make your notes look as beautiful and as distinct as you can. A nice file which is neatly organised will make you want to go to the folder.

Always write things in your own words. This is a good way to check that you understand what you have read or heard, and it is a good way to 'own' the information.

Sharpen your skills

If you find yourself still writing too many notes, try these exercises to sharpen your skills.

Fractionally speaking

Choose a set of notes you have already made and count the number of words you have used. Imagine that you have been told that the price of ink and paper is now so expensive you are only able to use half the number of words. Try condensing your original notes so that they take up only half as much space. See how many times you can repeat this process so that your notes still retain their original meaning. What does this process tell you?

Name that lecture

During the 1980s there was a game show where contestants had to guess the name of the song from as few of the notes as possible. Hold a competition with friends to see who can record the most effective notes in the fewest number of words.

Create a 'lift' statement

Imagine that you have to describe the content of a book, article or lecture to someone in the time it takes to enter into a lift and travel two floors.

Skills in practice

The Department of Health consultation document on Records Management states that:

> Records are a valuable resource because of the information they contain.
> High-quality information underpins the delivery of high-quality evidence-based health care. ... Information is of greatest value when it is accurate, up-to-date and accessible when it is needed. An effective records management service ensures that information is properly managed and is available when needed.
> (Department of Health, 2006: 8)

As a student on placement, you will make notes for two reasons. The first will be for the purposes of fact-finding, condensing information from case notes or ward rounds in much the same way as you did at university when reading or attending lectures. The second reason is to record information relating to your interventions with clients. Here the focus is communication. This purpose has a far broader remit. These notes are in the public domain and constitute a legal document. As such, every entry you make into paper-based or electronic record-keeping systems needs to be checked and countersigned by your placement educator. The entries you make will be used to communicate with other members of the team and provide a record of the client's condition over time, detailing the assessment, planning and delivery of the care provided and its evaluation. In doing so you will:

- provide an objective basis to determine the appropriateness, need and effectiveness of intervention

- demonstrate ... professional reasoning and the rationale behind any care provided

- highlight problems and changes in the service user's condition at an early stage

- facilitate better communication and dissemination of information between members of health and social care teams

- protect the welfare of service users by promoting high standards of care.

(College of Occupational Therapists, 2006: 2)

The remainder of this chapter explores how you can transfer your learning around taking notes in the classroom to your placement. It considers some of the different types of records you may be asked to keep, looks at how you will need to express your observations and some of the structures that you will follow. The challenge with a chapter like this is that the breadth of practice and local variation means it can only cover the broad principles. Take this as the starting point and build on it through your placements.

Be clear about what you need to record

The first step to successful record-keeping on placement is to be clear about what you need to record. This will be dependent on the overall purpose of the records. This list, adapted from the ideas of Sherry Borcherding (2005), provides a useful starting point:

Contact notes   A note is made each time an intervention or interaction occurs. This is not confined to face-to-face contact, but also refers to telephone conversations or meetings with other people.

Progress notes   As the name suggests, these notes document the progress the client has made towards their goals. If any changes are made in the intervention plan, these should also be recorded here.

Transition notes Written when the client is transferring from one setting to another, such as from an acute service to residential care.

Discharge notes These are made at the end of treatment, summarising the intervention and the progress made by the client to meet their goals. These notes include actions taken and recommendations or referrals to other services.

(Adapted from Borcherding, 2005: 7)

These will be used by staff and students across a range of professions in health and social care. There may be additional ones that are more common to nursing, which are outlined by Parkinson and Brooker (2004: 38–9):

Nursing assessment sheet – Contains a summary of biographical information, including name and address, past medical history, medication, details of admission, present nursing needs and important factors to be aware of, such as allergies.

Care plan – Provides a record of a client's needs and goals of treatment and the nursing interventions required to meet these goals. Care plans will also provide summaries of progress and dates where treatment has been reviewed, and when changes have been made, based on a reassessment of needs. Evaluation notes and discharge plans may also be included.

Vital signs – This is the chart where temperature, pulse, respiration and blood pressure are recorded. More complex charts may include further information and recordings relating to the functioning of other organs.

Fluid balance chart – A record of all fluid intake (drinks, intravenous fluids, infusions given) and fluid output (urine, vomit, diarrhoea, wound drains).

Medicine/drug chart – This includes a resumé of the client's biographical details and information that can impact on current drug regimens, such as the person's weight and allergies, and any contra-indications relating to medication. Space is then included on the chart to record the administration of medication. Different types of drug order are usually given separate areas on the chart.

Record information in a way that reflects the purpose it will serve

You will encounter a range of different note-writing formats and these will vary depending on your placement and the records management systems they adopt. In some medical settings you may come across a system of note-making based around the problem-orientated medical record system. These are called SOAP notes. SOAP is not something you use to get clean. It is an acronym that stands for:

Subjective – Where you comment about the client's perception of the situation
Objective – Where you detail your observations
Assessment/analysis – Your interpretation of the observations
Plan – Where you describe what happens next, identifying possible goals, actions or advice

This type of note-making was pioneered in the 1970s and sought to form a way of standardising how information was recorded. Although it is now out of fashion in many areas, it can be a useful structure around which to frame your note-writing. Here is an example:

S: Mrs X reported that she was anxious about making a drink in the assessment kitchen, stating 'I just know that I can't do this'.

O: Client seen in occupational therapy kitchen in the department. Mrs X mobilised around the kitchen independently without the aid of a walking frame. She sequenced the task of making a cup of tea appropriately, requiring one verbal prompt to remove the tea bag from the cup. She remained focused on the task and maintained a good level of concentration. At the end of the activity she stated that she felt tired but had enjoyed the activity.

A: During the kitchen assessment Mrs X demonstrated good sequencing skills and made a cup of tea with minimal prompting. She was extremely fatigued at the end of the activity and requested to be taken back in a wheelchair. Mrs X needs to build up her levels of stamina and confidence.

P: Referral made to occupational therapy weekly cooking group beginning on 15/05/08. Staff on the ward will invite Mrs X to make a hot drink at breakfast and at supper. On return to the ward Mrs X was informed of this. Further assessment in the occupational therapy kitchen to take place on 28/05/08.

Although this is a very specific framework, it can be easily adapted to provide a simple structure around which to base your notes when you begin to record information on placement. Here is a checklist of some of the things you may wish to include:

Date/time
The context of the meeting/contact/intervention including:
Why the client was seen, where they were seen, for how long

What you observed: *Chronologically or using categories*
                          i.e. physical health, mental health,
                          social interaction, mobility
                          Functional performance
                          Cognition (processing, perception)
                          Memory, concentration
                          Emotional and behavioural response
                          Warning! Avoid making
                          judgements or sweeping
                          statements (note that your
                          statements relate to a given
                          moment in time and a specific
                          situation)

The implications: *This could relate to physical health,*
                          emotional wellbeing, discharge,
                          independence, treatment planning
                          Progress and future plans

What next: *Continue course of action? Discontinue?*
                          Inform someone? Make a referral?
                          Specific intervention: who to contact,
                          when, frequency and duration of
                          treatment

Whatever system you use, notes should:

- Be based on fact, be correct and consistent

- Be written wherever possible with the involvement of the patient, client or their carer

- Be written in terms that the patient or client can understand

- Identify problems that have arisen and the actions taken to rectify them

- Provide clear evidence of the care planned, the decisions made, the care delivered and the information shared (based on Nursing and Midwifery Council, 2002).

Test your skills

The website that accompanies this book (www.skills4health.co.uk) contains a number of activities where you can put your skills into practice. The following exercise provides a short taster. Read the extract taken from a set of student notes. Identify any vague statements or emotive language. Can you identify the additional details required to give the notes value? Can you rephrase any statements to make the notes read more objectively?

I saw Mr Jones as requested. He had been too lazy to get dressed and looked very unmotivated. He is safe getting on and off the bed but required help to walk up the ward. He stated that he was tired but I think he was not completely honest. The plan is to see him in the department on a regular basis.

Patient much the same. Fell while walking across the ward. Query whether this was attention seeking. Checked out and taken to accident and emergency. Returned to the ward. Bathed during the evening with a bit of help.

Mrs Y is depressed. Refuses to do anything other than her knitting. Cries when asked to do otherwise. Very frustrating.

Record information clearly and legibly so that it can be understood

Your notes will be read by other people so if you are using a paper-based note system your best hand writing is required. There must be no doubt about what you have written, which means you need to spend time checking that your notes are legible. You might be able to read your hieroglyphics but others might struggle! Again the various professional bodies are very clear about what you should and should not do. Paper-based notes should:

- Be written in black ink (so that photocopies of the notes are readable)
- Be written clearly and in such a way that the text cannot be erased (no Tippex!)
- Be written in such a way that any alterations or additions are dated, timed and signed so that the original entry is still clear (do not scrub out amendments; rather, strike through with a single line)
- Be accurately dated, timed and signed, with the signature printed alongside the first entry
- Not include abbreviations (unless they are standard, agreed ones with accompanying interpretations*)
- Avoid jargon, meaningless phrases, irrelevant speculation and offensive, subjective statements
- Be countersigned (if you are a student) (based on Nursing and Midwifery Council, 2002).

*The comment relating to abbreviations is interesting as you will see abbreviations in the notes. However, this is not good practice and the guidelines issued by most professional bodies state that abbreviations should not be used. This is partly to ensure that there isn't any confusion as to the exact meaning of what has been written, and partly because under the Freedom of Information Act patients have rights to access and read their medical records.

Record this information in a timely fashion

The guidelines set down by the Nursing and Midwifery Council (2002) state that records:

- *Should be written as soon as possible after an event has happened to provide current (up-to-date) information about the care and condition of the patient or client*

This is echoed by standards for practice within advice provided by many of the professions allied to health and social care. The following examples are taken from the occupational therapy guidelines on note-keeping:

Timing and dating record entries: As with any factor of the care provided to an individual, the day and time that it occurred is important. Recording the date and time of an event allows the therapist to demonstrate that care was appropriate and as planned. It also allows the frequency of care to be monitored. Should the care provided be examined at a later date, the time and date of an event may be a vital piece of evidence.

Timely record-keeping: It is vital that records are accurate. The longer the time lapse between an event occurring and it being recorded, the greater the chance of inaccuracies or omissions in the records. (College of Occupational Therapy, 2006: 8)

Timing is of the essence. Entries into patient notes should be made as soon as an event or intervention has occurred. The written records you make are a means of communication between the multidisciplinary team members and will impact on the interventions offered by colleagues. Failure to do so can have frightening consequences for patient care. For example, failure to record a dosage of medication you have administered could result in a person receiving a double dosage, or an omission to record that someone had a fall during a home visit could lead to an exacerbation of the injury.

It can be difficult to document things straight away, but this must be a priority. Your entries will help promote continuity of care. If they are not up to date and you are unexpectedly sick or away from work, then another member of the team will have to come along and start again. If your notes are clear and up to date, your colleague will be able to literally pick up where you left off. Remember this simple fact: *If it is not in the notes then effectively it did not happen*.

Organise and file your information so that it can be easily accessed

At university you have to take responsibility in terms of devising ways to organise your notes. On placement it is highly probable that these systems are set down already. Again, you will encounter a number of different systems and much will depend on the placement setting. Here are some of the systems you may use:

- **Profession-specific files**. This is where records relating to your intervention are held centrally in your department. For example, notes relating to the physiotherapy intervention someone receives are stored securely in the physiotherapy department.

- **Integrated records**. Notes relating to a person are held centrally. Information is recorded by different professionals in the relevant sections of the record.

- **Under the single assessment process**. Notes are held centrally but rather than profession-specific information being contained in different sections, all professions make entries onto the same pages in a chronological order.

- **Electronic systems of record-keeping**. This is where members of the multidisciplinary team input information into the computer rather than recording this on paper. This information is then accessible to professionals across the different care sectors.

🌿 IN A NUTSHELL

This chapter has offered a number of ways to help you to develop your skills and confidence in the note-making and record-keeping process. You should be able to:

- Recognise that note-making is a tool for active learning

- Identify the strengths and limitations of how you currently record information

- Understand that the way you record information depends on the type of information and how you are going to use this

- Reflect on the purpose that notes fulfil in clinical practice, the differences and similarities between these notes and the notes you take in class

References and signposts to further reading and resources

Borcherding, S. (2005) *Documentation Manual for Writing SOAP Notes in Occupational Therapy* (2nd edition). Thorofare, NJ: Slack.

Buzan, T. (2006) *The Buzan Study Skills Handbook*. Harlow: BBC Active.

College of Occupational Therapists (2006) *Record Keeping by the College of Occupational Therapists*. London: COT.

Department of Health (2006) *Records Management: NHS Code of Practice*. London: Department of Health.

Garner, R. and Rugg, S. (2005) 'Electronic care records: an update on the Garner Project', *British Journal of Occupational Therapy*, 68 (3): 131–4.

Hoban, V. (2003) 'How to... handle a handover', *Nursing Times*, 99 (9): 54–5.

Nursing and Midwifery Council (2002) *Guidelines for Records and Record Keeping*. London: NMC.

Parkinson, J. and Brooker, C. (2004) *Everyday English for International Nurses*. Oxford: Churchill Livingstone.

13 Writing for information

 AT A GLANCE

This chapter is for you if

- You struggle to distinguish your essays from your reports

- You never seem to get the marks you feel that you deserve for your written assessments

(Continued)

(Continued)

- Your feedback includes comments such as 'you need to structure your work more carefully'

- You begin your assignment without ever really knowing what you are going to write

- You thought that a dissertation was something you ate after the main course

Writing is an important form of communication. In practice, notes, reports, discharge summaries, requests and leaflets are the main ways you will share information with clients, carers, other members of the multidisciplinary team and external agencies. To do this you will need to extract relevant information from a range of sources, decide on its accuracy and present this coherently in a way that is fitting to the situation and in a language that is appropriate for the audience.

The written work you will undertake at university will prepare you for these situations as well as offering you the chance to begin to influence practice more generally through your writing and research. It is therefore worth spending time developing your writing style and honing your skills.

Written assignments will take many forms, including short answers to set questions, essays, reports and dissertations, among others. Each requires you to develop and demonstrate a slightly different set of skills, including the ability to present information in different formats, build up an argument, select appropriate evidence to support your ideas using a range of sources, make connections between different subject areas and show that you are able to synthesise information to focus your thinking. It is the equivalent of performing mental yoga. The result will be a flexible practitioner who is able to make informed decisions and express these in a way that communicates clearly to the widest audience.

This chapter seeks to 'de-mystify' the writing process. It demonstrates that everyone has the capacity to write well if they follow a series of simple steps. The first part of the chapter focuses on ways to write and structure essays and reports, while the second half looks more specifically at some of the types of writing you will encounter in practice, focusing particularly on case studies and leaflets.

STARTING POINTS: WRITING WHIZZ OR WANDERER?

1 Many myths surround the writing process. Decide whether the following statements are true or false.

Statement	True	False
The ability to write well is something that you are born with		
Great writers are not born, they are made		
In order to write well you need to wait for inspiration		
When you write you should not use your own words		
Academic writing is different from other kinds of writing you may be asked to do		
It is important to back up what you say with evidence		
Most of the time you spend on an assignment should be used in planning		
Using other people's ideas without acknowledging them is plagiarism		
The reference list is another name for a bibliography		
Writing is difficult		

See page 193 for the answers.

2   Read the following comments tutors have written about students' work. For each statement, identify the mistake the student has made. And for each one you recognise in terms of your own writing, give yourself one point.

This is a good piece of work, but it is difficult to follow at times.
You see the wood and the trees all at the same time and seem to present both.
Be careful in terms of the length of your paragraphs.
You need to ensure that you support your arguments with evidence.
Make sure that you back up what you write.
Make sure that you reference all quotes.
Please answer the question.
I would like to have seen more of *your* ideas.
Try to shorten the length of the quotes used.
This assignment starts well but fizzles out towards the end.
Check your spelling and grammar.

Now, add up the number of statements you have ticked and see where you fall on the scale below:

Whizz										Wanderer
0	1	2	3	4	5	6	7	8	9	10 11

The writing process

Essays, reports, short answers do not just happen. They are the end result of a much longer process which includes research, reading and note-taking. A set formula or way of doing this does not exist – everyone is different – although generally it is safe to say that when you write, you will follow certain broad 'stages'. Again, the order that you do these stages in will differ depending on the subject area and on your preferred style. Generally, they will look something like this:

Responding to a question (perhaps seeking clarification)
Gathering information
Reading with your question in mind
Active note-taking
Pulling ideas together
Planning
First draft
Redraft
Proof-reading
Submit assignment
Reflecting on feedback to inform your next assignment

This description is very simplistic and is far from a linear process. For example, you may begin reading and then realise that you need to gather more information, or you may be planning your assignment at the same time as you are reading.

A good way of thinking about writing is to liken the process to putting together a jigsaw puzzle.

Writing an assignment is a bit like putting together a jigsaw puzzle

Step 1: Check the front of the box

The first thing to do is to check the front of the box so you are clear about what the end result will look like. If the image is a house, you do not follow instructions to put together a picture of a butterfly. Just as, in the same way, you do not write a report if you have been asked to write an essay.

Step 2: Make sure all the pieces are there

The next thing is to check that all the pieces are there. Before you are sure of this, there is little point in putting the jigsaw together. In the same way, when you approach your writing you need to assemble your information: notes from lectures, summaries of reading, general ideas.

If you discover that there are pieces of information missing, then you will need to do additional reading.

Step 3: Assemble the puzzle

Remember that preparation is key and you may need time to let your ideas form before starting to think about the strategy you are going to use to put this together. For example, are you going to start with the pieces around the outside edge first or put all the pieces together that are the same colour? It can be helpful to look at the picture on the front of the box and re-read the instructions, making sure you understand what is being asked of you and that you follow conventions for the particular type of writing you are undertaking. The equivalent of this in the writing process is pulling your ideas together and writing your plan.

Step 4: Build

Once you have completed the instructions watch your ideas fit together. This part is exciting. Once all the pieces are together you need to check that it matches the picture on the front of the box and that you have not made any silly mistakes. In essay writing, the message here is to proof-read your work and only print out when you are happy that it is free from errors.

Step 5: Sit back and enjoy

Things that can go wrong

You did not answer the question. This is the equivalent of creating a picture of a bicycle when the picture was of a sports car.

You did not follow particular writing conventions. For example, you wrote in the first person (I will describe…) instead of using a more academic style (the assignment will describe…) or you wrote an essay instead of a report. This is the equivalent of putting pieces of the puzzle in back to front so that their plain side is showing. This will completely change the nature of the end result.

Your work contains a number of spelling mistakes and grammatical errors. After you have finished the puzzle, check it against the original picture. Make sure that pieces are firmly in place so that it looks tidy and you know that if you need to move the puzzle it will not fall apart. Likewise, when writing an assignment you need to read through your work carefully. You may still get some things wrong because you are not aware that they are wrong but at least you can check for the careless mistakes.

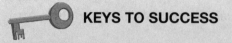

KEYS TO SUCCESS

The secret of successful writing hinges on the following:

- Take time to understand and address the question

- Decide on the format you are being asked to present the information in and the conventions that are associated with this

- Plan what you are going to write and structure what you want to say

- Support your ideas with evidence

- Think about language and style

- Proof-read your work

Take time to understand and address the question

It probably seems ridiculously obvious that the key to successful writing is to answer the question. However, you would be amazed by the number of students who do not perform well because they choose to ignore the question and write everything they know about a particular topic instead. This can happen for a number of reasons but most commonly it is a sign that the person has struggled to unravel the university-speak and understand what has been asked of them.

The first thing you need to do when you are given an assignment is to decipher the questions. You can do this in a number of ways:

- Unpick the question – decide what it is asking you to do

- Rewrite the question in your own words

- Interrogate the question. Climb inside the mind of the examiner. Ask yourself why the tutor has chosen to ask you this? Is there a line of argument that you can take or are expected to take?

- Study the marking criteria and see how they relate to the question

- Circle/underline key words

It is particularly helpful to circle key words as these tell you what you need to do with the information. For example, are you describing an idea or contrasting it with another approach? Successful writing hinges around the following statement:

It's not what you know, it is what you do with what you know…

There is a kind of hierarchy associated with these key words. This is based on something called Bloom's taxonomy. Let's say that these levels can be represented by a ladder. The words on the *bottom rungs* are all *descriptive*. These check your understanding of a subject, requiring you to recall, detail or outline information, retelling it in your own words. Examples of descriptive words include: describe, outline (give the main features of), identify (recognise), define (give a meaning of), explain.

The next rung or level up would be words that require you to do something with the information, whether this is *applying* it to a situation, or *contrasting* it with an idea, or *building* an *argument* that can be supported with *evidence*. Words associated with this rung of the ladder would include: discuss (look at different aspects), debate (strengths and limitations), examine (explore from different perspectives), question (interrogate), compare and contrast (identify similarities and differences), justify (provide a reason or reasons why, offer a rationale).

The highest rungs require you to make some kind of a *judgement* or *evaluation*, pull together ideas and make links and *connections* with other information. Examples of words associated with this include: critically debate, critically evaluate, synthesise (assimilate), appraise.

It makes sense that the rungs represent the differing levels of complexity and, by implication, the marks you can gain.

Illustration

This sounds fine in theory, but what does it look like in practice? Let's begin with a fun example. A group of students have been asked to complete an assignment about a box of chocolates. One student is describing, one is discussing and the other is evaluating. Read the following lines taken from their assignments and see if you can match what the student has been asked to do with the extract.

Beth.   *The vanilla cream is smooth in texture. It is a square chocolate, the size of a thumbnail. Its dark exterior contrasts with the light fluffy centre. The taste is sweet and it melts in the mouth. It is not too sickly.*

Mary.   *Overall the box is good value for money. In terms of pound-for-pound it is preferable to buy chocolates in this form rather than purchasing individual bars.*

Fran.   *The strawberry cream is much larger than the cherry crisp and feels much weightier. The drawback is that size is not always an indication of quality and the taste of the strawberry cream is more artificial than the rich centre of the cherry crisp. Overall cherry definitely wins the day.*

Beth describes the chocolate – how it looks, its shape, size and taste. She makes a tiny value judgement at the end when she states 'it isn't too sickly' but otherwise she focuses on what she sees as the facts. Mary, on the other hand, evaluates the box. She makes a value judgement that goes beyond description. This leaves Fran, whose emphasis is on discussion and evaluation. She is making judgements, weighing up the pros and cons, strengths and limitations before reaching a conclusion.

Repeat this exercise using the following examples, which are probably more typical of what you will encounter at university.

Mary. *Creek (2002) states that 'behavioural theories do not sit comfortably with client-centred philosophy'. There is an ethical question as to whether a person has the right to manipulate another's behaviour (Clancy and Clark, 1990). Dunn (2000) suggests that the reinforcer must be motivating to the child. If a child who is shy is sent to the group, they may feel uncomfortable being videoed and not repeat the behaviour so they are not chosen again. Conditional reasoning suggests that a range of interventions should be used and offering a 'one-size-fits-all' solution, such as an intervention that is not client-centred, as an alternative is not offered to those children who do not find the group motivating.*

Fran. *The client group is made up of school children aged 5–11 years old. Most children attending the school are from the immediate area, which is largely rented local authority housing. The school is of average size and includes children from a range of socio-cultural backgrounds.*

Beth. *There should be greater consistency in assessments by the staff at the school. Thorough training needs to be given and a regular newsletter can be used to encourage wider use of the group. A baseline of behaviour should be taken prior to implementing the intervention in order that its effectiveness can be evaluated. Other rewards schemes, such as stickers and team points, should be taken into account and perhaps tied in with attendance at sessions. When training people to run the group, the questioning skills are the crucial factor in order that the praise can be sincere and specific. Particular emphasis needs to be placed on practising using 'wow' words and open questions.*

This time Mary's focus is more critical. She is highlighting the strengths and limitations of the approach taken. The tone is discursive, looking at the intervention from different perspectives and drawing on evidence to support her ideas. Fran describes the setting of her placement. Notice how she simply presents the facts. Beth's emphasis is on evaluation. She is making a number of judgements and recommendations. This part would be strengthened if she made reference to the literature in order to support her ideas.

Decide on the format you are being asked to present the information in and the conventions that are associated with this

The second hurdle is to decide how you are being asked to present the information and to be clear about the format and conventions associated with this. At university, you will be asked to present information in a number of formats. Generally these will include:

- Reports

- Essays

- Reflective accounts

- Posters

	Essay	Report	Reflective writing	Poster
Purpose	Can be used to describe, debate or explore information.	Presents a summary of information on a given topic.	Offers a personal response to a situation and usually focuses on your learning.	Summarises and presents key information to a wider audience.
Structure	A continuous piece of writing. Information organised into paragraphs.	Very structured. Follows a set format, divided into sections with subheadings to guide the reader.	Less structured. Possibly a description at the beginning, what has been learned and the way forward.	Contains illustrations and pictures.
What does it test	Ability to develop an argument and to structure writing. It also looks at how to use evidence to support your ideas.	Ability to present information clearly, to offer 'the facts' as they appear, and to support these with evidence.	Your ability to see a situation from different perspectives and to demonstrate your learning through experience.	Ability to condense materials, to be succinct and make information eye-catching. Skills in using information technology.
Conventions	Adopts a formal style of writing in the third person: This essay... as opposed to 'I will be...'.	Follows a set format. Includes subheadings. Can include graphs, pie-charts and other numerical information.	It is subjective and is usually written in the first person (using the word I).	Tends to be A0 size. Text must be clear and readable. There are no real conventions, and plenty of opportunity for creativity.

Each requires you to follow a slightly different set of conventions which means that you need to exercise a range of skills. For example, an essay will test your ability to use information to develop an argument whereas a poster will require you to select with great care the information you can include in a limited physical space as well as thinking about the visual impact of the words.

If you are studying at degree level, it is probable that you will be asked to undertake a larger piece of written work based around a piece of research. This usually culminates in a dissertation or journal article. More details about producing the perfect poster and writing your dissertation are provided on the website that complements this book (www.skills4health.co.uk).

Plan what you are going to write and structure what you want to say

Once you have untangled the question, feel clear about what it is asking you to do and how you are to present this information, the next stage is to make sure you have a good plan.

The art of writing well hinges on your ability to make decisions. For example:

- What will you read?
- How will you record this?
- What will you include?
- What evidence will you use?

Plans offer you a framework for your thinking as well as your writing and make the writing process much easier. Time invested in planning ensures clarity of writing, clear direction and ordered thinking. Many students choose not to plan because they believe that this is time-consuming. However, the reality is it will save you time and earn you marks. How you choose to plan very much depends on your learning style and your personal preferences. Here are the approaches taken by a number of students:

I see planning as a two-stage process. I write the question in the centre of a large sheet of paper and begin by creating a giant mind map, sketching out my ideas with coloured pens, pictures, doodles. Anything goes. Making this a visual process enables me to look at things from a different perspective, physically make connections between areas and capture ideas that I might otherwise have missed. This is very much about thinking and reasoning.

The second stage is to recognise particular themes or trains of thought that have emerged and to see how these will create the thread of my argument and the stance I will take. Because I have wrestled with the thinking beforehand, it means that when I move on to more detailed planning, I am in a good position to do this because I am very clear in my mind about what I need to do. At this point I put together a more detailed plan, deciding what the main paragraphs will be. If there are holes in the argument, I go back to the reading so I can fill these in, so by the end of the process I am very clear about what goes into each paragraph.   Lesley

I approach the process quite methodically. I spend time reading the question so that I am clear about what needs to be done but then start with the learning outcomes. These spell out in more detail what I need to achieve to gain a pass and if they are written well they can offer ideas in terms of how to structure the assignment.   Richard

I use the reading list to find a text that offers an overview of the topic area and this reading, combined with the lectures and workshops, gives me a clear indication of the direction of the assignment and the main paragraphs it will include. At this point, I sketch out the main paragraph headings and the line of the argument the assignment will take.

I then go into 'detective mode'. I take five sheets of paper and on the top of each sheet I write down the 'theme' for that particular paragraph. I go back to the reading list and as I read the various journals and textbooks, I focus on extracting the necessary information and evidence that will go into each paragraph. I am very strict with myself and limit myself to a set number of books. At the end of this process I have five sheets of A4 paper with all the quotes, ideas and arguments you could possibly need. If anything, there is always too much information.

The final stage before I begin the first draft is to read through the sheets of notes and to work out how the ideas will 'flow'. For example, if my overall argument is against a particular approach, I write the paragraphs supporting the approach at the beginning (demonstrating I can see both sides of the argument) before dedicating the remainder of the assignment to annihilating this evidence and building up a really good case for not using this approach in practice. Or sometimes I begin by arguing strongly against the approach but include a couple of paragraphs extolling its virtues at the end, again to demonstrate that I am a rounded individual and that no argument is completely clear-cut. Once I am clear about this, then I can number the paragraphs and I am ready to begin writing. Rozena

There are many ways to plan but the students above seem to break the process down into two stages: the first is very much concerned with thinking and the second is more concrete, which is about getting to grips with the nitty-gritty and the organisation of the information. Perhaps it is possible to see these as two distinct but inter-related processes (Gocsik, 2005):

- Sketching

- Structuring

Structuring your assignment is about deciding how to organise information so that your ideas flow. Some students find it useful to write the themes of paragraphs on pieces of paper and to move these around a bit like you would a jigsaw puzzle. It might be that at this point you are also able to fill in the detail, the evidence you will use, the quotes you will include. If not, you will be able to identify where the gaps are and this will direct your reading.

Structure what you want to say

The structure of your writing will very much depend on its purpose and the format you have been asked to present this in. For instance, a report will have a very different structure from an essay because of the conventions it adopts.

Reports

Reports present information clearly and concisely. If a report was an item of clothing, it would be a suit and tie. They are very formal and tend to be written in the third person. Their purpose is to set out the facts in a highly structured and organised way. To this end, they usually follow a set format, and rather than being a continuous piece of writing, they include a series of subheadings. This signposting makes it much easier to dip in and out and to extract information very quickly. The subheadings will vary depending on the report and the audience for whom it is intended. If you are asked to write a report at university, your tutor will probably indicate what these subheadings are. They could include some or all of the following:

- Purpose of the report (why are you writing this?)

- Background/rationale (what are your motivations?)

- Methodology (how did you go about it?)

- Findings/results (what did you discover?)

- Discussion (what does this mean?)

- Conclusion (what did you decide?)

- Recommendations (what needs to happen next?)

A good report is concise, well-organised and presents information clearly. In addition to the various subheadings, it includes a series of stock phrases so that the reader is in no doubt about what the different sections contain. These signposts may include phrases such as:

- This report presents/summarises the findings of…/documents…/explores…/ investigates…

- The primary purpose of this report is to…

- The main findings of this… are…

- This report has highlighted that…

- In view of the main findings, the recommendations are as follows…

Diagrams, charts and tables can illustrate the points that are made.

Essays

Essays, on the other hand, present ideas and demonstrate a level of critical thinking. They are less formally structured and tend to be a continuous piece of prose divided by paragraphs. Most essays are written in an academic style using the third person. The exception to this would be a reflective piece of writing, which would be written in the first person. Essays will generally comprise:

- *A clear introduction*: This should set the scene and provide an overview of your assignment. Its function is to clarify, orientate and define key terms so that the reader knows exactly what you are going to cover, your stance and the direction of your argument. The introduction is a bit like a road map, indicating the desti-nation and the route you are going to take to get there.

- *A structured, well-thought through argument* supported with good reference to the wider literature

- *A series of paragraphs*: Paragraphs are self-contained units of information. The first line of the paragraph is usually called the topic sentence and should indicate what the paragraph is about. Paragraphs should be long enough to develop your ideas but not so long that your reader becomes lost in the detail. One-third to half a page of writing would be a reasonable length for a paragraph. Try the following structure, suggested by Gocsik (2005) to kick start the process:

first sentence (topic sentence) makes the main claim of the paragraph and tries also to link the paragraph with what came before

+ subsequent sentences: justify or illustrate the claim

+ final sentence sums up the paragraph (and perhaps tries to link the paragraph with what will come next)

- *Conclusion*: A well-written conclusion that summarises the main line of the argument. The conclusion doesn't offer anything new but allows the reader to consolidate their thinking. A good conclusion is like a dessert wine. It does not introduce a new course but helps to draw together all the flavours of the meal and leaves you with a good taste in your mouth, wanting more.

Let it flow

There is one final thing to mention about structuring. As you build up your written arguments you will follow a number of conventions, linking one sentence to the next and one paragraph to another. These link words ensure that your writing 'flows' and that your ideas move seamlessly into a cohesive piece of written work. Here are examples of common link words:

Cause and effect	above, as a result, hence, therefore, thus
Likeness link words	correspondingly, similarly, in the same way, also
Contrast links	but, however, nevertheless, on the contrary, on the one hand … on the other hand, yet, whereas
Reinforcement	again, also, and, further, furthermore, in addition, moreover, too
Illustration	for example, for instance, as shown, as highlighted
Focus	in particular, especially
Concession	granted, that is, it is true that, of course, naturally
Emphasis	in fact, indeed, of course, undeniably, inevitably
Order	finally, first, second, next, subsequently
Restatement	in other words, in similar terms, that is, that is to say, to put the point another way
Summary	all in all, altogether, in conclusion, to summarise
Time or place	later, simultaneously, so far, subsequently, there, this time, until now, above all, afterwards, at the same time, below, earlier, elsewhere, formerly, further, on, here, hitherto

Read the following extract taken from an essay written by a student about normalisation in the context of working with people with learning disabilities. Do not worry too much about what it means; rather, see if you can identify the link words used and how this helps the paragraph flow.

Emerson states that there is 'no such thing as the concept of principle of normalisation' (Emerson, 1992: 1). It is therefore essential to recognise that normalisation is not a static theory but one which has continued to evolve over time. Thus normalisation encompasses a range of ideas. For instance, the theories developed by Nirje regard the central idea as the right for individuals to 'experience normal daily routines' (Platts, 1993: 278). Wolfensberger, on the other hand, has redefined normalisation as social role valorisation.

Support your ideas with evidence

The mark of a good essay is the ability to develop a sound academic argument fully supported by the literature. Yet many students consider this to be a real sticking point and there is much confusion about what constitutes evidence and plagiarism. Some students are told 'you must not use your own words' and then receive feedback from assignments saying 'I need to see more of your own ideas. You need to demonstrate your ability to develop your own arguments.' Confused? Let's untangle what it means.

Essays offer you the opportunity to demonstrate that you can apply your understanding to a particular subject area. Some essays are more descriptive (identifying the main concepts), while others are more discursive (developing an argument). Either way, you will have built up a bank of ideas based around the reading you have been doing, the lectures attended, your own thought processes and, through this, will have formulated your own theories based on the collective sum of this knowledge. As part of this process you will have discarded some arguments in favour of others and will have pooled information. Although this represents the culmination of everyone else's ideas and takes into account their arguments, it essentially reflects your own particular 'take' on things. It is this 'take' that your tutors are interested in. They need to ensure that when it comes to adopting a particular approach or treatment you are able to survey the body of literature, weigh this up and make a decision based on the evidence.

An academic piece which summarises your ideas and is supported by the evidence is very different from plagiarism. Plagiarism is when you try to pass off something you have read as your own without acknowledging the source. Examples of plagiarism include copying information from a book without referencing the author, and copying and pasting information from the internet into your assignment and pretending that it is yours. Ways to avoid plagiarism are described on the website accompanying this book (www.skills4health.co.uk).

Using evidence

When you write, make every sentence count. You need to ensure that you back up all your ideas with reference to the literature. Whenever you make a statement (an assertion), say to yourself, 'How do I know this is true?' or say to yourself 'Prove it'.

Which of the following statements is evidence-based? What is the effect of including evidence to support the ideas?

1 Depression is common among older people.

2 Depression among older people is common. For example, a study undertaken by Jones (2008) found that as many as one in five people over the age of 65 have some form of depressive illness which requires treatment.

3 It could be argued that normalisation does not exist.

4 Evidence shows that chocolate is good for your health.

5 A randomised controlled trial undertaken by Craig (2008) argues that the incidence of depression is significantly lowered in individuals who eat more than two bars of chocolate a day. Indeed, she states that...

Statements 1, 3 and 4 lack the evidence; whereas statements 2 and 5 are supported by the wider literature. The difference between the two is clear: evidence substantiates the statements that you make and makes your arguments more credible as they support your writing.

You can make reference to this evidence in one of three ways:

- By quoting directly

- By paraphrasing

- By using a combination of the two

Quoting directly

This is when you use the exact words of the author. If the quote is shorter than 40 words, it can be embedded within your text. Enclose it within single quotation marks and acknowledge its source (I will say more about referencing later). As Craig (2008: 16) states, 'using evidence in this way couldn't be easier'. For longer quotes, start a new paragraph and indent the words (you don't need to use quotation marks when you 'extract out' quotes). Indeed,

It then becomes absolutely clear that this is a quote and stands out nicely. For longer pieces of writing it looks much neater and well ordered. However, you need to be careful not to use too many long quotes as this can result in an assignment which is all someone else's words and does not leave room for your own. (Craig, 2008: 42)

Paraphrasing

Paraphrasing is putting the gist of what someone has written in your own words. Again, you will need to acknowledge the source of the information. Here is an example: As the above examples illustrate, Craig (2008) offers a number of different ways of presenting quotes and provides sound advice relating to the length of these.

Combining the two

Sometimes you might choose to combine paraphrasing with a direct quotation. If I return to the above examples, I could say:

Craig (2008) offers a number of different ways to present quotes and provides sound advice relating to the length of these. She convincingly suggests, 'using evidence in this way could not be easier' (p. 16).

Return to the previous examples and decide whether the author is paraphrasing, using a direct quote, or a combination of the two.

References and bibliography

References guide the reader to the literature you have used. Every time you refer to a piece of evidence within the body of your assignment you will put down a marker that points the reader to where they can find a more detailed description of the reference. Depending on the system you are using, these take a number of forms. For example:

1   If you have been asked to use the Harvard or author-date system you will record the surname of the author, the year and the page number in brackets either 'directly after the quote' (Craig, 2009: 34) or as Craig (2009: 34) suggests, 'just before the cited material'.

2   If you are using the British Standard or Numeric system you will give the reference a number (the first reference is number 1, the second 2, etc.) and again you will place this 'by the cited source' (1) using 'appropriate brackets' (2).

The person reading your work can then follow these up by looking at the end of your assignment in the reference list. These offer a fuller description of the evidence, signposting the reader to the book, journal or website from where the evidence was taken.

For the *Harvard system* these are arranged in alphabetical order, with the surname of the author first. So, for example, the above reference may appear in the final reference list as follows:

References

Beevers, E. (2003) *Referencing made easy.* London: Lintott Publishers.
Craig, C. (2009) *Referencing for beginners.* London: Edison Publications.
Mayne, N. (2004) *Finding your reference.* Carlton: Island Publishers.

Note how the references include details of the title of the book, the place of publication and the name of the publisher.

The final reference list for an assignment using the *British Standard* would look something like this:

References

1. Mayne, N. *Finding your reference.* Carlton: Island Publishers, 2004.

2. Craig, C. *Referencing for beginners.* London: Edison Publications, 2009.

There are some variations around punctuation and different conventions in terms of how to reference different sources, such as websites and journal articles. Your tutor will usually provide advice and more detailed information about the system they would like you to use. Referencing is simply a formula and an easy way to pick up marks so it is worth spending time making sure you are clear about what is expected of you. The website accompanying this book (www.skills4health.co.uk) provides details of the most common forms of referencing you will encounter, with games and quizzes to test your understanding.

Your final reference list refers specifically to texts you have quoted, whereas the bibliography is the sum of your reading and contains materials you have not necessarily cited directly.

A good reference list:

- Demonstrates a breadth of reading (from a range of disciplines)

- Uses a range of sources (books, journal articles, websites)

- Uses relevant and reliable sources

- Includes a number of up-to-date references

- Follows conventions set down by the particular type of referencing adopted

- Goes beyond the reading list

In a 1,500 word assignment, you would probably be looking at a reference list of between 8 and 10 sources.

Think about language and style

Good assignments are won and lost on the style in which they are written. With the exception of reflective pieces which can use 'I', academic writing is written in the third person (the assignment, this essay). Here are a few dos and don'ts of academic writing according to lecturers:

Do	**Do not**
Write in a formal style	Use slang or write in a journalistic style (you know what I mean matey?)
Use the third person: This essay will discuss... It could be argued that...	Do not use the first person: I will discuss... I am going to argue that...

Make sure that if you are using an abbreviation that you write the word out in full first and then place the abbreviation in brackets directly after this	Use unexplained abbreviations SWIM (see what I mean)

Read the following sentences, which were all written by students in their assignments. See if you can offer suggestions for rewriting these so they reflect a more 'academic style'.

Statement	**Rewrite in a more academic style**
I think that it is important to consider	It is important to consider
Loads of factors were involved	
It is hard to work out	
In this essay I am looking at how…	
The books all say something different	
In my opinion	

Mind your language

Oppressive language is not acceptable and you will lose marks if you use it. Here are the five worst offenders:

Do not say	**Instead say**
Suffer (he suffers from depression)	He has (he has depression)
Wheelchair bound	Wheelchair user
Dyslexic	Person with dyslexia
Geriatric	Older person
Mental patient	Person with mental health problems

Proof-read your work

Finally, proof-read your work. Many assignments will include marks for presentation. An assignment filled with grammatical errors and spelling mistakes can detract from the overall content of the work. Proof-reading is a process where you read through your work to pick up on and correct spelling and grammatical errors. It also gives you the opportunity to ensure that your work 'flows'. You are probably already familiar with a number of tools that can support this process, for instance the spelling and grammar check on the computer. There are also different proof-reading techniques you can try. These are described in more detail on the website accompanying this book (www.skills4health.co.uk).

Before moving on to the section 'Skills in practice' here are the answers to the earlier writing quiz.

Answers to the 'writing whizz or wanderer?' quiz on page 176–7

The ability to write well is something that you are born with
Definitely **false**: Writing is a skill and a discipline.

Great writers are not born, they are made
True: Some people may find writing comes more easily than others do but academic writers are not born, they are made.

In order to write well you need to wait for inspiration
False: This is a common fallacy. The best way to write is to sit at a desk and to put your ideas on to paper or type them into a computer. It's a bit like doing a warm-up before you begin a race.

When you write you should not use your own words
False: Everything you write needs to be in your own words with the exception of when you use a quote to back up your ideas.

Academic writing is different from other kinds of writing you may be asked to do
True: Academic writing follows certain rules and conventions, particularly around the language and style of writing.

It is important to back up what you say with evidence
Very **true**: Every statement you make needs to be supported by evidence.

Most of the time you spend on an assignment should be used in planning
Probably **true**: The more time you spend on planning, the clearer your thinking will be and the easier it will be to write.

Using other people's ideas without acknowledging them is plagiarism
True: Plagiarism is when you try to pass other people's ideas as your own without acknowledging your source. This is a form of cheating.

The reference list is another name for a bibliography
False: Technically speaking, the references refer to books, articles and websites you have referred to directly, whereas the bibliography refers to sources of information you have consulted but have not specifically referred to in the main body of your writing.

Writing is difficult
It depends on your point of view. It can be difficult at first, but like everything else, it becomes easier with practice.

Skills in practice

You will be pleased to learn that you will not be expected to write essays on placement unless these are in connection with a piece of university or college work. Reports, notes, case studies and information leaflets for patients will be the basis of most of the written work you will do as a student and as a qualified practitioner. The remainder of this chapter focuses on reports, case studies and leaflets. Written notes are covered in another section of the book.

The keys to successful writing on placement are identical to those you require in the classroom.

Take time to understand and address the question

In practice it is highly unlikely that a referral from a consultant will read, 'write a 1,500 word essay on why Mrs X is being discharged'. There will not be a question as such, but the subject of your report will be inferred from its description. Just as you interrogated the title of an essay question, you need to be clear about what you are being asked to do in your writing and why. Here are some prompts that can help you get started:

- Is the purpose of this writing/report to justify my intervention?

- Is the purpose to describe what has happened, so other people can pick up where I left off?

- Is it to document something that happened?

- Is it to clarify the treatment approach taken?

- Is it to make recommendations as to the future care needs?

- Is it to summarise the intervention and care given?

You will need to make sure that your report/summary/written communication addresses the basic question. It can be helpful to start with the end point of what you want to say and work backwards. Your writing should leave the reader in no question about what your findings and recommendations are.

As a student, your placement educator will take ultimate responsibility for the reports and other official documents you write and these will need to be counter-signed before being submitted.

Decide on the format you are being asked to present the information in and the conventions that are associated with this

Again, this will depend on what you have been asked to do. Generally, on placement and in practice, you will encounter or be expected to undertake the following types of writing:

	Report	Case study	Leaflet/information sheet
Aimed at	Consultants, GPs, members of the MDT, other formal agencies	Can be used in assessment or as a teaching tool	Patients, clients, family members, carers
Purpose	To justify To summarise To document an intervention or course of action To provide continuity of service	To think through To reflect on To tease out To learn from To demonstrate reasoning	To inform To signpost To support To educate
Structure	Structured	Structured	Less structured
Language	Formal, written in the third person	Formal, written in the third person	Very informal language. Usually includes pictures

One of the best ways to learn how to write or produce these documents is to look at what is already in existence. Read through reports and case studies and look at patient leaflets and information sheets. Reflect on how they are structured. Spend time mentally evaluating these and identify good practice. Here are a few ideas to point you in the right direction.

Reports

In practice, a report is any document that formally summarises an event and makes recommendations for future action. Examples of reports include:

- Assessment reports

- Home visit reports

- Discharge summaries (whether this is an intervention or an admission)

- Accident reports

The report usually begins with an *introduction*, which outlines its purpose to the reader: This report summarises the interventions Mrs X received during…

Depending on the type of report you are writing, there may be a *summary* of the presenting issues or problems that resulted in this person coming into your service.

This is followed by *a record of your intervention* or what you did and perhaps a justification for this. It is important to be very precise, documenting dates and times. For example, the fact that the assessment took place six months ago could have a huge bearing on the case.

The findings come next. This section may be divided using subheadings. For example, an assessment report about a person with dementia could include subsections on cognitive functioning, perception, physical functioning and mood.

The *recommendations* follow, and these indicate what happens next. This is arguably the most important part of the document. If the person reading your report is in a hurry, this is the section they will focus on.

The report ends with *your name*, your *job description/title, where you are based* and the *date*. This is in case someone needs to contact you in the future.

You will find examples of reports on the website accompanying this book (www.skills4health.co.uk).

Case studies

A case study also takes the format of a report and follows a structure containing subheadings. However, because the aim is to demonstrate learning and highlight your thinking and reasoning processes, these subheadings are more numerous and quite different from other reports you will write on placement. If you are writing a case study as part of your assessment, you must remember to ensure that confidentiality is maintained at all times and that any details that identify the person are removed. You can lose marks and even fail a piece of work if you do not do this. Seek the person's permission beforehand.

The case study begins with *general information*: for example, the person's age, marital status, gender and diagnosis.

The next part presents a detailed and comprehensive summary of their *personal circumstances*, which may have a bearing on your intervention and describes the *background to the case*. Here you would include information about an individual's social history, education, work history, medical history and the reasons for the current referral as well as other significant personnel involved in client care. For instance:

Mr A is the youngest of a family of five children. At present he has two surviving sisters, both of whom live in the X area and one of whom he sees on a regular basis. The murder of his brother was a defining moment. … Mr A has a history of alcoholism…

A section is then included describing what has *happened from the person's perspective* – why they feel that they are there, their hopes about the future and the intervention. You may wish to include details here in terms of the level of insight they possess.

This is followed by a *summary of identified needs*.

Once you have built up a clear picture of the background and the associated factors that will influence the case, the next stage is to present your intervention. Your case study may therefore include sections on:

- *Assessment procedures*: descriptions of assessments undertaken, the findings of these, how these impacted on decisions made with regard to the treatment approach adopted.

- *Short-term and long-term goals*: what the person is working towards in the short and long term.

- *The resulting treatment interventions*: these should explain why one approach was adopted as well as why others weren't used. You may refer to the particular circumstances surrounding the case and draw on the wider literature.

- *The outcome,* or what happened: this part details the results of the intervention and describes what the outcomes were. Did the person meet their goals? Was the intervention a success? From whose perspective? Were the results different from what you thought they would be? If you started using one approach but for whatever reason it wasn't working and you changed direction, here is the place to justify your reasoning processes. You are demonstrating to your reader that you are able to see a far wider picture.

Finally, you will present a *summary of your learning*. What new insights have you taken away from this experience? How will this impact on future practice? What are the lessons to be learnt? This summary requires you to identify further areas for development, both in terms of your own learning needs and in relation to practice more generally.

Patient leaflets

Leaflets are, by comparison, far less structured. Again, a patient information leaflet will fulfil a specific purpose. Most are written with the intention of:

- Informing (providing information, education, facts)

- Giving instructions

- Offering advice, reassurance or encouragement

- Presenting a range of strategies

- Highlighting dangers

- Promoting a change in behaviour

- Signposting to further services or resources

When creating a leaflet, the first thing you need to do is to be clear about who your audience is and what you are communicating. Sometimes this means that you will have to create multiple leaflets on the same subject, each aimed at a different group. For example, a leaflet aimed at children about the splint they are wearing (to encourage) and a leaflet aimed at parents describing how to care for this (to inform).

Once you are clear about the purpose of the leaflet and its intended audience, you then need to decide upon the key message. A good information leaflet contains enough information to inform but not too much to overwhelm. It is a perfect illustration of when less is more and least is most.

The skills you will use when constructing the leaflet are exactly the same as for any other piece of written work.

In the *introduction*, the leaflet will state its purpose and include phrases such as:

This leaflet is aimed at…
It explains/describes/shows how to…

The *main body* of the leaflet will present information and is usually structured around a series of headings or subheadings to make it easier to read and to draw your reader in. Sometimes, these will take the form of questions.

What is dementia?
What do I need to ask my doctor?
If there is a problem, how…?

Finally, there will be some kind of a *summary* with *further information* and *signposting* to further resources.

This leaflet has explained where to go for help if you… For further information please telephone/contact/read…

The way you present information and your style of writing are crucial. It has to 'earn' the right to be read. To this end:

- Avoid jargon at all costs

- Address the audience directly using words such as 'you' and keep sentences short and simple

- Your leaflet will be reaching individuals who may find reading difficult for a number of reasons. Where possible, illustrate your text with pictures (particularly if you are giving instructions)

- Offer translations for individuals who do not have English as their first language

- Ensure that your font is large and clear enough for people whose eyesight is poor

Leaflets allow you to exercise your creativity; the bolder and brighter, the better. Remember that when you provide information in this way the person does not have the luxury of being able to ask you to clarify points or ask you questions directly. Information must be clear and accurate. If in doubt, check it out with someone.

There is no room for mistakes or misinterpretation of information. With this in mind, have fun!

Plan what you are going to write and structure what you want to say

On placement, it is vital that you present written information in such a way that it is clearly and coherently written. You will probably be working in a busy and pressured environment, where colleagues will not have time to read long and rambling accounts, trying to 'find' the gems of information you are attempting to include. You therefore need to ensure that what you write is clear and well structured.

While it is highly unlikely that you will have the same amount of time that you have at university to craft a detailed essay or assignment plan, time spent sketching out the key points you wish to convey on a piece of scrap paper before you begin to assemble your report, notes or leaflet will help you to structure your writing so that it flows in a logical manner and will save you time in the long run.

Where possible include signposts within your writing in much the same way as you do in essays at university. For example: 'This report will outline...', 'The findings of the home visit showed that...', 'Observations on the ward have highlighted...', 'In summary, it is recommended that...'. Remember that reading through existing documentation can help this process as it will enable you to see how other, more experienced colleagues approach this aspect of their work. The more opportunity you have to practise these skills the easier they will become, and over time your confidence and abilities will grow.

Support your ideas with evidence

When you are on placement writing formal reports and documents, you will still need to ground your writing using evidence. It is highly unlikely that this evidence will be from literature or textbooks. Rather, it will be focused on your observations, the results of assessments, statements made by patients and feedback from carers and other members of the multidisciplinary team. If you do not back up everything you say, your writing will lack credibility and others will be reluctant to act on your recommendations. Here are examples of the type of evidence you may wish to use to support your statements (the evidence is in italics).

Mr X appeared disorientated to time and place. *When asked where he was, he replied 'at the races'.*

The house was in a poor state of hygiene. *Bags of rubbish were found in the living room and rotting food was left on the floor.*

Mrs Y concentrated well. *She was able to sequence the task and remain focused for 30 minutes.*

Think about language and style

Language and style are just as important on placement as they are at university. The language you use within notes and reports, and your style of writing, will have implications in terms of the credibility of what you present and the gravity of what you say. Contrary to popular belief, writing well is not about using complex language and phrases; it is about recognising the audience that you are writing for and expressing yourself clearly. There may be subtle differences in terms of the formality of a report for a consultant and an information leaflet for a client, however both need to express ideas confidently and in such a way that there can be no confusion as to what you are trying to convey.

At all times remember that the clients you are describing in your report or notes have the right to read what you have written about them. It is completely unacceptable to use language that is demeaning or could cause offence. The rule of thumb here is that if you would not be happy to share your notes or report with the person you have written about, then you perhaps need to revisit what you have said in the first place.

Proof-read your work

Proof-reading is made more difficult as a consequence of the array of unfamiliar medical terminology, equipment and medication which your spell-checker will fail to recognise. However, *you must take time to do this*. Spelling mistakes at university make written work look untidy but on placement they carry more serious consequences. Always check the name of the person you are referring to and ensure that you include the right date of birth/patient number. For other tricky medical terms, create a small pocket glossary that you can carry with you (in your trouser or tunic pocket) to consult when necessary.

IN A NUTSHELL

Many students describe the process of mastering the written word as one of the most challenging aspects of their university course. However, spending time in the classroom developing skills and confidence in expressing ideas in writing can pay dividends in practice, and will ensure that you will be well placed to share information with your clients and with the wider multidisciplinary team, and ultimately to influence practice through your writing and research.

- Writing is a skill. It is like anything else, the more you write the easier it will become

- Make sure that you are clear about what you are being asked to do before you put pen to paper

- You will gain the highest marks for writing that goes beyond being descriptive and includes some form of critical discussion or evaluation

- Spend time planning what you are going to write. It will save you time in the long run

- Always back up what you say with evidence

- Reference this evidence according to the conventions set down

- Proof-read your work carefully and do not rely completely on the spell-checker!

References and signposts to further reading

Barrass, R. (2003) *Students Must Write: A Guide to Better Writing in Coursework and Examinations*. London: Routledge.

Cook, R. (2000) The Writer's Manual: A Step-by-step Guide for Nurses and Other Health Professionals. Oxford: Radcliffe Medical Press.

Gocsik, K. (2005) *Dartmouth writing program.* Available at: www.dartmouth.edu/~writing/materials.html (last accessed 01/01/09).

Pears, R. and Shields, G. (2005) *Cite Them Right: The Essential Guide to Referencing and Plagiarism* (2nd edition). Newcastle: Pear Tree Books.

Williams, D. (2002) Writing Skills in Practice: A Practical Guide for Health Professionals. London: Jessica Kingsley.

14 Thinking as a skill

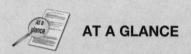 **AT A GLANCE**

This chapter is for you if

- Thinking gives you a headache

- You find it hard to see beyond the obvious

- Your assignments read: 'must be more critical'

- Decision-making brings you out in a cold sweat

- Your decision-making process currently consists of a pin, a blindfold and a list on the wall

> Thinking is the ultimate human resource. Yet we can never be satisfied with our most important skill. ... Usually the only people who are very satisfied with their thinking skill are those poor thinkers who believe that the purpose of thinking is to prove yourself right – to your own satisfaction. (De Bono, 2000: xi)

You may be intrigued to see that a full chapter has been devoted to the skill of thinking. Perhaps even now you are wondering if thinking fits into the range of competencies required for your future role and, indeed, whether it is possible to learn how to think. I would answer a resounding yes to both these points. The ability to examine evidence, to weigh up the facts and to form reasonable conclusions is a critical skill required by all health and social care practitioners.

This chapter begins by looking at some of the thinking skills you find will be useful in the classroom. You will learn how to identify issues, see things from different perspectives, weigh up the evidence and consider alternative solutions or ways of thinking and responding to questions and situations.

You will then learn how to transfer these skills into placement, focusing on how to appraise a situation, tap into your existing knowledge and develop strategies and solutions to enhance patient care. This complex decision-making process is called clinical reasoning, and is a skill you will develop and build on throughout your career.

I think, therefore I am .... I think

There are entire branches of psychology and philosophy dedicated to the art of thinking. It is not the aim of this chapter to delve into these but to offer a series of practical steps that you can take to gain the most from your reading and research and to consider how you can then translate these skills directly into practice. Our starting point is the university context.

University tutors will talk a great deal about critical thinking. They will tell you that the highest marks are gained for assignments that contain a degree of criticality. However, the term can seem a little elusive and it can be hard to understand what they mean. The problem lies with the word 'critical'. We often associate this with a fussy parent or teacher. Yet the term in fact refers to quite a reflective process, where you think about the information with a view to making judgements regarding its accuracy and what you believe.

Price and Maier (2007) describes this as a process of 'interacting' with information, questioning, reflecting on and evaluating the content of what you are reading or hearing. So the next time your tutor asks you to critically examine an issue, you need to weigh up the evidence, think and examine this from different viewpoints and develop your own perspective or argument as opposed to accepting what you read or hear at face value. To visualise the different types of thinking, imagine a series of building blocks.

At an unthinking, descriptive level you might describe the building blocks, simply repeating what you see: 'There are six building blocks labelled C, D, A, L, B, T.

To move beyond this and look at the situation more critically you might compare your observations with your previous understanding or you might examine the blocks more closely. For example, on first appearance, it seems that they contain the letters but on closer examination you will see that they have letters on six sides and are different sizes.

Based on this examination you will make some simple decisions. For example, you may choose to discard some. You may then step back and look at what you have, pulling in additional information: 'Three appear to be the same size and are made of the same material. These seem to form a natural order.'

Finally, you reassemble and rearrange the blocks based on what you have found. This final stage is called synthesis: 'When these are placed together they spell the word 'cat'.

You will follow a similar process when you read a book or an article or listen to a discussion. You focus on the detail, examine what is under the surface, and test this out to check that it is true. Then, based on what you already know to be true, you will pull in additional pieces of information to adapt and develop your thinking to construct new perspectives or offer a different view.

KEYS TO SUCCESS

To engage in a process of critical thinking when reading an article, a book or listening to an argument you need to:

- Identify the desired outcome
- Define the issues/argument
- Look at the information from different perspectives
- Decide on a way forwards

Identify the desired outcome

Critical thinking is an active process. The first stage is to decide what you aim to achieve by engaging with the information. Do you hope to:

- Build up a clearer picture
- Think about the subject in a different way
- Explore an argument
- Find 'the truth'
- Compare what you have read or heard with information from different sources
- Decide the credibility of the information

Define the issues/argument

The next stage of the process is then to define the issues or argument. Try to summarise this in short sentences in much the same way that a journalist writes a newspaper headline. Ask yourself 'What is the bottom line?'

- The author thinks x
- X argues this and Y argues that

Try this for yourself. Read a short chapter in a book or a journal article and see if you can summarise the main thrust of what the author is saying. This is your starting point.

Look at the information from different perspectives

The next stage is to engage with the information, looking at the information from different perspectives. This is where the critical thinking process really begins. Edward De Bono (2000) pioneered a method of parallel thinking called '*Six Thinking Hats*'. The approach requires you to look at an issue from a number of clearly defined perspectives. We will describe these in more detail later in the chapter.

The following activity is a variation of the technique. Rather than using hats, this approach uses different coloured pens. Read an article or listen to an argument several times, and as you do imagine that you are making notes.

Imagine that you are holding a *violet* pen. For the purpose of this exercise, the violet pen is the critical pen. It looks for flaws in the argument and detects inaccuracies. It homes in on assumptions, picks up occasions where bold statements are made without the necessary supporting evidence and detects inconsistencies. When you use the violet pen, you ask: 'Is the evidence trustworthy?' 'Can these results really be generalised to a wider population?' 'Did the researcher use an appropriate method and measure what they said they would?'

Now imagine that you are holding a *brown* pen. The brown pen represents growth, like the earth. The brown pen seeks out alternative ways of looking at the issues or evidence to generate new ideas. It asks: 'Can I think about this in a different way?' 'Is it possible to reach a different conclusion using this evidence?'

The *orange* pen peels back the layers and looks underneath. When you make notes with the orange pen you are asking: 'Does this author have a personal investment in this line of argument?' 'What is their track record and are they an expert in this field?' 'Who was the research funded by and is it biased?' 'How current are the ideas?'

Pink is the colour of romance. The *pink* pen denotes relationships. When you use the pink pen to make notes or to highlight information ask yourself: 'How does this relate to what I have read before?' 'What is the relationship between X and Y?' 'How can I relate this to what I have observed on placement?' 'What are the implications of this for practice?'

The *gold* pen is extremely positive. When you use the gold pen highlight the strengths of an argument.

The *blue* pen is the pen of decisions. When you hold this pen you draw on all the other pens and, weighing these up, position yourself in relation to the arguments. The blue pen challenges you to look at the bigger picture. Ask yourself: 'Where does this line of thinking lead?' 'What was my standpoint/viewpoint at the beginning and where is it now?' 'Do I need any further information before I make a final decision?'

Decide on a way forwards

The blue pen is a useful pen to end with as the final stage of the critical thinking process is to decide your next step. For example, if you are critiquing an article or a chapter in a book, you may choose to:

- Make a judgement based on your reading

- Find more information and widen your research

- Clarify the evidence

- Formulate your standpoint and start to plan your assignment

If you are listening to a verbal argument, you may:

- Respond with a counter-argument

- Ask more questions

- Keep quiet

Problem-solving

The other skill you will hear quite a lot about at university in relation to thinking is that of problem-solving. Problem-solving begins with a challenge or an issue and the aim of the process is to generate possible solutions and find the best way forwards. If problem-solving was a shape, it would probably be a diamond. You begin with a problem, *generate* lots of potential solutions and then narrow this down to a way forward.

The processes of critical thinking and problem-solving may seem very different but I would like to argue that they require similar skills and that the steps to success can be equally relevant. Here is a worked example.

You are required to complete a piece of group-work by the end of next week but your group is finding it very difficult to meet and you are running out of time.

Identify the desired outcome
Once again the starting point is to identify the desired outcome so that you have a direction in which to work and a measure to demonstrate whether or not you have been successful. It is helpful to write this down. In this instance one possible outcome might be:

To work together as a group and submit the work on time.

Define the issues
The next stage is to identify and map out the issues. An issue could be a problem, an obstacle, a puzzle, a question or a situation where something could be improved or developed. In this example the problem could be defined as:

Possible failure to meet a deadline.

However, this is quite superficial and you may want to untangle this further, elaborating the issues. In the following example, these might include:

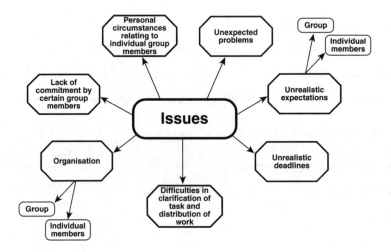

The more time you can spend untangling what the issues really are, the higher the chance of reaching a successful outcome and avoiding this pitfall in the future.

Look at the information from different perspectives

De Bono's 'Six Hats' are very useful here, particularly if you are engaging in group problem-solving. De Bono argued that we become confused because we try to see/do everything at once. He suggested that 'emotions, information, logic and creativity all crowd in on us. It is like juggling too many balls' (De Bono, 2000: xi). This technique works very well when engaging in group problem-solving activities as all group members are invited to think in a particular way at any one time. For example:

White hat thinking: invites the group to focus on the facts
Black hat thinking: focuses on the limitations of an idea
Yellow hat thinking: emphasises the positives
Green hat thinking: invites the group to generate new ideas
Red hat thinking: invites the group to look at the emotional view
Blue hat thinking: exercises control on the thinking process

Begin with the green hat, which allows you to generate lots of possible ideas (based on experience of previous problems and experiences). Then work through these ideas using the different ways of thinking as a means of evaluating their respective drawbacks and merits.

Here is the list of ideas generated by green hat thinking:

- Use a group discussion board
- Break down the large activity into smaller components and give everyone the responsibility for one each
- Discuss where lack of commitment comes from
- Identify respective strengths of group members
- Look to support mechanisms
- Speak to the tutor

Select each idea in turn and subject it to the 'six hat thinking' process. Here is the beginning of that process for using the discussion board. Try to complete the remaining boxes.

Colour hat	Type of thinking	
Black hat	Limitations	Not everyone has access to the discussion board. Recently, the site containing this has been down. Varying degrees of confidence among group members.
Yellow hat	Positives	This will save everyone coming to university. It is possible to print off the comments and this can provide evidence for the assignment.
Red hat	Emotional view	
White hat	Focus on the facts	
Blue hat	Best combination of ideas	

Decide a way forwards

Finally, make a decision as to the best way forwards. Remember, you do not have to confine this to one thing. The best way forwards might be an amalgamation of all your ideas: a combined approach. Once you have reached a decision you can start the process of planning to put your decision into practice.

Skills in practice

> Clinical reasoning [is] the process used by practitioners to plan, direct, perform and reflect on client care. (Schell and Schell, 2008: 443)

The decisions you make on placement and in practice will have huge ramifications in terms of patient care. The process of identifying the needs of the individual and developing an intervention or a programme to meet these needs is complex and fraught with challenges. You will be confronted by multiple perspectives, conflicting evidence and difficult environmental and organisational constraints. Chapter 10 on researching information highlights some of the processes you will need to work on when sifting through the evidence. It is fair to say that there is no such thing as one solution. You need to understand the factors impacting on the decision-making process and also what led you to arrive at your present course of action.

The term given to this process of thinking and decision-making is 'clinical reasoning' and is a key skill used by professionals in practice. If you can master this, you will be able to:

- Step outside the situation and understand the factors impacting on your decision-making processes

- Consider different ways of thinking about a situation which in turn opens up more possibilities to improve patient care

- Articulate your actions more clearly

Your experience in the classroom will provide a firm foundation in this process. It is possible to transfer the keys to successful thinking in the classroom to clinical decision-making in practice.

Identify the desired outcome

This can be a tricky one, as it may not be immediately apparent. It will also depend on your perspective. For example, if you are a paramedic arriving at the scene of a road traffic accident, from the paramedic's point of view the desired outcome will be to save as many lives in that situation as possible. From the perspective of one of the people who is injured, the desired outcome is that they survive. Similarly, for the person with dementia, their desired outcome is to return home, whereas for their carer it might be that they go into residential care. In all your interactions with patients, remember that your duty of care lies with the client. Sometimes the desired outcome will be a compromise based on a combination of the following factors:

- The wishes of the client

- Medical factors

- Constraints of the wider service

Define the issues

Again, this will very much be dependent on your particular professional role. For example, if you think back to the paramedic arriving at the scene of an accident, on arrival he will be weighing up the situation, deciding what the issues are in terms of who is most at risk and their priorities as a consequence of this. On the other hand, if you are the social worker putting into place a package of care for a person with dementia, you may be trying to understand the issues in terms of family members and looking at factors that might prevent the person from returning home. Either way, you will need to quickly assimilate a great deal of information based on a range of sources, including the patient's narrative, test results, assessments, information from carers and the person's past medical history. We have already likened this process to 'being a detective'.

When you first meet a client you will need to listen to what they say. You will then pull together and synthesise this information within the context of your previous experiences and the evidence gathered from other sources (e.g. assessments, tests, accounts by family and carers). From this you will begin to gain a sense of the main issues involved. However, a word of warning here. You may find that the issues change, that they are hard to uncover and sometimes do not even relate to the patient but rather to the service in which you work or to the dynamics of the team (e.g. a lack of resources).

Look at the information from different perspectives

People are complex. Happily, we are more than a combination of chemicals, organs and neurons. As such, we will all experience health and illness in very different ways. Our response will depend on the condition, our psychological response, our existing coping mechanisms, support networks, general health and the length of time we have experienced the condition (adapted from Kitwood and Benson, 1997). Add to this, conditions beyond your control – environment, resources, economic situation – and you will begin to see that the decisions you make in relation to patient care will be governed by a whole range of factors and ultimately will rest on the perspective you choose to take. Let's begin with a non-clinical example to illustrate a decision-making process.

You come home from placement and you are hungry. Your choice of meal could be governed by

1. What is in the fridge

2. What kind of a day you have had and your cooking skills

3. Your knowledge of the nutritional content of certain types of food

4. How you feel (and yes, the tub of ice cream looks very tempting)

5. What certain types of food mean to you

Each type of thinking is given a label.

(a) Making a decision based on practicalities, e.g. available resources, is called pragmatic reasoning (what is in the fridge?).

(b) Making a decision based on a person's present situation and life context is called conditional reasoning (the kind of day you have had and your cooking skills).

(c) Making a decision based on the textbook approach in respect of your professional knowledge is called scientific or procedural reasoning (nutritional content).

(d) Making a decision based on the emotional response of the person and their relationships is called interactive reasoning (how you feel).

(e) Making a decision based on a person's life history or story is called narrative reasoning (the meanings associated with the food).

Now let's take an example from practice:

You are a student on a busy medical ward in a large general hospital. You have been working with a client who has sustained an injury on a fishing trip, resulting in severe upper limb weakness. Feedback from staff is that he is reluctant to take part in any therapeutic intervention and appears unmotivated, sometimes tearful when anything is suggested. Fishing was his life and without this he sees no future. The ward is an acute ward and there is a pressure on bed space and the consultant is suggesting that he should be discharged into residential care. He is appalled by this, as he has lived in his house since he was born and has a large number of friends who live locally. The textbook intervention is to work proximally to distally (from his shoulder to his wrist and hand), increasing his passive range of motion. However, this would take over six weeks.

Use the space below to make a list of all the different issues and factors that will impact on the decision you make.

The table on the facing page contains a list of the different types of reasoning and the questions associated with these.

Decide a way forwards

This is easier said than done. As you can see from this example, there is no definitive way of looking at a situation. You need to take into account these different perspectives and their respective strengths and limitations before making a decision. In many cases there is not a simple right or wrong answer.

Type of reasoning	Possible questions
Scientific or procedural reasoning	What do I know about this condition? What is the prognosis? What does the evidence say is the most appropriate intervention? Is there evidence for other approaches that could work? What further information is required?
Pragmatic reasoning	Is there another ward where he could receive rehabilitation? Will increasing input from therapy reduce the amount of time he needs to spend on the ward? Are there any further staff or resource implications? How could I overcome these?
Narrative reasoning	What does this accident mean to this person? What does residential care mean? What previous life experiences may have impacted on how he is experiencing this current admission? What is his story? How does he see his future story?
Conditional reasoning	Is there a way to tap into his previous lifestyle to help him? Are there other networks available? Does he have any family? What is his job? Are there other interests we could use? What about his interest in fishing? How might his home situation impact on the intervention?
Interactive reasoning	He seems angry and resistant to change and by the same account very tearful. How is he coping with this emotional response to the accident? How can I find out what he really feels? Will this emotional response be a barrier to treatment or can it be harnessed?

However, being aware of these different reasoning styles, and the perspectives they offer, will inform your thinking and will maximise the range of possible treatment options and media that are open to you. Use these options as a framework to talk things through with your educator. In doing so, you will take into account all that is available and this will ensure that your client has the best possible outcome.

Clinical reasoning is a complex process and it will take time to feel confident in using the different styles of reasoning in practice. However, your placement educator is there to support you and your weekly supervision sessions offer an ideal opportunity to discuss the complexities of the decision-making process and to develop skills in applying a full range of professional learning styles to the situations you encounter. The resources at the end of this chapter will also guide your thinking.

IN A NUTSHELL

This chapter has illustrated something of both the importance and the complexity of the thinking and reasoning skills you will develop on your course and beyond. The key messages are as follows:

- Thinking is a core skill required by all health and social care professionals

- Thinking skills begin developing in the classroom

- Critical thinking is a way of looking at a situation and weighing up the evidence

- Clinical reasoning allows you to look at complex situations from different perspectives and to choose the solution that best fits the needs of the person within the confines and resources of the organisation in which you are working

References and signposts to further reading and resources

Carr, S.M. (2004) 'A framework for understanding clinical reasoning in community nursing', *Journal of Clinical Nursing*, 13 (7): 850–7.

Cottrell, S.M. (2005) *Critical Thinking Skills: Developing Effective Analysis and Argument*. Basingstoke: Palgrave Macmillan.

De Bono, E. (2000) *Six Thinking Hats*. London: Penguin.

Fairbairn, G.J. and Winch, C. (1996) *Reading, Writing and Reasoning: A Guide for Students* (2nd edition). Buckingham: Society for Research in Higher Education/ Open University Press.

Healey, J. and Spencer, M. (2008) *Surviving Your Placement in Health and Social Care: A Student Handbook*. Maidenhead: Open University Press McGraw-Hill.

Higgs, J. and Jones, M. (2000) *Clinical Reasoning in the Health Professions*. Oxford: Butterworth-Heinemann.

Kitwood, T. and Benson, S. (1997) *Dementia Reconsidered: The Person Comes First*. Buckingham: Open University Press.

Price, G. and Maier, P. (2007) *Effective Study Skills: Unlock Your Potential*. Harlow: Pearson.

Schell, B.A. and Schell, J.W. (2008) *Clinical and Professional Reasoning in Occupational Therapy*. Baltimore, MD: Lippincott, Williams and Wilkins.

Thompson, A. (1996) *Critical Reasoning: A Practical Introduction*. London: Routledge.

15 Preparing for and performing well in pressured situations

JARGON-BUSTING

MCQs: An abbreviation for multiple choice questions.

Open book: An examination where you can take your textbook or a series of notes in with you.

OSCEs: Objective structured clinical examinations: a practical form of assessment.

Viva: An oral examination.

AT A GLANCE

This chapter is for you if

- You feel that you have the memory span of a goldfish

- You struggle to recall information when it really counts

- You feel that your marks in exams do not reflect your knowledge, abilities and skills

- You try to learn information in exactly the same way

- You lose sleep worrying about exams

- You never perform as well in exams as you do in coursework

- You find that your mind goes blank when you are working under pressure

Pressure is part of life in the twenty-first century. In health and social care practice it may stem from the complexities of meeting patient needs and can be exacerbated by a lack of resources, outcomes and performance-driven targets. At university, these pressures may also take many forms: juggling multiple roles, coping with change, balancing personal budgets. These will probably be constant throughout your course and we have already considered some of the strategies and techniques you might use to cope with the stresses arising from these situations.

However, there is another level of pressure that relates specifically to your ability to recall information and work in a very exact and precise manner within tight time constraints under the gaze of others. This might be when performing a specific clinical procedure, undertaking an assessment and recalling your observations, feeding back at a case conference with close questioning by the consultant or even taking a person's medical history and remembering the questions you need to ask. These situations will test your memory, your ability to recall and process information and to apply your learning to a range of situations.

Written examinations, practicals and assessed presentations at university will help you to begin to prepare for these situations in the context of health and social care practice. They will enable you to demonstrate your understanding and your competence to practice. This chapter looks at a range of strategies that can help you to make the most of your memory and to recall and apply information when you need to in order to perform at your best. It particularly addresses the area of examinations in university and practical skills on placement.

STARTING POINTS

What kind of a memory do you have? Before you even begin to look at techniques for remembering information, it can be helpful to play to your strengths and tap into your natural affinities. At the heart of this process is deciding what kind of a memory you have. Are you the kind of person who likes to picture the information you need to remember or does your memory thrive on words sounds, rhythm and rhyme? Alternatively, are you someone who learns by doing?

Now you have considered some of the skills you already possess, let's look at the types of examination you might face.

Types of examination

Examinations are not about learning and regurgitating everything there is to know on a given topic. They are about having a good understanding of a subject area and demonstrating your ability to select and apply this understanding to a range of given situations, choosing appropriate evidence to back up your ideas. It is therefore useful to have a clear idea about what these situations are and what exactly you might be facing.

The following is a list of some of the examinations you might come across during your university career. They come in all shapes and sizes and can take on a number of different guises.

Essay examination

An examination based on essays requires you to recall, structure and order information and develop a sustained argument in response to a question or series of questions. The number of questions you will be expected to answer within the time will vary, but should be no more than 4 questions in a 2–3 hour period.

Short answers

Short answers are less detailed than essay questions but still require you to structure your ideas clearly. In short answer questions examiners are looking for breadth of knowledge and your ability to express your ideas succinctly. Sometimes a short question can contain multiple sections.

Multiple choice questions

These are often abbreviated to MCQs. Here you are presented with a list of possible answers in response to a question. You need to choose and indicate the correct response.

Gapped questions

Gapped questions have spaces in the text requiring you to insert a missing word. In some instances several technical terms are supplied and you have to select the right one for each gap.

Open book examinations and seen papers

These test your ability to apply information rather than your ability to recall facts and figures. The key to an open book exam is to check how many texts you can take into the room with you and make sure that you are very comfortable in finding your way around these. If the rules say that you can annotate your text, it would be well worth purchasing a copy of the book and using a highlighter pen to denote particular themes. Work out a system so that you know where key information is located. However, avoid making this over-complicated. For seen examinations, you may also be allowed to take in a page of notes. Again, the key to a seen paper is to research the subject well and to learn a detailed essay plan. If you write and learn by rote the introduction prior to the examination, this will save you valuable time and help to give you confidence as you tackle the rest of the paper.

Objective Structured Clinical Examinations

These practical examinations are also known as OSCEs. You will go to a series of work stations manned by an examiner where you will be given a patient scenario. After reading a set of instructions describing what you need to do, you will then undertake the specified task. This might relate to reading a measurement, looking at an x-ray, interpreting or undertaking an assessment, or it could require you to perform a simple procedure such as taking a blood pressure, mobilising or interacting with a client (often played by an actor).

Viva

This is short for *viva voce* or oral examination. During a viva you will be asked questions by your examiner and will be required to give verbal responses. For example, you might have been asked to learn a range of 'conditions' and then, on arrival for the examination, will be given a case study describing a person with one of those conditions.

Oral presentations

In an oral presentation you will be required to speak for a specified length of time on a topic. Ordinarily, you would be given a title beforehand. Preparation is the key. It is not necessary to revise lots of information, but you will need to be methodical as you approach the question. Refer to Chapter 16 on presentation skills for additional pointers.

KEYS TO SUCCESS

In order to do well and succeed in examinations you need to:

- Be clear about what you need to learn
- Be aware of how you will need to recall and apply this information
- Translate the information into a format that makes it easier to learn
- Develop specific techniques to aid recall
- Plan ahead
- Manage your nerves

Be clear about what you need to learn

The first step in the revision process is to decide what you need to learn. Condensing copious notes into a manageable form will save time and energy and make learning more effective. Review your work, making sure that you understand the material and look at past examination questions to identify recurring themes. Then make lists of topic areas. Use this process to prioritise your learning, dividing information into the following categories:

- Information vital for the examination

- Information that is not vital for the examination but would be nice to learn

- Information not required for the examination

Remember: you need to be brutal. In an ideal world you would revise everything you have been taught but the chances are you will be working within a set timeframe. In order to make the best use of this time you need to be as focused as possible. It is far better that you have a good grasp of relevant information than a hazy recollection of lots of vague facts.

Be aware of how you will need to recall and apply this information

It is worth getting this straight at the beginning as it can affect how you decide to approach the process. Sometimes, depending on the type of examination you are sitting, you might not so much need to learn specific information but know where to locate it. The following table provides a summary of the issues you need to take into account when revising.

Type of examination	Types of things it is testing	What you need to take into account when revising
Unseen paper: essay questions	Question analysis Information recall Depth of understanding Ability to structure and order information Ability to develop and sustain an argument and support your ideas with evidence Ability to work under pressure within time constraints	The number of questions Do you need to revise everything equally well or do you know that particular subjects will definitely come up, in which case can you narrow down the number of subjects you are going to revise? How much can you feasibly write in the time allocated?
Unseen paper: short questions	Information recall Ability to focus and write succinctly	The number of questions you are expected to answer Will you have a choice of questions and

(Continued)

(Continued)

Type of examination	Types of things it is testing	What you need to take into account when revising
	Time management: ability to allocate time across questions Breadth of knowledge	do you know what possible topics may crop up? If you answer one topic from one section does this limit your choices of other topics from different question sets?
Multiple choice questions	Ability to recall information Reasoning skills Ability to make decisions when under pressure	The range of subjects you will be examined on The number of questions you are expected to answer and the time in which you have to complete these. Will you be penalised if you answer a question incorrectly? (e.g. two marks deducted for every incorrect response)
Gapped question	Information recall Understanding of specific terms and ability to use specialist vocabulary	Does the exam contain a list of the specialist vocabulary for you to choose from or will you be expected to recall this from memory?
Viva	Information recall Reasoning skills Ability to articulate ideas Ability to work under pressure	What form will the viva take? A case study presented beforehand? The results of an assessment? The findings of a test?
Presentation	Ability to structure ideas Ability to sustain a verbal argument supporting ideas with evidence Ability to plan ahead Ability to communicate information to different audiences	What is the question? How long do you have to speak? Who is the audience? What audio-visual equipment is available?
Open-book examination	Ability to locate and use information Ability to work under time constraints Ability to select and use appropriate resources	How many texts can you take into the examination room? Can you annotate these?
Seen examination	Ability to focus your revision Ability to plan ahead and work under pressure	Are you allowed to take a page of notes into the examination? Is it worth learning an essay plan? Is it worth writing and learning an introduction to the essay?
OSCEs	This type of examination tests your competence to practice under pressure as well as to interact and communicate with a client	What are the practical activities you will be expected to perform? Will you have access to the scenarios beforehand?

Translate the information into a form that will make it easier to learn

Once you have decided what you need to learn the next stage is to translate your notes into a form that will aid your revision. This will very much depend on the subject area, your learning style and the type of examination you are sitting. However, as a rule of thumb, revision notes should be:

- Portable

- Visually attractive

- Mirror the type of examination you are sitting

- Reflect your lifestyle and learning style

- Contain an element of fun

Condensing your copious notes into a format for revision may seem time-consuming, but this way of interacting with the information is a way of making learning active and will form a key part of the revision process as a whole. Here are top tips to making revision notes you want to read:

1. Condensing notes on to small index cards or slips of paper makes these infinitely less intimidating to read and far more portable compared with carrying a huge ring binder full of information.

2. The more visually attractive the notes, the more you will want to read them: diagrams, photographs, cartoons, pictures from magazines, images from the internet can all increase your motivation to look at the information and will also help you to make connections in your visual memory.

3. The best notes mirror the type of examination you are sitting. For example, if you are revising for an anatomy examination or a piece of legislation that takes the form of multiple choice questions, a useful technique is to write questions on one side of the card and the answers on the other. That way you can test yourself at given points.

4. To maximise your learning, ensure that your notes reflect your lifestyle and your learning style. Identify pockets of time that you can make good use of. For example, if you are an auditory learner, commit your notes to an audio-tape or your mp3 player and listen to these while walking the dog, washing the car or doing the ironing. If you are a visual learner, pin information to the back of the toilet door, inside cupboards, above the kettle, make key words out of fridge magnets so that every time you go into the kitchen you will be reminded of what you need to learn. You will also be able to visualise these in the examination.

5. Make your notes memorable. Cards cut into the shape of bones with stickers representing sites of origins and insertions, a skeleton made out of cardboard, and a three-dimensional brain made from plasticine will all help to reinforce the information you need to learn.

6. Make learning fun. Put information in your own words, use text speak, transform your notes into a song, make playing cards from key information, turn flow charts into jigsaw puzzles. Use any means to make your revision notes something you want to interact with and return to again and again. In doing so, you make it easier to involve family and friends so that revision is not such a lonely process.

7. Make your notes distinct. Colour, scent (perfume, aftershave) will all engage the senses and make learning memorable.

Develop specific techniques to aid recall

So, you have made a decision in terms of what you consciously need to remember and you've put this into a format where you can begin to rehearse information in order to commit it to memory. The next stage is to encode the information so that it becomes stored in the long-term memory. Tony Buzan is an expert at creative learning techniques. He likens the brain to a giant filing cabinet and suggests that to be memorable information needs to be:

- Well organised

- Accessible

- Associated with items or thoughts already stored in the memory

- Outstanding or unique as this appeals to the imagination

- Appealing to the senses: taste, touch, sound or sight

- Linked to your particular interests

  (Buzan, 2006a: 104–5)

Encoding translates information into memory patterns. The more patterns and associations we can make, the greater the chance we will be able to recall the information. Buzan recognises that the senses play a key role in this process so you may remember something because of the way it sounds (auditory) or how it looks (visual). You may make a connection because of the meaning of the words (semantic), or through the physical or emotional response something evokes in you (kinaesthetic). It can also help to organise information. Here are some simple techniques you can try to aid memory recall.

Make learning visual

Pictures, drawings, doodles, cartoons, images can all help to commit your ideas to visual memory. When you are faced with a question, all you have to do is to recall the image and this will help you to make the connection with the information.

Shapes are also extremely useful as they contain a distinct number of sides. For example, you can associate the different types of anti-depressants with a triangle: each side representing a different category (tri-cyclics, SSRIs, MAOIs).

Make learning ordered

The brain thrives on order. Try chunking information so that information is organised in 'categories'. For example, if you are trying to learn about the impact of a piece of health policy, you can structure it around 'themes': social, economic, demographic, physical or psychological. If you have an anatomy exam and are trying to learn the bones, you can organise your thinking around first letters: coccyx, clavicle, cranium, pelvis, patella. Once in the exam, you think of the letter and your brain makes the association with the word.

Give learning a rhythm or a sound

If you are an auditory learner, make your revision into a song or give it a rhythm. Rap is a perfect revision aid as it carries a strong beat. Alternatively, find a song that you know well and substitute the information you need to learn into the words of the song.

Make it silly

We remember things that are fun or exaggerated. That is why we often find it easy to remember jokes. Try giving complex medical terms a silly name. I like to invent characters. For example, the French Lord who finds it impossible to stand up: Sir E bellum (cerebellum) and his dog 'Pons' or the jungle animal with an excellent memory: 'hippo' campus. They don't have to be exact (so long as you remember the proper term in the exam). For example, the famous three-times world champion cyclist (tricyclic) Annie Trampoline (amitryptaline) renowned for her ability to make everyone laugh (anti-depressant).

Create a story

Tony Buzan is a great advocate for using stories to improve memory. You may need to use your artistic licence here. For example, how about this as a way of remembering the anatomy of the upper limb?

A cook with a huge cap (**scapula**) fell over. Everyone thought this was quite humorous (**humerus**) given the **radius** of her waist. One of the other cooks Una (**ulna**) said to everyone what are you carping (**carpals**) on about? We were lucky that she had her marbles (**metacarpals**) about her and cooked the stew. It could easily have been the flan (**phalanges**) that got it.

Try familiar revision techniques

Mnemonics are a good aid to memory. These comprise sayings or phrases where the letters of the words mirror key ideas or concepts. A common mnemonic to remember the bones in the hand is: Sally left the party to take Cathy home (scaphoid, lunate, triquetrum, pisiform, trapezium, trapezoid, capitate, hamate).

There are other techniques you may want to try (method of loci, activities based around taste, teaching someone else). The key to using these is to find what works for you.

Plan ahead

To revise well you need to be strategic. Gone are the days when you locked yourself in your room and crammed solidly for two days and two nights until the day of the examination dosed up on strong black coffee. The problem with this method is that:

- It is extremely bad for your health
- You will probably remember very little of what you learnt

When you are training to be a health and social care practitioner you are in it for the long haul. Everything you learn will have a direct bearing on the quality of client care you are able to give and you will need to get to the point when recalling this information is second nature. The good news is that if you plan ahead, you need not ever pull an all-nighter again. Your planning encompasses two elements: first, you need to think about how you will organise your revision; and secondly, you will need to think about how you are going to approach the day.

Planning your revision

The key here is to make a revision timetable. Begin by making a simple list of all the tasks you need to do. List all the subjects you need to revise and then allocate your time for each subject under the headings:

- Making revision notes from notes (preparation)
- Committing information to memory (learning)
- Practise (rehearsal)

Working backwards from the date of the examination, decide how much time you can dedicate to each topic area. This will be based on the simple equation:

Time for revision/total amount to revise + practise = length of time spent on each topic

Now focus on the detail and *divide your time* into study blocks. Imagine that each day is split into three: 9.00–12.00, 1.00–4.00 and 5.00–8.00. You should aim to do some form of revision in two out of the three periods. Any more than this would be pointless as you would struggle to absorb this amount of information. Within these periods, have a short break (about 10 minutes) every 40 minutes. Indeed, Buzan (2006b) suggests that you are most receptive to learning at the beginning and end of a revision period. Studies have also demonstrated that returning to the same information at regular intervals will boost your memory so build time to revisit revision topics into your plan (Sisson et al., 1992).

Set yourself *clear revision goals*. These can be on a daily or weekly basis. Setting SMART targets will enable you to keep track of your progress. It is also useful to build in slippage time in case issues arise that impact on your study.

You will also need to *prioritise your learning*. You can do this in a number of ways. For example, if you are the kind of person who finds it difficult to get down to revision, try starting with subjects you find interesting or easy. This can help to build your confidence and increase your motivation. Alternatively, identify subjects that are certain to come up and begin with these. Once you have these under your belt you can look at subjects that have arisen on past papers less frequently.

Finally, keep *revision interesting*. Stop revising from becoming a chore by making it a sociable activity.

Make revision sociable

Revision does not have to be a solitary activity. Do not feel that you need to do this on your own. Identify and draw on the resources around you. For example, could a group of you share the task of making revision notes so you each focus on one topic area? Could you work together sharing strategies to aid memory and recall? Could you identify a 'study buddy' and test each other?

Here are some of the ways my students have blurred the boundaries between work and leisure and turned revision into a sociable activity:

Revision darts

As a group, work out one piece of information connected to each of the numbers on the dart board. When you throw a dart you have to recall the information, depending on where that dart lands.

Revision Scrabble

Play Scrabble with a twist. Choose a subject that you and your friends have revised. Then play the game in much the same way as you usually would with the one difference being that all the words have to relate to your revision topics. If you use a word that does not seem directly related, your team mates can challenge you, but if you are able to link this to your learning in some way then your word stands.

Make the most of your time: revise anytime, anyplace, anywhere...

The moral of this story is not to assume that revision only happens behind closed doors. Fit it into your lifestyle, identifying those pockets of time that you can use to learn bite-sized pieces of information. You will be surprised to discover how much you will remember without even trying. This will appeal to all kinaesthetic and visual learners and bring new meaning to the term multi-tasking.

Planning for 'e' day

Many students make the mistake of believing that the revision process ends here. The student has learned a series of facts and has committed them to memory. Yet still they perform poorly. This can be for a number of reasons:

- Examiners are looking at how you are able to apply your learning. It is not enough just to regurgitate a list of key facts, figures and theories. You need to demonstrate that you understand what you have learned and that you can apply this to a range of situations. It is the equivalent of thinking that you can pass your driving test by learning the *Highway Code* and reading a car manual. Take time to practise past papers, demonstrate procedures and talk through case presentations. Ask for feedback and continually hone your skills.

- The second reason relates to technique. If you were about to run a race you would not turn up to the track without having a plan of action. Many students arrive in the examination room without having given much thought to how they will tackle the mechanics of the exam. They are often tired and stressed, having stayed up late the night before. If you were about to run a race, you would have a clear strategy about how you were going to approach it. The equivalent in examination terms is to become an exam animal.

Steps to becoming an exam animal
Well before the exam date:

- Have a plan

- Stick to your plan

- Practise past papers (if possible in the room or the building, under time constraints)

- Decide your cut off point for revision

- Make sure you are in peak physical condition: have a good night's sleep for at least the two nights leading up to your exam, have plenty of exercise, watch your diet (avoid junk food, sugar and caffeine and alcohol at all costs)

The day of the exam:

- Have a good breakfast (avoid a high sugar breakfast: this will give you a sugar rush but you will then experience a dip in energy)

- Wear comfortable clothes (there is nothing worse than being uncomfortable, too warm, too cool, too tight)

- Arrive early, check you know where the exam is taking place and double-check the time

- Make sure that you have your equipment (calculator, pen, pencil, pencil sharpener, eraser) and that everything is in working order

- Avoid all people who will stress you out with the words 'I haven't done any revision' and then proceed to tell you about interventions you are unable to pronounce

- Go for a walk, steady your breathing and get into the 'exam zone'. Visualise yourself turning over the exam paper and writing, picture yourself sitting back at the end of the examination feeling pleased

Have a strategy for how you will manage time within the examination

For example, spend 5–10 minutes checking the instructions: How many questions do you need to answer (check)? Which sections do these need to come from (check)? Are you clear about what the question is asking (check)? Have you checked the word count (check)?

Have a clear idea of the order in which you will answer the questions. For example, if tackling essay questions, you might choose to answer the easiest first (this gives confidence and gets rid of exam nerves), then the question you can answer the best (you are now in full flow), and finally your poorest question last (it is not the end of the world if you fail to finish it). On the other hand, if you are approaching a set of multiple choice questions, you may choose to answer those you definitely know first so that you have time to concentrate on those you are less sure about before offering a wild guess at those you really do not know the answer to.

Be clear about how you are going to allocate your time within each question

For example, if you have 50 minutes to answer an essay question, you could think about it in this way.

50 minutes: 5 minutes planning, 5 minutes for the introduction and 5 for the conclusion leaves 35 minutes. I will probably write 5–6 paragraphs in this time which gives me about 5–6 minutes per paragraph. This leaves five minutes to read through the question at the end.

Be clear about how you are going to use your time. I once invigilated an examination where I noticed a person had stopped writing. Candidates needed to answer three questions in three hours so I knew that it was unlikely that she had finished. I looked at the person with a puzzled expression. She raised her hand to ask whether she could go on to the next question.

Stay for the whole time in the exam room

Do not on any account (with the exception of a fire alarm or using the bathroom) leave the room. Stay for the duration of the exam. Once you have left the room you cannot return. Read through your answers and check that your writing is legible, make notes. Whatever you do, stay.

Have a contingency plan

Be clear about what you will do if you are seized by panic or things go badly wrong. Here are a couple of examples:

- If you turn back the paper and cannot answer any questions you can:

    (a) Scream
    (b) Weep, or
    (c) Stop for one moment. Take a number of deep breaths and look at the question again. Identify possible information from your revision that you can apply.

- With ten minutes to go before the examination is due to finish you have only written three out of the six paragraphs you had planned. You can:

    (a) Give up
    (b) Continue to write frantically and complete one more paragraph, or
    (c) Make detailed notes for the remaining two paragraphs in order to maximise your chance of gaining as many marks as possible

Starting to get into the swing of things? Think of further scenarios and possible actions you could take.

After the exam

After the examination, do not, on any account, spend hours mentally dissecting your answers or agonising over things you cannot change. This is wasted energy and will increase your anxiety levels. Instead, do something nice to reward yourself – go for a coffee or a meal out with friends and take an evening off if you can. When you feel able to reflect on the experience, focus on the following questions:

- What did you learn about yourself?

- What did you do well?

- What did you do less well?

- What will you do differently next time?

Manage your nerves

It is completely normal to experience some degree of anxiety prior to an examination. The Yerkes-Dodson law (1908), which measures the relationship between motivation and performance, suggests that in order to perform well a moderate amount of stress is necessary. Without this you are unlikely to put in the effort required to do the work. Indeed, one of the reasons why tutors set assignments and examinations is to see how you rise to the challenge, respond and work under pressure.

However, if this level of anxiety is too great, the immediate effect is that your ability to concentrate is impaired and it is highly likely that you will have difficulties in remembering and recalling information. This can impact on performance. Indeed, research has shown that '15–20% of college students experience lower grades due to the effects of test anxiety' (Kelman and Straker, 2000: 160).

It is therefore in your best interests to find a way to control and channel your nervous energy so that it works to your advantage. The good news is that a range of simple strategies exist to enable you to do this. Begin by revisiting Chapter 7 on managing anxiety and then read the following list of further ideas you may wish to try.

Build up your personal resources: examining your lifestyle

Stress has both a physical as well as a psychological impact. In order to minimise its effect, it therefore makes sense to keep physically well. Spend time examining your lifestyle. Eat a nutritious diet and exercise regularly as this can minimise the effects of stress as well as boost your immunity. Recognise the importance of a good night's sleep and avoid stimulants such as caffeine and nicotine, which can raise your heart beat and contribute to feelings of anxiety. Finally, avoid excess alcohol at all costs. Not only does it fail to remove the stressor, but can make matters worse by compromising your immunity and may lead to additional problems.

Reframe and rename the situation

Turn the situation on its head so that you begin to think about it in a different way. Consider the following scenario: you go for an interview but instead of feeling that you are being interviewed by the organisation, you go instead with the attitude that you are going to find out whether the organisation meets *your* requirements. The situation is exactly the same but you are in the driving seat. Follow the same process with exams. See these as a chance for you to find out what you know or check your understanding. Better still, rename them so that an exam becomes a 'quiz' and a presentation becomes the chance to 'share and tell'.

Finally, if you are worried about examinations, this is how you make yourself incredibly nervous:

- Leave revision until the last minute

- Listen to the horror stories of others

- Recall every time you have done poorly in an exam and dwell on this

The secret of managing your nerves is to plan ahead, focus on what you know as opposed to dwelling on what you have not had time to learn. Avoid stressful people at all costs. Focus on your performance, making sure that you do not let others distract you or undermine your confidence.

Skills in practice

A quick recap

This chapter has highlighted that:

(a) As a rule university lecturers are not sado-masochistic ogres who invent examinations in order to torture students and make their lives difficult

(b) Many examinations (OSCES, practicals, presentations) mirror the kinds of things you will be doing in practice and enable you to rehearse these skills and build confidence

(c) Examinations which might not seem to be directly relevant (multiple choice questions, etc.) also help you develop skills you will require on placement. For example, recalling specific information, performing in front of an audience, working under tight time constraints, making split-second decisions, recording information very precisely and concisely within a short timeframe.

Nonetheless you may be thinking: 'In practice I will not have to do formal assessments unless I am on a course or updating my CPR training.' This is true. However, you will have to recall information, make split-second decisions and work in highly pressured situations on a daily basis. The remainder of this chapter therefore looks at how you can transfer the keys to success into placement situations and a work setting.

Be clear about what you need to learn

The first step to preparing for and performing well in pressured situations on placement is to identify the subject matter you need to learn. This may be easier said than done, particularly if this is your first placement or you are unfamiliar with the practice area. The placement will test you on a number of levels, including:

- Your ability to remember, relate and apply knowledge and skills learned at *university* to the placement context

- Your ability to remember and apply knowledge and skills learned on the *placement* to the placement context

In addition you will also be required to recall and follow procedures and processes relating specifically to the placement you are on.

There are a number of ways to approach this. If you know the placement setting or specialism beforehand, you should spend time reading through your university lecture notes and make a record of terminology or factual information you find difficult to remember. A pre-placement visit can also direct your reading and revision. At the very least, this will help you identify a starting point where you can focus your energies. As your placement progresses, you can then keep a running record of new information as it arises and the contexts where you need to apply this. Your educator will also be able to offer support and guide you to additional areas you should address. Here are some examples identified by students on placement:

It is worrying, I know, but I struggle to remember the stages of CPR (cardio pulmonary respiration) and the number of chest compressions to breaths.

I am hopeless at home visits. There have been occasions when we've got to the house and I've realised that we don't have a key or the burglar alarm has been activated the moment we have stepped over the threshold and I look blankly at the OT.

*When we were in theatre the surgeon said 'pass me the ****' and I paused for just a second. It is difficult because in theatre every second counts.*

Assessing for equipment is my nightmare. It is remembering what I need to measure before I prescribe it.

I have dyslexia and my main challenge is spelling some of the complex terms under pressure.

I find it difficult to feed back information at the ward round or at handover. It isn't so much what is happening for each person as who individuals are. It is making sure what I report back relates to the actual person.

Be aware of how you will need to recall and apply the information

The above quotes highlight two things:

- The wide breadth of information you may need to access and recall while on placement, ranging from specific medical information and procedures to names of patients and clients

- The challenge of predicting the situations and contexts where you may be required to apply these skills and demonstrate your understanding

It will take time to identify how you will be required to recall and apply this knowledge, particularly if this is your first placement or you are unfamiliar with the area or specialism. You will need to draw on your acute observational skills, making a note of situations as they arise. For example, will you be expected to present information verbally? Or turn theory into practice and undertake a complex multi-stage procedure? Alternatively, will you have to produce written information within a short timeframe?

At this point you may find it useful to jot down the type of information you are expected to recall, the circumstances where this might occur and additional stressors that may increase the pressure you experience. Examples may include performing the procedure in front of others, working within a specified time, using complex terminology, being put 'on the spot', or speaking to a wider audience. Use the following grid to record your own experiences.

Situation	Information/content	How the information is applied (practical, written, spoken)	Additional stressors
Ward round	Recalling patients, understanding terminology used, verbally presenting information	Spoken	Speaking in front of a group. Answering questions from other members of the team

The grid will serve a number of purposes. It will help you to identify situations where you may be required to perform in a pressured situation and you will therefore be able to mentally prepare for these.

Translate the information into a format that makes it easier to learn

The next stage is to put this information in a format that is memorable. Again, it will depend on your individual learning style and the type of information you need to recall. The rules, tools and techniques used in the classroom apply directly to place-ment. For example, if you need to remember the exact order in which to perform a procedure, information in the format of a flowchart can be useful. To remember terminology, create glossaries on small index cards. Carry the index cards with you and take advantage of spare moments to recap or use the cards as prompts.

Develop specific techniques to aid recall

By now you should be an expert at a range of techniques that support recall. Do not forget to use colleagues on placement as an additional resource as they will also have their own strategies to share with you. Here are tips from the experts:

When it comes to nursing a critically ill patient, I still use the mnemonic ABCDE which stands for airway management, breathing, circulation, dysfunction (neurological) environment/ everything.

When I need to measure a patient for a walking stick, I imagine that the walking stick is a stylish cane, a bit like the one owned by Fred Astaire. This reminds me that I need to measure from the styloid process.

I always jumbled up section two and section three of the Mental Health Act. I knew that one was detention for assessment and one for treatment. To help me remember, I picture these two words. The word assessment contains two pairs of the letter 's'. Two pairs = section two. Treatment, on the other hand, contains three 't's. Three 't's = section 3.

When I look at the x-ray I still focus on the shape of bones to offer me clues to their names. Only the other day when I was reporting to a colleague on an x-ray of the carpal bones I commented on how the hamate looks like a little hammer.

Plan ahead

When you undertake an assessment at university you will at least know the time, place and broad subject matter of your examination. You may not have this luxury on placement, although you will probably be able to identify potential situations where you will need to demonstrate your skills before they arise.

The best way forward is for you to take control of the situation. During supervision, discuss the areas where you have concerns and adopt a graded approach. Begin by observing others undertaking assessments and procedures or feeding back information to the team, and begin to model your approach on these. Negotiate with your tutor opportunities where you might carry out particular tasks under supervision. During the initial stages, access situations which are not time pressured or in front of large audiences. As you become more confident, put yourself in increasingly challenging situations, drawing on the support of your supervisor and the wider team. This approach will enable you to gradually gain mastery over these situations.

Manage your nerves

When you try anything for the first time you are bound to feel nervous. However, the more you repeat the process, the easier it becomes and the less self-conscious you will feel. De-sensitisation is the name given to a technique where you repeatedly face an anxiety-provoking situation to the point where the situation becomes common-place and the anxious feelings subside. The best illustration of this is driving. Do you remember initially when you had to think about every manoeuvre? You may have felt anxious as a result of this. However, the more you drove, the more confident you felt and the less anxious you became. This is the same with most other situations: speaking in front of others, performing procedures, writing notes. The more you repeat these, the less frightening they become.

The secret here is to practise. Do not put yourself under too much pressure to begin with. Start small, in front of one or two supportive colleagues in situations where you are not assessed and where too many time constraints do not exist. Then gradually build this up, increasing the pressure so that when you need to perform on the day you will not even have to think about it.

IN A NUTSHELL

Even the mention of the word 'examinations' is enough to strike fear into the bravest of students. This chapter has hopefully helped you to demystify the process and to learn the keys to success. Remember:

- Examinations and timed assessments at university help you to prepare for working under pressure in practice

- Break revision down into bite-sized pieces, find ways of learning things that work for you and have fun

- Do not forget to think about how you need to apply your learning to different situations and make sure that you give yourself time and space to practise

References and signposts to further reading and resources

Acres, D. (1994) *How To Pass Exams Without Anxiety: Every Candidate's Guide to Success* (3rd edition). Plymouth: Northcote House.

Buzan, T. (2006a) *Brilliant Memory: Unlock the Power of Your Mind*. Harlow: BBC Active.

Buzan, T. (2006b) *The Buzan Study Skills Handbook.* Harlow: BBC Active.

Cottrell, S.M. (2007) *The Exam Skills Handbook: Achieving Peak Performance*. Basingstoke: Palgrave Macmillan.

Harden, R.M. (1988) 'What is an OSCE?', *Medical Teacher*, 10 (1): 19–22.

Hendry, C. and Farley, A. (2003) 'Examinations: a practical guide for students', *Nursing Standard*, 17 (29): 48–53.

Sisson, J.C., Swartz, R.D. and Wolf, F.M. (1992) 'Learning, retention and recall of clinical information', *Medical Education,* 26: 454–61.

Yerkes, R.M. and Dodson, J.D. (1908) 'The relation of strength of stimulus to rapidity of habit formation', *Journal of Comparative Neurology*, 18: 458–82.

16 Presenting yourself well

AT A GLANCE

This chapter is for you if

- You have difficulty communicating ideas to large groups

- You find that during verbal presentations you lose your train of thought and tend to ramble

- You have the urge to purge before you speak

- You feel that your audience immediately turns off the second you open your mouth

- You sport a 'bunny in the headlights' look when facing a group

The previous chapter briefly described how presentation skills are sometimes used as a means to assess your ability to articulate your understanding of a subject area. The emphasis placed on this form of assessment is not surprising given that your ability to communicate information verbally with the wider team will have a direct bearing on the quality and coherence of care a patient or client receives. The clarity and coherence of your communications about the assessments undertaken or particular observations made to your placement educator, immediate colleagues and the wider multidisciplinary team will be the difference between a *client receiving the intervention they require or being offered a less appropriate treatment or course of action.*

This chapter looks at a range of techniques you can use to present yourself well. It invites you to think about the ingredients that make up a good verbal presentation and explores a series of tools and techniques you can apply to presentations at university and on placement.

Health warning: This chapter provides you with a communication tool-kit but the only way to develop your presentation skills is to practise these skills and volunteer for situations that involve presenting to a wider audience (debates at the students union, speaking in church).

STARTING POINTS

1 Try this simple quiz to see whether you are a 'premier' presenter.

What would be the largest number of people you would feel confident about speaking in front of?

(a) 20–200 people
(b) 5–15 people
(c) 2 people (at a push)

When your tutor asks you to feed back your group's progress to the class, do you...

(a) Jump at the chance and volunteer?
(b) Say 'I'll do it if someone else will help me'?
(c) Grab the pen, thrust it into someone else's hand and push them to the front of the room saying 'if you insist'?

Do you equate giving a presentation with...

(a) Something pleasurable, like chocolate or beer?
(b) Indifference: a bit like watching a poor reality TV show?
(c) Pain and anxiety: akin to root canal work?

When you picture yourself giving a presentation, do you imagine...

(a) Being centre of the stage: holding your audience in the palm of your hand?
(b) Giving a solid performance: nothing too sparkling but OK?
(c) Sobbing in the corner of the stage?

What is your biggest worry about giving a presentation?

(a) Not wanting to leave the stage
(b) Fluffing your lines
(c) Completely drying up

If you answered mainly (a), you are someone who relishes the opportunity to share your ideas with a wider audience – a bit of a performance junkie. Your presentations probably exude confidence, and because you are confident your audience wants to listen to what you say. With so much charisma and power you need to check your facts and be careful not to get too carried away.

If you answered mainly (b), you have a good balance. In the main you are very confident at presenting your ideas, although this is not something you necessarily enjoy or seek out. This chapter will give you a few pointers to help you tweak your presentation style and to ensure that you have maximum impact.

(Continued)

(Continued)

If you answered mainly (c), presentations terrify you and, unless you master your fear, this could hold you back on placement. On the positive side, learning how to speak in front of others is a skill and this chapter will give you lots of ideas and pointers so that by the end of the process you will appear as confident as everyone else.

2   Over the next few weeks make a note of what makes a perfect presenter. Observe lecturers and fellow colleagues and see if you can develop a checklist of the ingredients that make up a good presentation.

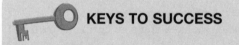 **KEYS TO SUCCESS**

Now that you are clear about what makes a good presenter you can start to develop these skills for yourself. The first part of the chapter focuses on giving presentations in the classroom. Remember, good presenters are not born, they are made, and everyone has the potential to give a good presentation. All you have to do is use the following keys to success:

- Be clear in terms of what you need to communicate

- Pitch it at the right level: know your audience

- Be a smooth talker: use signposts and scaffolds

- Check out the parameters

- Know your audio-visual aids

- Say it with confidence

Be clear in terms of what you need to communicate

Begin by deciding what you need to say. The best presentations are focused with a clear aim and the information is relevant and addresses the topic or question. Less effective presentations are those talks where the presenter includes everything they know.

The content will be guided principally by the brief or question you have been given. Use the assessment or marking criteria to structure your ideas, noting how marks are distributed. There is little point spending most of your time talking about one aspect if this only carries a tiny percentage of the overall marks.

The best way to keep to task is to answer the question. As a tutor, there is nothing more disheartening than listening to a presentation where the student appears to have read your question and then decided to answer their own. Yes, you might feel that you would rather talk about something far more interesting, but you need to save this for another time if you want to pass. During this initial stage it can be helpful to sketch out a mind map, noting the areas you will cover and the information you will include. This way you can identify any gaps that require further research. Spend time deciding how you will use the information. Essentially there are three types of presentation:

1 **Information-giving.** This is predominantly descriptive, giving or summarising information. You may be asked to do this as part of a mini-teaching session, sharing theoretical or factual information. Here the tutor is looking to see what you have understood and is relying on you to extract the main facts from your reading and to relay these to the group. You will need to make decisions about what information to include.

2 **Discursive.** Here you will need to debate the strengths and limitations of an approach or develop an argument, exploring and weighing up different perspectives, challenging your audience to accept a different viewpoint. For this, you will need to decide your 'angle' – are you for the intervention or against it? Pull your audience in, challenge and confidently debate.

3 **Demonstrative.** This type of presentation tends to be used in the context of training: for example, when demonstrating your ability to illustrate your understanding of a technique or teaching a practical skill to others.

Pitch it at the right level: know your audience

The one sure way to deliver a presentation flop is to pitch it at the wrong level. As Raveenthiran (2005: 353) states:

It is boring to talk about what the audience already knows.
It is futile to talk about what the audience cannot understand.
It is arrogant to talk about what you know and ignore the interests of your audience.
It is dangerous to talk about things you are unsure about.

At university it is probable that your audience will comprise your fellow students and tutors. However, it is possible that, with the increasing levels of service-user involvement, you may also be talking to people who are not familiar with the subject area. Generally, it is always better to begin your presentation by briefly outlining things your audience may already be familiar with before leading them gently into the 'unknown'. Pay attention to non-verbal communication (fidgeting and yawning are sure signs that the information is pitched at too high or low a level) and if you are unsure, ask whether they are already familiar with particular facts as you go along.

In doing so you are demonstrating that you are receptive to their needs and can make adjustments accordingly. One final point here: mind your language and avoid jargon at all costs.

Be a smooth talker: use signposts and scaffolds

This does not mean that you have to sound like James Bond. Being a smooth talker is about thinking of ways to structure your ideas so that you move seamlessly from one point to another. A good presentation is like a good essay. It will comprise a series of key ingredients, including:

- An introduction, outlining the aim of your presentation and the areas your talk will focus on

- The main body, containing the substance of your talk and developing the ideas outlined in the introduction

- A conclusion, drawing together the main points and containing the 'take home message' for the audience

You are probably familiar with the following mantra: Tell them what you are going to tell them (intro) tell them (main body), then tell them what you've told them (conclusion).

A good model for this is the *News at Ten*. Note how the main events are summarised on each bong of Big Ben. Then the news presenter introduces each one, starting with a catchy headline followed by plenty of detail. Finally, the programme pans back to the main presenter who says something along the lines of: 'Tonight...' and gives a summary of the main issues.

Here are some pointers offered by university and college tutors:

Talk your audience through the structure so they are mentally prepared. I liken this to giving someone a map. If they can gain an overview of the journey, they will be able to enjoy the journey. This is far better than not providing any clues and then suddenly saying 'Hey, we're here!'

I begin by giving a broad overview, describing exactly how many areas we will be looking at. An example of this was a lecture I gave about anti-oppressive practice last week. It began something like: Today we are focusing on three main areas: first, I'll begin by outlining... Then we'll look at... And finally,... After each section I take them back. So we've looked at... now we are going to focus on...

Do not forget your ending. If someone has been asleep throughout the presentation it's their chance to take away the key message. I spell this out in no uncertain terms 'in conclusion', 'finally', 'to sum up' are stock phrases.

The rule of three

Some authors are quite prescriptive in their approach. For example, Richard Hall (2007: 32) suggests that you should: *'limit your thinking to the rule of three: a simple technique where you are never allowed to use more than three main points'.* This can be helpful in focusing your ideas and ensuring that you are clear in what you are arguing. The best approach is to decide your 'bottom line' – the key message that you want your audience to take away – and then work backwards from this so that everything you include leads to this conclusion.

Finally, some of the most memorable presentations tell a story (Hall, 2007). Anecdotes, narratives and personal experience offer fantastic structures on which to hang your presentation and offer an effective mechanism with which your audience can identify and understand what you are saying.

Check out the parameters

One final point to make at this preparation stage: check out the bigger picture. Make sure that you know:

- How long you are speaking for

- What the environment is like

- The time of day when you will be speaking

Let's look at these points in turn.

Avoid the Mickey Mouse syndrome

There is no point preparing an elaborate presentation if you only have 10 minutes in which to deliver it. Speaking at break neck speed and sounding like Mickey Mouse is not conducive to putting your point across. Be selective in terms of the information you will include. If you have a 15–minute presentation, plan to speak for 12–13 minutes. That way you can take your time and articulate your ideas clearly. If there is time left over, use this for questions.

Check out the environment: cavern or coat cupboard?

Check out the environment beforehand if you can. Make a note of acoustics, temperature and space. Decide how you will use this to your advantage. For example, if the room is very large, standing at the front will enable you to project your voice to the back. On the other hand, smaller spaces are more intimate and standing may make your audience feel as though you are towering over them. In these instances it is far better to sit on a chair or perch on a desk.

Time and timing

Find out when you are going to deliver your presentation. The danger spots are immediately before or after lunch and last thing in the afternoon when your audience may be distracted by thoughts of food or the journey home. During these times, the more interactive your presentation can be, the greater the chance your audience will be alert and engaged.

Know your audio-visual aids

Make sure you are aware of the range of the audio-visual aids that may be available on the day and what they have to offer. Here is a brief outline of some of the tools and the accompanying rules that will enable you to gain the most from these.

Audio-visual aids: the tools

PowerPoint. This is a computer presentation package. It is generally easy to use and the presentations generated using PowerPoint have a highly professional finish which is visually appealing to larger audiences. Handouts can be created from the slides.

Overhead projector. This has largely been replaced by PowerPoint. The overhead projector allows you to project the content of your presentation on to a screen. You can either print or hand write the information using a special pen on the acetates.

Flip chart. Although this is considered to be low-tech by many, it is ideal to use with smaller groups. The main advantage lies in its flexibility. So, for example, you can prepare notes beforehand or use the flip chart to record ideas as they emerge.

Slide projector. Photographic slides add a visual dimension to your presentation. Take time to prepare these beforehand and have a quick dress rehearsal to make sure that they are in the correct order and the right way round.

Posters. Posters combine images and text to summarise your presentation. A poster can be any size but A0 is the most visually striking. If you are using a poster, make sure that you make clear reference to its content and exploit its potential to the full.

Video. These are often embedded within the presentation. If you have the facility, video is worth using to illustrate what you say as it is very engaging and 'three-dimensional'. It also takes the pressure off you for a moment. Make sure it is relevant. Your audience may find it hard to make the link between *Match of the Day* and the function of the skin. Also, be careful not to overuse video. Your audience will feel cheated if they end up seeing more of the video than you.

Handouts. These are useful for your audience to refer to. If you are using PowerPoint, you can use the 'print off slides as handouts' facility. It would be a mistake to hand these out at the beginning if you wanted your audience to hang on your every word. Alternatively, if you want to take the focus away from you, then the earlier these are distributed, the better.

Audio-visual aids: the rules

The following points mainly apply to PowerPoint presentations and those delivered using the overhead projector. Ways to put together the perfect poster can be found on the website accompanying this book (www.skills4health.co.uk).

Keep slides simple: avoid clutter at all costs
Focus on font: san serif fonts, such as Arial, are the most readable
Size matters: use a 36 point for titles and a 28 point for body text
Make a case: use title case for headings and lower case for information. Never use upper case and avoid underlining and italics
Be bold: a dark background (deep blue or black) and light coloured text (white or yellow) for contrast will make your words stand out
Less is more: less than 30 words per slide, 5–6 words for headings
Keep it moving: keep the number of slides down to one per minute or even one per 40 seconds
Do not overshoot: a maximum of five bullet points per slide
Picture perfect: an image can speak a thousand words
Make your graphs graft for their place: avoid 'busy' graphs and tables
Be constant: ensure that your slides are consistent. Do not suddenly switch fonts half way through. You may not notice but your audience will

Check it out

As a student you are well placed to learn from the example of others. When attending lectures and listening to tutors or other students presenting information, note the presentations that are more visually appealing, and what makes them so. Categorise strengths and limitations under the following headings. Feel free to add your own 'crimes against presentation'.

Wanted for crimes against presentations

The good	The bad	The ugly
Clear uncluttered fonts	Over-complicated graphs	Distracting animation Sounds Gimmicks

Say it with confidence

(… or how to appear like a swan when you feel like a duck)

The secret to giving a stress-free presentation is to practise at every opportunity:

- In the bath

- In front of the mirror

- In front of friends

- In front of family

As you practise, check out your timing and make adjustments to your presentation as necessary. You need to decide whether you are going to use any prompts above and beyond your slides to remind you of what to say. Avoid reading your entire presentation from a script as this can make it difficult to engage with and make eye contact with your audience. If you are concerned about losing your thread of ideas, make use of cue cards containing key words which can act as prompts. There is also a notes facility in PowerPoint. Finally, make sure that you face your audience and read from the computer in front of your rather than turning your back to read things from the screen, as this makes your voice sound muffled.

On the day ...

It's not what you say, it's the way that you say it: use your voice

Your voice is an incredible tool. Some authors have estimated that on average 7% of what we understand comes from the words that are used within our verbal interactions, compared with 38% of information resulting in tone of voice and 55% being dependent on non-verbal cues (Mehrabian, 1981). Use this to your advantage. Make sure you project your voice to the back of the room. Try to vary the tone of your voice and the speed or pace of delivery to give emphasis to different parts of what you say. Use silence to your advantage. A short pause can give emphasis to a point you are making. If you are nervous and you hear yourself making a 'clack' sound and your tongue sticks to the roof of your mouth, take a drink of water.

Sound enthusiastic

Content is important but you will have sat through lectures packed full of useful information that you can no longer remember because the lecturer was dull, boring, spoke in a monotone and went on and on and zzzzzz... Be enthusiastic about what you have to say. If you fail to show any interest, there is little chance that your audience will be engaged. Smile, move about, make eye contact and draw people into your talk.

Watch out for those non-verbals

Hand gestures and facial expressions can be used to your advantage to emphasise particular points. Politicians are masters of this. However, treat these with caution because inappropriate gestures can also interfere with your presentation and detract from what you say. Here are the top 12 non-verbals to avoid:

- The hipster: hands on hips – can be quite intimidating

- The windmill: flamboyant gestures – can be distracting

- The shuffler: pacing – can be hypnotic

- The drummer: taps their fingers on table – can be particularly annoying

- The avoider: hides behind the script and refuses to make eye contact – looks suspicious

- The defender: arms folded – can look very aggressive

- The philosopher: yhhmmm, ahhhh – can also be very distracting

- The dodger: hands in pocket – can look suspicious, difficult to trust

- The giggler: laughs uncontrollably at their poor jokes – can be vaguely annoying, particularly if the jokes are not funny

- The rooster: struts from side to side with small jerky movements – can be distracting

- The mumbler: does not look at the audience and speaks to the floor, covers their mouth at times, making it difficult to hear – can be hard to follow

- The gabbler: speaks too quickly – can also be hard to follow

When it comes to giving presentations you may feel the least confident person in the world. The good news is you are not alone. Some of the most eloquent speakers will tell you that they also experience nerves just before they are about to present, but rather than letting this hinder them, they use the adrenaline to give them the edge. Preparation helps, but here are a few additional tips from students of ways to overcome nerves:

The secret is to script and learn the first few lines of your presentation. This will boost your confidence and help you get into the swing of things.

My advice would be dress to impress. Wear something that makes you feel good about yourself. If you feel good, you will project confidence and a stage presence. My motto is: 'They may not remember what I say, but they will remember my fantastic shoes!'

I have a simple routine that works wonders. Before I go on, I smile, take a deep breath in and drop the shoulders. Automatically my body goes into relaxed mode.

Talk yourself into it. Say in your head: 'I'm really going to enjoy this.' Your audience looks to you in order to decide how they should feel. If they see you enjoying it, they will too.

Essentially, when you give a presentation you are acting a role. I'm not a very confident person but when I present I play someone who is confident. I swear, sometimes when I come out to the front I can hear my voice saying 'Tonight, Matthew, I'm going to be...', as though I am a contestant from Stars in Your Eyes.

If you are doing a presentation as part of an assessment, enlist the help of your friends. Get someone to time you and to give you the heads up five minutes before you are due to finish and prime them with questions or comments they should make.

Have a contingency plan. If the worst thing that can happen is that you dry up, then bring a copy of your talk with you. That way, in the very worst case scenario, you will read from a script. That's not so dreadful, is it?

Remember, you are in control. It is a bit like being a conductor.

My advice would be to have fun and don't expect it to be perfect.

After the presentation...

You may think that the presentation has ended, but most presentations allow time for questions. If your presentation is part of an assessment at university, the questions will be the time when your tutor invites you to demonstrate your learning by offering you additional opportunities to add to or develop what you have to say. Listen carefully, as it can indicate areas which needed to be developed further. The secret here is to clarify what the person is asking, do not be defensive and if you are unsure of the answer, give it back to the audience. Something along the lines of 'before I answer this, it would be interesting to hear the views of the audience' always works well.

Finally, once it is all over, mark yourself on your own performance. Give yourself marks for:

- Content: relevance of information, use of evidence

- Structure: clarity and flow of ideas, timing

- Delivery: voice, language, engagement with audience

- Use of audio-visuals: appropriateness, clarity, ability to enhance presentation as opposed to dominating, confidence in using these

Use this as the basis to identify areas for improvement and work on your skills.

Skills in practice

Presentations on placement come in all shapes and sizes, ranging from relatively informal feedback sessions about particular clients to the wider multidisciplinary team to a full-blown case study and possibly conference presentations. You will need to be clear about what the purpose of the presentation is and the nature of your audience so that you can adapt your presentation style and language accordingly. However, while the context will vary, the skills for success will remain broadly the same as those you have used to present your ideas in the classroom at university. This part of the chapter will explain what these new situations entail, what is expected of you and how to use the keys for success to unlock your skills and articulate your ideas clearly and coherently.

Be clear in terms of what you need to communicate

The first rule of good presentations is to be clear about what you need to communicate. On placement this could include:

- Sharing information about services to a client and their family

- Feeding back on a client's progress or the results of an assessment

- Demonstrating a technique at an in-service training session

- Disseminating research

- Providing information relating to an assessed case study as part of your university course

It will take time to gain a feel for these situations and understand what is expected of you and the nature of the information you will be presenting. The secret is to attend as many of these meetings as possible when you begin your placement and use these as opportunities to uncover:

- The type of information shared in these meetings (views and opinions, technical details, summaries of interventions or teaching on a particular condition)

- Particular conventions used (language)

- Whether it is structured in a particular way or follows a certain format

Supervision can also offer you the time and space to talk through your observations with your educator.

Pitch it at the right level: know your audience

As you gain a feel for the different situations where you will be expected to present, you should start to recognise who the audience will be. This will enable you to ensure that you pitch your presentation appropriately. You will quickly see that communication in these situations occurs on two levels. On the one hand, you will be required to adopt the formal, sometimes technical language associated with the area of practice when presenting to colleagues, consultants and practitioners. This is particularly true of medical settings. On the other hand, you will need to be able to change your language when speaking to clients and carers, explaining the information in a clear and non-technical way, and avoiding jargon. In these instances, you need to take into account additional communication needs, such as visual and auditory impairments. Finally, do not assume that everyone has English as their first language.

Here is a brief overview of some of the contexts on placement where you may be called upon to use your skills.

Situation	Audience	Type of information you may present	Formality rating
Case conference	Consultant, members of the MDT; the patient and carer are usually also invited	Providing information. Summarising interventions and reasons for the decisions made, making recommendations for future care based on assessment of need	***
MDT meeting or ward round	Consultant, members of the MDT; the patient may also be invited, depending on the area (more usual in mental health settings)	Providing information to other members of the multidisciplinary team: presenting results of assessments, feeding back observations regarding progress	***
Handover	Members of the team	Providing information to ensure continuity of care, highlighting any issues that staff on the following shift should be aware of	**
Client/carers groups	Clients, carers (informal and paid), families (can include younger carers)	Teaching: providing information, demonstrating skills, ways to use equipment, techniques to manage a 'condition'	*
Case study presentation	Members of the multidisciplinary team (and your tutor if this is in connection with a university assessment)	Providing information: summary of your work with a particular patient, presenting issues and reasoning processes for the purpose of teaching. Will also	***

Situation	Audience	Type of information you may present	Formality rating
		include reflections and future recommendations	
In-service training session	Colleagues, care staff	Teaching: imparting information, demonstrating a skill or technique	**
Journal club	Colleagues and peers	Teaching: offering opinion, summarising, critiquing research papers	*
Abstract presentations	Colleagues and peers	Disseminating research through a short formal scientific talk	***

Be a smooth talker: use signposts and scaffolds

The great advantage of many of the presentations you will give on placement is that they tend to follow a set format. Signposting what you have to say is therefore much easier. For example, if you were feeding back about a home visit at a multidisciplinary team meeting you would probably base this around the following headings:

- Date of visit

- Social situation

- Tasks undertaken and level of functioning: physical, mood, cognitive functioning

- Potential risks

- Recommendations

The key here is to be completely clear about what you are saying so that the team is in no doubt. Remember the mantra: tell your audience what you want to tell them, tell them, then tell them what you have told them.

Check out the parameters

Case study and abstract presentations, and in-service training and patient groups will be allocated a significant amount of time and use a format with supporting visual aids that you will be familiar with. Feeding back at case conferences, handovers and multidisciplinary team meetings, on the other hand, is a completely different matter. Here, time is of the essence, particularly if there are a number of clients being discussed. The art to presenting yourself well in these situations is to say what you need to say as succinctly as possible while still providing enough detail.

Try these simple techniques:

- Be concise. Begin with the main message. If time is tight, a long rambling introduction will frustrate your colleagues.

- Be as precise as possible. Ensure your facts are straight and exact.

- Make use of summaries and recommendations.

- Written prompts can help you focus.

- Be clear about when you are expected to give feedback so that you are prepared and know when it is your turn to speak.

Know your audio-visual aids

The experience of giving presentations at university means that by the time you are on placement you will know your flip chart from your PowerPoint and the relative strengths and limitations of a range of audio-visual aids. The key to placement is to find out what is available and the conventions associated with different meetings in respect to this. While it is highly probable that in-service training sessions will utilise flip-chart and PowerPoint slides for quite formal presentations, it is highly unlikely that this will be the case when presenting in most case conferences and multidisciplinary team meetings. These usually take place in an office in the department where you work, and although the meetings are formal, the team will be seated. In these instances, it is probably more acceptable to provide short notes or a formal report to which the team can refer.

Say it with confidence

The key to speaking confidently on placement is to practise. Take every opportunity to rehearse what you want to say and gain feedback from friends and colleagues. Attend other meetings so that you are clear about how other staff members approach this and you know what to expect. Keep within time constraints but do not let anyone hurry you. You might be a student, but what you have to say is important and needs to be heard. Finally, pace yourself, speak slowly and clearly and do not forget to smile. Things will not always go smoothly but over time you will find your own style and as a result your confidence will grow.

IN A NUTSHELL

Many students identify the act of giving a verbal presentation as one of the most nerve-racking aspects of their course. There is the assumption that being able to speak confidently in front of others is a gift people are born with. However, the key message of this chapter is that everyone has the ability to present themselves well and, like everything else, giving presentations is something that can be learned and developed through practice. We will give a poor presentation at some point, just as we will all write a less than convincing essay or flunk an exam. The secret is to learn from the experience and then give another presentation at the earliest possible moment. The worst thing you can possibly do is dwell on the experience and mistakenly, let this be your defining moment. If you can master the art of presentations, not only will this earn you extra points in the classroom and enable you to shine at interview, but it will also allow you to be the strongest advocate for the clients you work alongside. Above all, remember:

- Formal presentations allow you to present your ideas/thoughts to a wider audience

- You need to be clear about what you are presenting and who your audience is

- Spend time before the presentation planning what you are going to say. The brief you have been given will help you to do this

- Use audio-visual aids to enhance and emphasise content and to engage the audience

- As far as you can, relax and have fun

References and signposts to further reading and resources

Cottrell, S. (2003) *Skills for Success: The Personal Development Planning Handbook.* Basingstoke: Palgrave Macmillan.

Hall, R. (2007) *Brilliant Presentation.* Harlow: Pearson Education.

McCarthy, P. and Hatcher, C. (1996) *Speaking Persuasively: Making the Most of Your Presentation.* St Leonards, New South Wales: Allen and Unwin.

Mason-Whitehead, E. and Mason, T. (2007) 'The art and science of presentations', *Journal of Postgraduate Medicine,* 46: 193–8.

Mehrabian, A. (1981) *Silent Messages: Implicit Communication of Emotions and Attitudes.* Belmont, CA: Wadsworth.

Prasad, S., Roy, B. and Smith, M. (2000) 'The art and science of presentation: electronic presentations', *Journal of Postgraduate Medicine,* 46: 193.

Raveenthiran, V. (2005) 'The ten commandments of oral presentations', *Student BMJ,* 13: 353–96.

Whitehead, E. and Mason, T. (2007) *Study Skills for Nurses.* London: Sage.

17 Working with others

JARGON-BUSTING

Case conference: A meeting of professionals to discuss how best to support a client's needs.

CPA: An abbreviation of care programme approach, which calls together a range of professionals involved in patient care to ensure that different community services are coordinated to meet the individual's needs.

Forming: Part of the group process described by Tuckman and Jensen (1977) where group members first come together.

Group dynamics: Describes the group processes and interactions that reflect how the group evolves and develops.

Ice breakers: Introductory activities used to help group members get to know each other.

Key worker: The member of the multidisciplinary team responsible for coordinating care.

Norming: A term used to describe the point at which the group has cohesion.

Performing: The point at which the group is functioning and is actively working towards its agreed objectives.

Storming: Part of the group process described by Tuckman and Jensen (1977) where group members face conflict as they seek to establish their place within the group.

Warm-up: An introductory exercise to orientate group participants to the main focus of the session.

AT A GLANCE

This chapter is for you if

- You find it difficult to speak in front of others in group situations

- You tend to shy away from working with more than one person

- You avoid meetings at all costs

- You develop a 'lemming syndrome' in group scenarios, following the crowd even if you disagree with the decisions that are being made

- You dread assignments that include an element of group work

- You worry about facilitating your own groups

Definition: A group consists of a number of people who meet together to follow a chosen activity. (Maslin-Prothero, 2005: 127)

Groups offer many opportunities within health and social care practice. They can foster a sense of belonging, offer support, reinforce identity, provide a vehicle for developing skills and create a forum for collective problem-solving. During your time at university you will experience at first hand the benefits and challenges of working with others in a range of situations, including tutorial groups, classes and year groups. Your course may also include modules that look at group-work and the complexities involved in managing their dynamics. These experiences will lay the foundations for working as part of a multidisciplinary team and for establishing, developing and facilitating your own therapeutic groups in practice.

This chapter provides an overview of the skills required for effective group work. It offers you the opportunity to reflect on the range of groups you are already part of, and the role you play within these groups, before looking at ways to manage and gain the most from group-work situations in the classroom and on placement.

STARTING POINTS

Groups come in all shapes and sizes, ranging from spontaneous, informal gatherings to those containing highly organised and complex structures. During your lifetime you will have participated in a range of different groups with varying degrees of success. Try the following exercises to discover what you already know about group-work and uncover your deepest, darkest group-work secrets.

(Continued)

(Continued)

1 Read the following statements and circle the ones that relate to you:

Often the first time I notice that the group is not working well is when one of the members runs from the room sobbing.

I love the sense of power being in a group gives me. I like to take control and watch others squirm.

I start to think about what I want to say and as I do this I feel my heart beating in my mouth, but then the moment passes me by and I feel a failure.

I sit quietly but frequently have the urge to say or do something completely outrageous.

I do not rate group work highly. I turn up, sit there for an hour, say a few things then walk away.

As soon as conflict arises, I am out of the room.

I think that groups are pretty pointless really. I go through the motions but do my own thing anyway.

Group work is just another way weaker students end up being carried through their course by the stronger ones.

It does not really matter what happens in the group so long as I am OK.

Group work is boring.

If you circled 0–2 statements, excellent. It sounds as though you are a bit of a group guru. You value the importance of group work and understand the possibilities it offers. You recognise that the mark of a good group leader is someone who brings out the best in others and enables others in the group to thrive.

If you circled 3–6 statements, hmm, it sounds as though you have mixed experiences and views about group work. Read through your statements. Do your answers relate to lack of confidence or over-confidence? You will find it helpful to look at the sections in this chapter that relate to the group-work process and group facilitation.

If you circled 6–10 statements, you definitely have group goof-type tendencies. As long as you believe that the group is there for you and that you are the most important person within the group, you will struggle with the group-work process. Being a group leader is not about being on a power-trip. It is about supporting other group members and enabling individuals to gain the most out of working together.

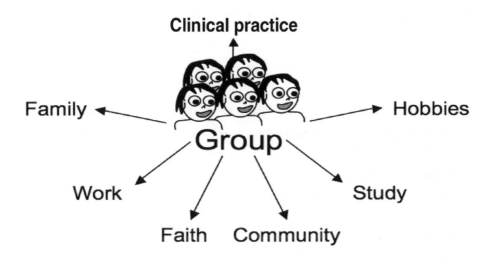

2   Complete the diagram above, recording particular groups you have been part of under these broad headings and roles you have played within these groups.

Based on the diagram: what are the top five things you gain from being part of a group?

1

2

3

4

5

3   What are the main three challenges you face?

3

2

1

4   Look at the following list of group conditions. Circle those you see as being necessary ingredients for success in groups.

clearly defined roles	fluid structure	routine	spontaneous
tight focus	heated debate	rigour	free speech
relaxed	flexibility	fun	focused
listening	controlled	friends	colleagues

Now you have started to think about your experience of, and response to, being part of a group the next stage is to focus on group work in the classroom.

Six reasons why you should take part in group work

Groups allow you to:

1 **Pool resources**, allowing you to potentially cover a greater breadth of information.
2 **See the information from different perspectives,** enabling you to think more broadly and more critically.
3 **Share and develop** new skills.
4 **Learn how other people approach tasks,** offering you the opportunity to model good ways of working.
5 **Give and receive** support.
6 **Develop skills** in summarising information, in speaking and listening, collaboration and cooperation, and ways of dealing with conflict.

Group work as an active process

Being part of a group is an active process, more so in the classroom where you will be working with people whom you have not naturally chosen to be with and who may not share your interests or synergies. It will be necessary for you to find and establish your role, learn when to take an active part and when to sit back and listen to others. Conflict will inevitably occur, and it will require you to work together to find ways of managing this so that over time you can establish a group identity and maintain a positive dynamic. You need to acknowledge that the success and failure of the group is your collective responsibility and you all have a role to play. This experience offers rich learning: the best way to learn how groups work is to be part of one.

KEYS TO SUCCESS

Successful group work requires you to:

- Be clear about the purpose of the group, its destination and the conditions required for success
- Recognise the skills of group members and the potential role they could play in the group's success
- Organise and shape group meetings to make best use of the time available
- Recognise and respect the group process
- Acknowledge and deal with conflict

Be clear about the purpose of the group, its destination and the conditions required for success

A group's success will to a large degree be dependent on how clearly its primary purpose is defined and the extent to which individual members sign up to a set of commonly agreed goals. At university you may be part of a number of different types of groups, including:

- **Task focused groups**: where you have been given a specific piece of work to complete

- **Study groups**: with a mainly supportive role, focusing on sharing ideas about different subjects and working together to build skills in order to complete assignments or coursework

- **Support groups**: for example, tutor groups. These tend to be a place where you can share your concerns and worries

- **Problem-based learning groups**: small groups where students work together to 'solve' a problem or scenario that acts as a trigger for learning

- **Action learning sets**: a group of 4–7 students who get together to identify issues or questions they have and use these as the basis of their learning

The first thing you need to do as a group is to establish what you are about and what you hope to achieve. You need to work together to reach a consensus and define your primary purpose. This is not to say that if you are a task-focused group and someone is having a difficulty that group members should not offer support. However, if your task-based group regularly becomes a place where personal difficulties are discussed to the detriment of completing the work, then it is unlikely that you will have a satisfactory outcome.

The following exercises can help this process.

Group mission statement

Aim: To establish the purpose of the group.
Resources: Slips of paper with the words 'The main purpose of this group is…' printed on them (you need enough for everyone), pens and pencils, a container.
Instructions: Group members take a slip of paper and complete the sentence. These are collected and placed in a container. The container is passed around the group and each person draws out an answer and reads it aloud. When all the results have been shared everyone then works together to create a mission statement to describe the purpose of the group based on this collective understanding. Consideration is also given as to how the group will fulfil these aims.

Illustration

Here is an example of a mission statement created by a group of radiography students:

The purpose of this group is to complete the assignment on time to the best of our ability. We will do this by sharing our resources, attending all sessions and being open in our communication.

And another created by a group of paramedics:

The purpose of this group is to offer each other support in the build up to our examinations. We will do this by making this a space where we can be honest with each other about our feelings and shout, cry and scream as we feel appropriate.

Ground rules

Aim: To establish a set of agreed standards of behaviour developed by the group to which group members agree to subscribe.
Resources: Two sets of Post-it notes (different colours or different shapes), pens, a sheet of flip chart paper.
Instructions: Group members take two sets of Post-it notes. On one set they write down things they want to happen in the group and on the other, things they do not want to happen. The sets of Post-it notes are collected, the different statements are discussed and a list is agreed. This is copied on to a sheet of flip chart paper and displayed during group meetings, thus acting as a reference point and a visual reminder.

Illustration

Here is a set of ground rules created by a group of occupational therapy students (note the use of positive language):

We will all

- Play an active role in contributing to group tasks.

- Listen to what others say.

- Maintain the confidentiality of the group: information discussed within the group stays within the group.

- Respect a person's right to have an opinion without being judged.

- Give everyone the space to speak.

- Be punctual, attend meetings whenever possible and when we are unable to do so, let other members know in advance.

An alternative way to approaching this activity is for the group to choose from a list of pre-written rules. An example of one such list is provided on the website accompanying this book (www.skills4health.co.uk).

Pre-empting problems

It can also be useful to enter into a broad discussion about possible penalties if the rules are broken and how the group will manage this. If you do this at an early point it can feel more objective and less personal than devising such rules after issues arise. For example, if a group member repeatedly fails to turn up to group sessions without explanation it might be decided to:

- note this in the minutes

- ask the group chair to discuss the issue with the person in question

If the group is working on a joint assignment and the person continues to behave in this way, you might also agree to:

- involve the tutor in the discussion

- request marks be deducted from this person's individual score for the overall piece of work

Recognise the skills of group members and the potential role they could play in the group's success

A group can offer a safe place where individuals can identify strengths, share skills, experiment with different roles and discover new ways of working. The real strength of group work is that, as a collective, you will possess a range of skills and abilities that you are able to pool in order to achieve your goals. The starting point, therefore, is to undertake a skills audit in order to:

- Recognise the skills of the group members and how they can potentially contribute to the aims of the group

- Identify any gaps and decide how to address these

- Consider skills individual members feel that they would like to achieve and explore opportunities to support their development

There are lots of ways to do this. From formal published tools such as the Belbin (1981) group role questionnaire through to informal skills audits. However you approach this task, the secret is not to be shy. False modesty is pointless if it means that other people in the group do not hear about what you can offer. The following exercises are a good starting point.

Skills audit

Aim: To determine the skills you possess as a group.
Resources: Small pieces of card.
Instructions: Group members take a number of blank pieces of card and write down the skills they possess. These may relate to technical skills, for example using a particular computer application or being able to structure an assignment or speak in front of others. They may also relate to personal qualities, such as being an encourager or a problem-solver.

The group look through the cards and note down the range of skills they can draw on. Any gaps are highlighted and possible resources that can be used to meet these are identified.

Skills swap

Aim: To use the group as a vehicle to share existing skills and develop new ones.
Resources: Two sets of Post-it notes (you can distinguish these by using different colours or shapes).
Instructions: Group members take two sets of Post-it notes. On one set they record skills they already possess and are willing to share. On the other set they write down skills they would like to develop. The Post-it-notes are initialled so that they are easily identifiable.

The notes are collected and the group match up skills and needs. If by the end of the exercise there are still needs that cannot be met, they look at possible resources they can tap into.

Fulfilling group roles

Once you have undertaken your skills audits you may find it helpful to then identify particular tasks that individuals will take responsibility for. Within most groups there are a number of fixed roles you will need to consider. These include:

Chair

Being a chair is like being the captain of a ship. Your role is to guide the group, manage the dynamics and ensure that everyone has a chance to contribute. You will need to have an air of confidence and authority as you have to keep the group on task.

There is a skill to making the group a safe place to be, knowing when a situation is escalating and finding the right moment to step in. A good chair is someone who is fair, is able to listen well and put the needs of the group first.

Here is some advice offered by students on the subject of chairing a meeting:

Set the tone
Arrive early, dress for the part, invest time and effort. It is your responsibility to see that things run smoothly. This isn't about friendship or being a student, it is business.

Keep an overview
Identify group members who are not contributing or who find it difficult to say anything. Praise their contributions, use specific questioning techniques and help them to feel comfortable.

Be prepared
Know the subject area. Read what you can beforehand so that you have a good idea of the direction you are moving in. Other group members will be looking to you to take a lead.

Note-taker

Your role is to record what happens in the group and identify who is responsible for individual tasks. You need to listen very carefully to what individuals say and record information quickly and accurately. A certain degree of confidence may also be required when seeking clarification from group members. You will require good organisational skills in order to summarise information and present it in an acceptable format at the appropriate time.

Here students share the secrets of good note-taking:

Make sure that you are well equipped
Ensure you have the tools for the job. A well-sharpened pencil, a pen that works and enough paper to see you through the session. There is nothing worse than having to rummage through your rucksack, writing on tiny scraps of paper with a pen that you continually have to shake to make the ink flow.

Revisit your notes at the earliest possible moment
Revisit your notes while the meeting is still fresh in your mind. Read through what you have written and make sure that your writing is legible.

Work at your pace
Do not worry if you find it difficult to keep up with everyone. It is much easier to speak than to write and at all times you need to remember that you can set the pace of the meeting. Seek clarification at appropriate moments, read back summaries and seek validation so that the group 'owns' the notes. It is better to do this during the meeting than afterwards when no one can remember.

Sharing roles

It is often best to rotate these roles among group members in order to give everyone an equal opportunity to experience how it feels to take responsibility and develop the underpinning skills that are required. This helps everyone to take an active role and feel part of the group. It also prevents the same individuals from dominating the proceedings.

Further roles

The chair and the note-taker are two of the more easily identifiable roles within the group. However, there is a whole series of other roles that are less formal and transparent. Read the following examples and decide whether the role may help a group to achieve its aims or whether it would hinder the process. See if you can identify any roles you have played and identify others that are not listed.

Questioner	Seeks out information and looks for clarification of facts or questions assumptions that have been made.
Silent member	Says very little. Attends meetings but does not offer an opinion. Can be quite passive.
Mediator	Intervenes during periods of conflict to find an acceptable way forwards.
Pacifier	Pours oil on troubled water. Prevents arguments from escalating.
Elaborator	Takes ideas and expands or builds on these.
Clown	Appears not to take anything seriously. Turns everything into a joke.
Time keeper	Keeps the group on track.
Bully	Overtly or covertly dominates the group, imposing their opinion on others. Particularly focuses on weaker members and undermines their confidence.
Aggressor	Verbally attacks other group members. Continually expresses disapproval.
Encourager	Recognises and praises the contributions of others. Can play a key role in keeping the group motivated.
Scapegoat	A person who is blamed when things go wrong, even if it is not their fault.
Gossip	Does not always respect ground rules and will share information outside the group.
Anecdote teller	Has a story for every theme or idea the group discusses. Constantly relays personal experiences to group members.

We will all play different roles at different times. Some are definitely not conducive to effective group work and others, such as questioner, will depend on the purpose you will serve. For example, if your role as questioner is to clarify thinking at the beginning of the process, this can be helpful. However, if over-questioning leads to the group going round and round in circles, this is less useful. It can be useful to reflect on the reasons why you play the roles you do. Try the reflective exercise contained on the website accompanying this book (www.skills4health.co.uk) to explore this further.

Organise and shape group meetings to make best use of the time available

Research by John Adair (1986) found that groups who sought to build their team, achieve the task and respond to individual needs were those who functioned most effectively. Here are some of the techniques that may support you in this process:

- Make sure the session has a clear direction. Work together to clarify the purpose of the meeting and work towards this agreed goal. Divide work fairly.

- Make the most of the time you have available. An agenda or group meeting sheet can help to keep you focused. When actions are recorded, make a note of who is responsible for given tasks. Be clear about deadlines.

- Establish routines and rituals so that sessions have a shape or rhythm. For example, some kind of greeting or introduction, followed by a main activity, then agreement regarding the actions required for the next meeting.

- Ensure that everyone has the chance to speak.

- Strive to maintain a sense of organisation but also build in some flexibility so you can cope with the unexpected.

Here is a short description by a student of how they manage the group-work process.

Our course uses problem-based learning so we need to be quite organised and work closely together as a group. We have found the best way to do this is to set and follow an agenda for each meeting. One of our ground rules is to arrive on time. The first five minutes are spent catching up and then we get down to business. The chair of the meeting reads out the aims of the session, what we hope to achieve by the end of this, and we add anything we might need to at this point.

We have found a group worksheet very helpful. This has space to record the issue discussed and the time allocated. We stick quite closely to this. We have a timekeeper to support the chair and this helps to keep us on track. The note-taker records everything and as we identify further subjects or topics to look at we note these down and record who has responsibility to fulfil this task.

There are tensions sometimes and on one occasion we called a 'crisis meeting' with the sole aim of sorting this out before it escalated. We found that the best way to prevent this from happening again was to include space on the agenda at every meeting to give feedback about how we think the group is going. Every third meeting we have a more formal feedback session, looking at strengths and limitations of the process and identifying what we need to change to make it more effective. This acts a bit like a pressure cooker, letting off steam before it explodes.

The final part of the group meeting is spent deciding the agenda for the next meeting and who is responsible for what. The note-taker makes sure that this is recorded on the sheet and we use this as the basis of the next meeting.

Recognise and respect the group process

The group process can be seen as a journey: a number of individuals come together united by a common purpose. They work to achieve this task and the group ends. The group will experience various highs and lows along the way. Tensions will arise at different points, there will be conflicts as group members vie for position, seek to establish their role and cope with various pressures as they arise. If the group is strong enough, these conflicts will be resolved and they can, in turn, act as catalysts to allow for the strengthening of relationships and bring the group together so that it works more effectively. If they are not resolved, the group will fragment and drift apart, with its purpose only partially realised.

Understanding the underlying process will allow you to identify what is happening in your group, to step outside the group, view events more objectively and to take the necessary steps to help the group to work more effectively together.

The group journey has been described in various ways, for example, by Yalom (1985) and Bion (1961). The most well-known of these studies is Tuckman and Jensen's 'Stages of small-group development revisited' (1977). Tuckman and Jensen suggested that groups go through the following stages:

- Forming

- Storming

- Norming

- Performing

- Ending

Forming

This happens at the beginning of the group process. This is the stage where you are sizing everyone else up and perhaps feeling anxious in terms of your place within the group. You will probably be asking yourself such questions as: What if they don't like me? Where shall I sit? It is also the time when you are looking for someone to lead the group. This is a bit of a honeymoon period and at this point, by and large, individuals are pretty polite and may not be showing their true colours.

Storming

According to Tuckman, and Jensen (1977), storming occurs when group members start to seek out their position or role within the group and vie for power or control. This can be a crucial point in the group process and a time when the group is most vulnerable. If feelings of hostility that arise from competitiveness or conflict are not resolved, the group can possibly fragment.

Norming

This is where things settle down. At this point individual members have found their niche and the group begins to take on an identity.

Performing

This is when things really come together and the group starts to produce the goods. Everyone is pulling together, taking responsibility and committed to achieving its purpose. You are no longer a number of individuals who are working separately, but a cohesive whole with a clear identity. Being part of a group at this point can feel great.

Ending

If the group has been working well the ending of the group can be a difficult experience. The pleasure of having achieved your goals will be weighed against feelings of loss in terms of no longer being part of the group and losing your identity and role.

This is simplistic formulation and in reality it will not be a linear process. For example, a group might be working very well and then something happens, such as a group member being away or a change in the nature of the task, leading the group to revert back to the storming process. Technically, the more times this occurs, the quicker the group will work through the stages.

Acknowledge and deal with conflict

Conflict can occur within a group for many reasons. It is not unnatural and it should not necessarily be regarded as something that is negative. There are two kinds of conflict. The first kind of conflict is energising – it generates excitement, challenges preconceptions, revisits 'truths' and can move thinking on/forward. The second type of conflict is destructive, very personal, prevents people from wanting to be part of the group, leads the group to be inward-looking and can tear it apart.

The biggest mistake that students make is that they confuse group work with friendship. Friendships can emerge from groups, but the primary reason you are meeting is business, not pleasure. Groups at university prepare you for a professional role, and part of being a professional is being able to make and express professional judgements so that, as a team, you can work together to ensure that you are meeting your client's needs. Sometimes what you have to say will be difficult and challenges the status quo. However, the alternative is unthinkable. Imagine the following scenario…

You have assessed a client and found that they require further in-patient rehabilitation. Your colleague doesn't agree. You like your colleague and so as not to upset her you agree with what she says and do not share your results.

Yet, as unacceptable as this may sound, you will find yourself in group-work situations at university where you agree with another person not because you feel this or believe it, but because you want to 'please them'. There are dangers here as you can be sucked into a 'lemming' culture where everyone agrees with everyone else and you never really achieve any critical depth to your thinking or actions. Alternatively, you can end up with the formation of subgroups or cliques, which can be counterproductive. Such groups are often indicative of power struggles that have not been resolved.

Tips to cope with conflict

Keep it professional: Develop clear ground rules at the beginning of the group-work process and do not be frightened of reverting to these. When you start to work as a group, spend time looking at and agreeing how you will tackle potential problems and issues should they arise. This way everyone agrees that particular behaviours carry identified consequences.

Avoid making it personal: Focus on the behaviour, not the person. Instead of saying 'You have caused a problem', say 'how can we work as a group to move forwards?'

Keep it open: If someone 'only wants to talk to you', try to encourage them to talk to other people in the group too. The danger occurs if subdivisions form and group members establish themselves in opposing 'cliques'. This can be very divisive, waste a lot of energy and cause the group to malfunction.

Distinguish between aggression and assertiveness: There is nothing wrong with a group member expressing their opinion and sharing what they think or believe if it is done in an open manner. This will enhance the group process. The problem arises if a participant continually tries to impose their ideas or exercise power over other people in the group. Examples of aggressive behaviour include open physical or verbal hostility and more subtle manipulative behaviour, including sulking, loud sighs when someone contributes to the discussion and generally making comments that undermine others.

Build in time to step back and talk about the group: It can be difficult to broach issues when the group is in the middle of a period of conflict, particularly if comments are critical. If you build in time to talk about how things are progressing as part of a regular group 'health check', participants feel that they have permission to talk about issues as they arise. If this is done on a regular basis, problems can be quickly addressed before they escalate. Whenever you engage in this process try not to dwell on problems, but rather look for solutions.

Identify your resources but only use these when you really need to: Problems will inevitably arise. You will find that not everyone is committed to the group: individuals will turn up or arrive late, will either not contribute or actively seek to undermine others. If you can work together to resolve these issues, then your group will be stronger as a consequence and you will be in a stronger position to take this learning forwards into group-work situations in practice. However, there will be times when you may need extra support, and during these times you need to identify additional sources of support, usually from your tutor, who may be able to act as a mediator in the situation.

Skills in practice

Teamwork is a feature of health-care practice. Decisions are made in multidisciplinary teams where different professionals pool expertise in order to coordinate care. When these group processes work well, patients benefit from the sharing of multiple perspectives and the combined knowledge and skills of each professional. However, if the group breaks down, care can become fragmented and patient safety can be compromised. You need only think of the case of Victoria Climbie, a little girl who died because of a breakdown in communication between different members of the multidisciplinary team, to understand the importance of effective group work in practice.

As a student, you will be part of a number of groups and it is vital to understand their purpose and the respective roles you and other members of this team play within these. The remainder of this chapter therefore looks at how to gain the most from groups on placement, focusing particularly on the multidisciplinary team.

Be clear about the purpose of the group, its destination and the conditions required for success

You could be part of any number of groups on placement, including:

- Student support groups

- Your immediate team

- Your professional group (e.g. nursing, operating department practice (ODP), paramedics)

- A journal club

However, the most common group you will encounter is the multidisciplinary team (MDT). The purpose of the multidisciplinary team is to 'bring together experts in different specialities to discuss the management of patients with a given condition or disease' (Rattay and Mehanna, 2008: 1). The overall aim of the group is to reach a consensus as to the best course of action for the patient/client. However, the group will meet together for different reasons:

MDT meeting: this is a regular weekly or monthly meeting to discuss patients' progress. This can involve all members of the team. Each patient is discussed in turn and the interventions are reviewed. Results of tests, x-rays, assessments such as home visits and treatment regimens are shared and in light of these further interventions are planned. Patients and their family members are often invited to be part of this.

Discharge meeting: This occurs at the end of a given period of treatment or intervention. The aim of the discharge meeting is to make sure that things are in place. For example, if a person is being discharged from hospital, colleagues from community services will be invited to ensure a smooth handover.

Case conference: This may not comprise the whole multidisciplinary team. Case conferences are called in order to discuss the needs of specific clients. This can be in response to a crisis.

Review: The purpose of a review meeting is to explore the progress the person is making and to decide whether to maintain or change the current treatment regimen.

CPA: For some clients with mental health needs, future care requirements can be extremely complex. The Care Programme Approach coordinates care and sets down very detailed plans of the resources and support required.

Handover: This is a feature of in-patient settings. It describes the sharing of information when staff from one shift hand over to another.

Recognise the skills of group members and the potential role they could play in the group's success

As a student you will be joining an established team with pre-formed roles. The chair or lead will depend on the area of work. For example, in a clinical setting this role is usually played by the consultant. The make-up of the team will depend on the setting. If you are working in a mental health setting, the multidisciplinary team may comprise:

- Consultant psychiatrist

- Nurse

- Social worker

- Occupational therapist

- Dietician

- Community psychiatric nurse

- Psychologist

On the other hand, if you are working on a cancer unit, the team can include:

- Surgeon

- Oncologist

- Radiologist

- Pathologist

- Clinical nurse specialist

Again, the skills of the group members will be determined by their professional expertise. It is a useful exercise to clarify your understanding of the different roles team members play. For example, do you know the difference between the occupational therapist and the physiotherapist, or between the social worker and the community psychiatric nurse?

Activity

Try the following exercise. Look at the areas below and see if you can identify possible team members:

- Which professions might be involved in a multidisciplinary team meeting for a person involved in a road traffic accident?
- Which professions might be involved in a multidisciplinary team meeting for a woman who experienced a fractured pelvis during a complicated birth?
- Which professions might be involved in a multidisciplinary team meeting for a person who has been diagnosed with dementia?

Work your way through the scenarios and identify the contributions that each team member would make to the person's care.

In addition to their specific, professional skills, individual members will also have a number of personal skills that they bring to the group experience. Examples of these may include an ability to organise the group, or to keep others on track, or an ability to summarise information. When you are on placement it can be useful to spend time observing how members of the team use these skills, and where teams are functioning well, how the group enables this to happen.

Organise and shape group meetings to make best use of the time available

The shape of the group meeting will very much be dependent on the reason why it has been called, and the way that groups are organised will reflect the context of the placement setting.

Multidisciplinary team (MDT) meetings tend to follow a set format dictated by the chair of the meeting. Everyone will assemble at the given time and the chair (usually the consultant or key worker) will present a summary of the case history and the issues that have arisen. Relevant members of the MDT will then be invited to contribute information, for example, findings from tests and x-rays, assessments, and home visit reports. Based on this information, the team will then decide the best course of action, identifying who is responsible and the timeframe in which this is to be achieved. For instance, Is further assessment required? Will a person's medication be changed? Do other services need to be involved? Decisions are made in relation to the long-term goals relating to patients. Is the focus on getting someone home or is it in the best interests of the person to go into residential care? These are big decisions and clients and their families are frequently invited to attend the meetings. If the MDT is focusing on discharge, then emphasis will be given to ensuring that everything is in place to meet the person's future care needs. It is therefore important that actions are carefully documented. Notes are taken throughout. The time and place of the next meeting is agreed. After the meeting, notes are written up, referrals to other agencies are made, letters are composed and the paperwork is updated.

As a student, it is highly unlikely that you will chair a group meeting but you will be expected to contribute and you will play a part in the smooth running of the proceedings. Here students describe some of the things they have been asked to do.

I was responsible for setting up the room, making sure that the case notes were in order.

My supervisor asked if I would telephone the person's family to let them know the time and the place of the meeting.

My role was to present the x-rays and to discuss what they showed.

We had undertaken a number of home visits and I verbally reported back the findings of these, highlighting possible safety issues.

I fed back my observations about how Mrs X had been on the ward since her admission.

I was responsible for taking notes throughout the meeting and feeding these back to my nursing colleagues at the next handover.

It is worth going to a meeting just to gain a feel for how it is organised so you are then more prepared for when you are asked to take an active role. Here is an account given by one student:

I will never forget my first MDT meeting. My placement educator asked if I would 'present' a person I had been working with, describing the assessments undertaken, my findings and recommendations. I arrived at the meeting and was really taken aback at the speed at which things flowed. I was a bit shocked by its formality. Of course, when it was my turn to speak I was completely unprepared. I had made a few brief notes but these weren't nearly as detailed as they needed to be and I completely fluffed the questioning. I felt bad because I really slowed down proceedings and there were other embarrassing moments when the consultant asked me to talk about other patients on the ward. Even though I had worked quite closely with some people, my mind went blank and I stuttered my way through the whole thing. Overall, I was unprepared but the consequences of this are huge. Big decisions about patients' futures are riding on this information.

I reflected on the experience and the next time I made sure that I was ready. I made a list of each person on my caseload, treatment aims, a summary of the interventions carried out, my observations and recommendations. I then compiled a detailed report for the person I had been asked to 'present'. When the consultant began his questioning I could really do each person justice. My educator complemented me, and for the first time I felt as though I had made a real contribution to the long-term needs of the clients in my care.

Recognise and respect the group process

Your experience of being part of a group at university will have provided you with plenty of opportunities to understand the journey most groups travel and the shifting dynamics they experience. Placement will offer you additional insights to recognise what might be occurring within the group process. The challenge that many hospital and community teams face is the rapid changes they experience both in terms of staff turnover, either through shift patterns, rotation of personnel, or the organisation or re-organisation of departments and, within many teaching hospitals, the presence of student practitioners. One of the consequences of this is that teams are constantly evolving and moving through the various stages of group formation. Even your presence within the team will impact on the dynamic of the group and how individuals interact. Use your reflections to consider the role you play within the team and how you personally cope as the group evolves. Seek to understand factors that both help and hinder this process and then see how you can use these insights to inform the group-work you undertake back in the classroom at university.

Acknowledge and deal with conflict

A group of professionals passionate about the patients they work with; different philosophies of care; external pressures on beds and waiting lists; complex decision-making processes. All these factors mean that conflict is inevitable. There will be clashes and different parties will argue furiously about the treatment approach adopted. At times you may be required to present information that may be in conflict with the general consensus of the other team members. For example, the occasion when there is pressure on beds and your assessment has shown that the person requires further rehabilitation and needs to remain on the ward. However, you need only think back to your experience in the classroom to remember that this is not personal; it is business and it is in the best interest of the client for you to voice your findings clearly and with confidence. After all, the purpose of the multidisciplinary team is to share these different perspectives in order to build up as clear a picture as possible as to the best way forwards to support the individual within the resources available. A team where everyone was constantly in agreement would not work effectively. When channelled appropriately, professional debate can generate new ideas and create innovative solutions to challenges.

To end this chapter, here is some advice offered by a community mental health team about how to manage the group conflict in practice:

The first point is to keep it professional. Debate is part of the function of the team and it is not personal. If team members take comments relating to the clinical decision-making process to heart, then problems occur. We function well because we recognise and accept that everyone has a valid contribution to make and we value the diversity of the team. To this end, we always build in five minutes at the end to give feedback, have a coffee and to generally leave the business behind. There is nothing worse than if someone dashes from the meeting feeling that their point of view has not been accepted or that they have not had the chance to air this opinion.

Avoid making judgements and saying negative things about people behind their back. This feeds into the development of cliques and can be very divisive within the team. As a student, keep well out of the politics. Becoming involved will serve no purpose and will drain your energy.

If an issue arises, then discuss it with the person involved outside the group. Again, if you are on placement, then the best person to talk this through with before taking any action is your educator. It can be a valuable learning experience to address such issues in a professional manner.

Learn to be a good listener. Remember that, realistically, the team meeting will represent a minute fraction of the time you are working in the area. True teambuilding occurs in the spaces behind formal meetings, in the tiny gestures you make to contribute to the effective working of the group, the indications that you are willing to play your part and to take the time to show that you care.

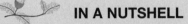

IN A NUTSHELL

This chapter has described group work in two very different contexts. However, in each context the do's and don'ts of effective group work are surprisingly similar:

- Do make sure you are clear about the purpose of the group and why you are meeting
- Do plan ahead and organise how best to use your time
- Do take time recognising the skills that individual members bring and ways you can tap into these
- Do build in time to reflect on your progress and identify ways of moving forwards
- Do not ignore conflict or let things escalate out of control
- Do not expect to play a passive role in the group-work process
- Do not over-rely on others to intervene at the slightest problem
- Do not avoid group work hoping that it will go away

References and signposts to further reading and resources

Adair, J. (1986) *Effective Team Building*. Aldershot: Gower.

Belbin, R.M. (1981) *Management Teams: Why They Succeed or Fail*. London: Butterworth-Heinemann.

Bion, W.R. (1961) *Experiences in Groups*. New York: Basic Books.

Jaques, D. (1992) *Learning in Groups*. London: Kogan Page.

Maslin-Prothero, S. (2005) *Bailliere's Study Skills for Nurses and Midwives* (3rd edition). Edinburgh: Elsevier.

Rattay, T. and Mehanna, H.M. (2008) 'Multidisciplinary team meetings', *Student BMJ*. Available at: http://student.bmj.com/issues/08/07/education/278.php (last accessed 18/08/2008).

Tuckman, B.W. (1965) 'Developmental sequences in small groups', *Psychological Bulletin,* 63: 384–9.

Tuckman, B.W. and Jensen, M.A. (1977) 'Stages of small-group development revisited', *Group and Organisation Management,* 2 (4): 419–27.

Yalom, I.D. (1985) *The Theory and Practice of Group Psychotherapy* (3rd edition). New York: Basic Books.

Part IV Planning and preparing for the future

18 Gaining your dream job

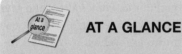 **AT A GLANCE**

This chapter is for you if

- Your friends are getting jobs that have failed to even feature on your radar

- You think a person spec is someone who wears glasses

- You fill out lots of applications but never make it to the next stage

- You would like to know how to dazzle at interviews

This chapter is about looking towards the future and taking the first steps towards gaining your dream job. Up to this point everything on your course has been geared towards preparing you to be the best practitioner you can possibly be. The moment you have passed your course you can apply for registration with the relevant professional council or body and then you are qualified to be let loose on the public and to work as a fully-fledged, wage-earning health professional. This is a fantastic moment. You have the qualifications, the motivation. All that is left is for you to find your dream post. Unfortunately, dream jobs rarely jump out and find you. You will need to put time and effort into thinking about where you want to be and how to get there.

This chapter shows you how to pull together the skills covered in this book and apply them to the job-hunting process. It shows you how to read a job description, untangle a person specification and put together an application in such a way as to maximise your chances of success. Finally, it looks at how to present yourself well and gain the most from the interview process.

STARTING POINTS

Before you start your job hunt in earnest it can be useful to clarify your thinking and to tie down the type of job you are interested in. The following activities can help this process.

Use the mind map opposite to explore your thinking about your dream job. Where will it be? How much will you earn? Who will you work with? How many hours will you work? What kind of boss will you have? Who will the client group be? When you wake up on a morning what will you look forward to? Are you looking for the breadth of experience which can be gained through something like a rotational post, or are you looking for a more specialist post which will offer you the depth?

Right, a quick reality check. Are you surprised by anything you have written? What strikes you in particular?

Back to fantasy mode… Imagine that your fairy godmother comes along and says that she can grant you your wish but because her magic is not powerful enough you can choose only two of the characteristics of your dream job. Which two would you select? Again write these in the space below:

Characteristic one   Characteristic two

Again, are you surprised by your answer?

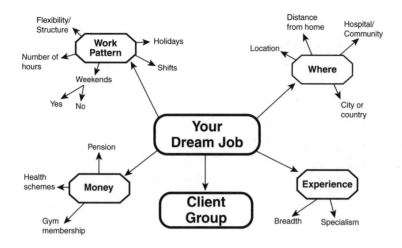

Now for a different tack. This time we will use a housing analogy. When you buy a house there are factors known as deal-breakers. These are things about the house that you simply could not live with, compromises you are not prepared to make. For example, it might be that you could live with dry rot but not noisy neighbours. Similarly, there are things about jobs that have the same effect. For instance, a job could be perfect in every way but if you had to drive 50 miles to get there or if parking cost £5.00 a week this could be the one factor that prevents you from applying. Use the space below to list your potential deal-breakers.

These exercises are useful as they help you to clarify your thinking. One final thing to consider: Are you prepared to accept a post that you are not particularly interested in as an interim measure in order to develop skills and act as a spring-board to a post you really want, or are you able and willing to wait until a preferred post comes along? This will very much depend on your personal circumstances and the job market in general. There are pros and cons to both approaches.

To wait or not to wait that is the question…

Points in favour of taking a post in the interim
- Money
- Helps to maintain confidence and skills
- Can be easier to find a job when in employment

Points against
- Boredom
- Disillusionment
- Grow complacent and may not leave

KEYS TO SUCCESS

Finding your ideal job is underpinned by the following keys to success:

- Know where to look and how to search
- Look good on paper
- Present yourself well
- Reflect on your performance

Know where to look and how to search

Sadly, if a job is a dream job to you, it will be a dream job to everyone else. A highly competitive job market requires you to adopt a methodical approach and have a search strategy, planned with military precision.

The first thing to do is to find out where jobs are advertised. Look in professional journals, websites, local newspaper and the university intranet (some employers approach universities about potential opportunities). Do not be frightened to explore other avenues. For example, many students have personal contacts built up through placement or as a result of friendships with graduate students who are now in employment.

If you are serious…

- Start looking early. Popular posts can be advertised as early as Christmas with start dates held from June onwards.
- Develop a routine of looking on a regular basis.

If you are very serious…

- If something catches your eye but you feel that you do not meet all the criteria, telephone for details.
- Be proactive and organise a job fayre where you invite local employers to the university to talk about the opportunities that exist within their Trusts.
- Join a professional interest group: a good way to network.
- Bookmark job websites.
- Identify resources in the university that can help, e.g. the careers service.

If you are super-serious…

- Send for details about a particular job or jobs at an early point of your course. Note the skills required and start to gain the experience in order to build that CV.

- Become an active member of the local group of your professional association.

- Contact places where you would like to work who have not yet advertised posts. Send your CV expressing your interest and ask to be kept informed of any opportunities as they arise (if you do this, remember to enclose a stamped addressed envelope).

- Think outside the box. An increasing number of opportunities arise in non-traditional areas of practice. Make sure that you thoroughly investigate all possibilities.

- Undertake voluntary work in the area.

The job advert

Most posts are advertised though a job abvert. A job advert provides a thumbnail sketch. It will state the job title, the location, the level or banding, the pay-scale and then a few details about what the job entails and the experience required. The advert is like an aperitif to a meal and whets the appetite. Read it with a critical eye and ask yourself: 'What does it not say?' 'Is it a fixed-term contract or permanent?' 'Are there support structures in place or not?' 'Are you expected to assume a great deal of responsibility or do you feel that you are being asked to do a reasonable amount given the grade of the post and the experience requested?'

To find out more you will either need to telephone for a job specification or download the details from the internet. Additional information will include:

- A job description

- A person specification

These serve quite different purposes.

The job description

The job description tells you what the job is about. It outlines the main duties and responsibilities of the post and includes practical details such as the hours of work, location, lines of accountability, who you would be answerable to and where the post sits within the wider organisation. You need to read this from two different perspectives. On the one hand, you need to decide what you will bring to the post and whether your current skills and experience match the requirements. On the other hand, you will need to develop your own checklist to weigh up what the job has to offer you. Your checklists could include the following:

- Do I feel excited about the post?

- Is it challenging/stimulating?

- Does it offer support?

- Is there the opportunity for mentorship?

- Are there opportunities for training/personal and professional development?

- Does the post relate to my 'bigger picture' and plans for the future?

- Do I have the necessary skills and experience?

- Can I fulfil the main duties?

- Are there particular specialisms required?

- Is training offered with regard to these specialisms?

- Is the post supervised by a fellow physiotherapist/occupational therapist/social worker/ operating department practitioner/paramedic/nurse/midwife or would I be managed by a person from a different professional group?

This is a very useful process. It can clarify thinking and support the decision-making process. The secret is to be honest with yourself. If the job description is asking you to do something beyond your present capabilities, you need to decide whether the gap between your current skills and the skills or knowledge required is too large at this point. Make a mental note of what you might need to work towards in the future. This is the equivalent of seeing a house that is beyond your budget. Do you decide to put in an offer or walk away and save hard?

The person specification

This lists the key duties associated with the post and the qualification/skills/ experience required. It is often presented in the format of a grid with boxes indicating whether particular attributes are essential or desirable and how they will be assessed. This may be through application, interview or both.

This is an important document. Think of the person specification as being like the learning outcomes on an assignment. The first hurdle you need to jump with any job application is to make sure that you evidence each of the criteria. Employers operate strict equal opportunities policies. Be careful not to assume that just because you have been somewhere on placement that the person reading your application will automatically know that you have a particular skill. The first stage of the sifting process involves practitioners sitting with a pen marking your application against the set criteria. Only applicants gaining a certain score will be invited to interview. You therefore need to make sure that you evidence each of the points marked as essential, otherwise your application ends here.

Look good on paper

Once you have researched the job market thoroughly and identified the post you are going to apply for, the next step is to complete an application to get that all important interview. Your application must:

(a) Demonstrate that you have the skills required to fulfil the advertised post

(b) Relate these skills to relevant experience

(c) Demonstrate that you have read the description of the post and are committed to and enthusiastic about the job described

(d) Offer something that makes your potential employer want to find out more

Be discerning. It is not necessary to write everything on the application form – there probably isn't the space. Remember, your application will form a starting point for discussion and give you a chance to elaborate on your ideas.

The art of selling yourself

Students often describe the hardest part of the application process as the completion of the personal statement. The challenge is achieving the balance between being too modest and sounding arrogant. This is not as complicated as it might initially sound. The first stage is to sketch out your ideas. Try these fun and creative activities to start this process:

Imagine you are writing a 'lonely hearts' column but instead of seeking a person you are seeking an ideal post. Here is an example:

I am an intelligent, conscientious, reliable paramedic. I rwtp (respond well to pressure). Seeking a challenging first post with a supportive team.

Complete the following in relation to your skills, experience and attributes:

I have good/very good/excellent…
I have experience in…
I have undertaken a range of…
College/university tutors have commented on…
Placement supervisors have commented that…
I am interested in… because…
On placement I…
Group work is…
I am conscientious/hard working/reliable…
I am involved in…

At university I have enjoyed...
On placement I have enjoyed...
I welcome the opportunity to develop…
My main strengths are...
I have not had the opportunity to... however, I have... (similar experience)
An example of when I demonstrated x is…
A particular strength is…
I work well…
I can…

Next, circle the adjectives/nouns in the list below that apply to you:

Adaptable, bright, caring, computer-literate, communicator, completer, conscientious, creative, decision-maker, determined, effective communicator, entrepreneur, flexible, grounded, group player, group worker, hardworking, honest, initiative, innovative, integrity, intuitive, jovial, knowledgeable, leader, listener, motivated, motivator, negotiator, organised, problem-solver, questioning, reflective, reliable, self-reliant, sensitive to the needs of others, team player, understanding of others needs, versatile, visionary, willing to learn (add your own)

Structuring the personal statement

Once you have sketched out your ideas, you are ready to sit down and structure these in much the same way that you would plan an assignment. Imagine that the essential and desirable criteria are learning outcomes that you need to evidence. Draw evidence from placement, voluntary work, additional roles undertaken (course rep, member of specialist interest group). Here is an example of one way you might do this

	Academic	Professional (placement and previous work)
Written communication skills	Marks for written work, types of written work undertaken: essays, reports, dissertations	Keeping accurate documentation on placement, writing reports, summaries, compiling treatment plans, producing leaflets for clients
Verbal communication skills	Examples of presentations given as part of your course, modifying your presentation style to meet different audiences,	Examples of speaking at ward rounds, handover, conferences, communicating with clients with complex communication needs.

	Academic	Professional (placement and previous work)
	working in small groups, chairing meetings	Evidence of undertaking initial interviews, experience of using specialist communication equipment. Building a rapport with clients. Evidence of listening skills
Organisational skills	Ability to meet assignment deadlines, to set goals and work towards these	Managing a case load, time management, skills in problem-solving
Clinical skills	Examples of practical skills developed during your course in clinical skills suites, simulations, expert knowledge gained through undertaking an option or carrying out your research study	Carrying out a particular intervention. The range of your placement experiences. Specialist clinical skills (e.g. splinting, respiratory, emergency medicine)
Teamwork/ teamplayer	Examples of participating in and facilitating groups during your course (learning sets, small groups)	Examples of being part of a multidisciplinary team or your professional group on placement, and instances where you have facilitated groups on placement
Technology	Word-processing assignments, using particular statistical packages, accessing research databases, using the internet	Electronic record-keeping, using technology as part of an assessment or therapeutic intervention
Personal qualities: adaptability, flexibility	Engaging with a range of different learning styles: lectures, problem-based learning, conscientious attitude, determination, motivation. Comments made by tutors	Flexibility: working across a range of areas, gaining experience of a range of different client groups in a number of geographical areas during practice placement learning. Comments made by supervisors about your honesty and conscientiousness

Additional pointers when writing your application

- Make sure that you do your skills justice but always be honest. When you have drafted your personal statement, ask a friend or colleague to read it and identify what they believe to be the essential criteria of the job for which you have applied.

- Reflect on your efforts. Put yourself in the interviewer's shoes for a moment and imagine that you are reading your application for the first time. Based on your reading, ask yourself whether you would offer this person an interview. List the reasons for your decision. If you are not happy rewrite the parts that are unsatisfactory.

- Once you are happy with your draft, transfer this information on to the application form. If you are handwriting this and are worried that you will make mistakes, write it out using a feint pencil to begin with before using a black pen. You can always rub out the pencil once you have done this.

- Proof-read your work. An application that is full of spelling mistakes and grammatical errors creates a really bad first impression which is difficult to ignore.

- Before you post your application be sure to take a photocopy. This way when you get an interview you can remind yourself about what you have written and prepare yourself for questions that your interviewers might want to ask, based on what you have said.

Here is a worked example. It is an extract from a supporting statement written by a student for a job in a specialist education school. Read through the statement and identify where she has supported her statement with evidence.

I am extremely interested in the post of X within your specialist school. I undertook one of my placements there and was impressed by the quality of care offered to the children and the person-centred ethos of your institution.

I am currently completing a BSc in occupational therapy at X university and will qualify in July 2009.

I have experience of working with young people of secondary-school age in hospital and social care settings and have been actively involved in youth groups within church for many years. I am committed to seeing individuals, particularly young people, reach their potential and feel that this post will enable me to do this.

I have excellent communication skills. While on placement supervisors have commented that communication with clients, carers and colleagues is my strongest area and I am confident in working with individuals who have complex communication needs. At present I am on my final placement with the X Learning Disability service, where effective communication is crucial to enable positive outcomes for the client. My role requires that I work closely with external agencies and service providers, both statutory and voluntary, within health and social care. I regularly give feedback at multidisciplinary team meetings about the progress of individuals I am working alongside, and I have a good understanding of other people's roles in the team.

My experience on the course and on placement has enabled me to develop skills in facilitating groups as well as working on a one-to-one basis with individuals in order to help individuals to develop skills, structure time effectively and to support the development of leisure, work and self-care. I am confident in using and undertaking a range of assessments to identify individual needs and to formulate interventions to support skills development. I have facilitated a range of groups, including anger management, coping with anxiety, social skills development, building self-esteem, life skills (cooking, independent living) and have used a range of therapeutic and creative media to enable the individuals I have worked alongside to reach their goals. I have also facilitated a range of support groups for families and carers which have explored coping strategies and ways to diffuse the difficult situations they may face at home.

My experience across a range of areas has meant that I have developed good working relationships with a number of different resource providers. With this overview, I have enjoyed using creative approaches to problem-solving and to finding alternative solutions to situations. Being on a community placement means that I am able to work well on my own and to use my initiative as well as being part of a group.

I am extremely conscientious and hardworking. Managing university, placement and family commitments requires a great deal of time management and I have excellent organisational skills and am able to work under pressure. Indeed, while being at the university I founded a student group called X. The aim of the group was to enable students to keep up to date with current best practice and professional development. This group has grown in size to approximately 80 students and I coordinate six teams who engage in a range of projects.

Curriculum vitae and covering letter

Some employers require a curriculum vitae (CV) and a covering letter as opposed to a formal application form. A CV is a brief resumé, a snapshot of your qualifications, skills and experiences relevant to a post. Because it is a brief resumé, most CVs fill just one side of A4 paper. The skill here is to provide just enough information to make the person reading it want to find out more from you.

Various formats exist and a range of templates you may wish to use can be found on the internet. Most CVs will contain the following sections:

Personal details: Name, date of birth, nationality

Contact information: Address, telephone number, mobile phone, email address

Educational history and qualifications

Employment history

Summary of professional activities, skills and competencies

Interests and achievements

Other information (e.g. driving, IT skills, details of referees)

Your CV needs to be accompanied by a covering letter. This is your opportunity to demonstrate why you are interested in the post and reiterate the particular skills that you will bring to the post. Make sure that somewhere in the letter you include the name of the post for which you have applied. Examples of covering letters are found on the website accompanying this book (www.skills4health.co.uk).

Present yourself well

Going for the interview

The final hurdle is the interview itself. To have got this far means that you have ticked all the necessary boxes and your potential employers have seen something in your application that they like. This must give you confidence. The secret now is to keep your cool. The following exercise can help you to get into the 'zone' as you begin to mentally prepare for the big day.

Activity: Moving into the zone...

Begin by putting yourself in the place of the interviewers. Use the space below to describe the kind of person you would like to work with. What would be the key qualities you are looking for? Someone who is enthusiastic? Intelligent? Thoughtful?

What clues will you look for in your interviewee in terms of what kind of a person they are?

What might the following suggest?

- A person who arrives late
- Someone who does not make eye contact
- An individual who mumbles
- Someone who is unkempt or not dressed smartly

Most interviews consist of a short presentation or a task where you can demonstrate your skills, followed by a set of interview questions. For example, you might be asked to give a short oral presentation at the beginning of the interview on a subject relating to current practice or a piece of recent legislation. It is usual for you to know this in advance. This is your chance to make a good impression and get ahead.

Remember that you have a wealth of experience based on all the presentations you have already given at college and university. The same rules apply:

- Make sure that you fulfil the brief

- Keep the presentation focused

- Keep the presentation relevant

- Stick to the time

You do not have to elaborate on every tiny detail. If your interviewers are interested, they can ask you to give more details during their questioning. It is worth checking beforehand to clarify the audio-visual aids you will have at your disposal. There is nothing worse than arriving on the day with your PowerPoint presentation on a memory stick only to discover that the department has nothing more up to date than a flip chart.

Things to do in the build-up to the interview

Preparation is the key. Here are a few practical pointers of things to do in the run-up to the interview offered by employers and students.

This sounds embarrassingly obvious, but the first thing you need to do is to read the letter inviting you for interview. I am constantly dismayed by the number of applicants who arrive without the key documentation we require. To 'forget' a passport or a copy of the qualifications we have asked for speaks volumes about your organisational skills. (Employer)

First impressions count. Your interview begins the moment you walk into the building. (Employer)

Dress for success. Wearing something smart but comfortable is the order of the day. You feel more confident if you are dressed for the part. (Student)

My top tip would be to wear something that does not easily crease or that is so tightly fitted that it shows up unsightly sweat rings. I left the house looking immaculate but the combination of a long journey and pre-interview nerves meant that by the time I arrived I looked as though I had been dragged through a hedge backwards. (Student)

Remember that interviewers are human too. We know that sometimes things happen that are just out of your control. In these circumstances we are more interested in how you cope with these. For example, if someone has had the foresight to bring the telephone number with them so that they can let you know if they are going to be a few minutes late, this can only count in their favour. (Employer)

Make sure your mobile telephone is switched off. My boyfriend telephoned when I was in the middle of my interview to wish me luck and I just felt as though I wanted the ground to swallow me up. (Student)

Activity: Preparing for the interview

For a moment, imagine that it is the morning of your interview. You are sitting on the low settee that you have been shown to, waiting to be invited in to your interview. You can hear the murmur of someone talking in there although you can't quite hear what is being said. Close your eyes for a few moments and imagine how it might feel. After about two minutes open your eyes and read on...

The door opens and the previous candidate is shown to the door by the interviewer. They shake hands, making good eye contact. 'They seem to have a good rapport', you think. The interviewer turns to you and smiles. Would you like to come in they say. You sit in the chair you have been offered and smile. The questions begin. Sitting right where you are, respond to the following questions:

Welcome, did you have a good journey?
Now, would you like to tell me a little about your experience?
Why have you decided to apply for this post?
What skills do you think you could bring to it?
What do you think is your greatest strength? Your greatest weakness?
Can you give an example of when you have worked with a group?
What can you bring to this team?

How did that feel? You will not be able to anticipate all the questions but the more you can identify and rehearse the areas that could potentially crop up, the more prepared you will feel. Here are some of the general topics you may wish to think about:

Questions about you

- Your interests

- Your course/career to date and any changes in direction or gaps in employment history

- Skills you possess

- Skills you would like to develop

- Your past experience and future career hopes and ambitions

- Strengths and weaknesses

Questions in relation to the post you have applied for

- Motivations and interests: why have you applied for this post

- How you might handle particular aspects (managing staff, long hours, weekend work, shifts)

- Specific skills and competencies required to fulfil the role

- Evidence of your ability to use your initiative

- Evidence of your ability to work under pressure or deal with difficult or challenging situations

- Evidence of your ability to work with others, on your own, with supervision or with minimal supervision

- Group work skills; working as part of a team

- Scenario-based questions (if x happens, what would you do?)

- Questions relating to documentation (e.g. black pen, single line through mistakes and initial)

- Questions relating to procedure (e.g. if a person refuses to return from a home visit, what would you do?)

- What personal qualities will you bring to the post?

Questions relating to or impacting on practice

- Current policy and legislation (e.g. How might the Mental Capacity Act impact on your practice?)

- What do you know about Skills for Health? What is clinical governance? What do you know about the National Service Framework for...?

- Recent advances in practice

- Evidence-based practice (e.g. reasons why you might use one particular technique over another)

Questions relating to your commitment to continuous professional development (CPD)

- How you intend to manage the transition from student to practitioner

- Your thoughts and expectations about supervision

- Examples of CPD opportunities accessed over the previous year

- How you have utilised critical incidents to inform reflections

- Discussion around your CPD portfolio (it is a good idea to bring your CPD portfolio along with you)

- Support and training required

The 'any questions' question

This is your opportunity to clarify points you are unsure of and to demonstrate that you have thoroughly researched the post. Avoid asking a question for the sake of asking a question if the information has already been provided. Finally, remember to thank your interviewers for their time and smile.

Further tips

Treat the person specification as a friend. It will signpost you to more detailed questions. Remember, if a skill, attribute or qualification is identified as being desirable or essential and it was not assessed in the application, then it will be determined by the interview.

For each question, decide key points you need to cover. Illustrate your points but do not waffle. Ground your answers in practical examples from placement, the classroom and employment. For extra brownie points refer to experience 'above and beyond', including examples of voluntary work or membership of an interest group.

Then practise, practise, practise. Invite your friends to give you a 'mock interview'. If you have been given a presentation to prepare, then rehearse it.

Here is some advice about interviews from students.

My advice is to be honest. If you have not worked in the area before do not be frightened to say, but then draw on other experiences from similar placements or voluntary work you have undertaken to illustrate your answers. Feedback from my interviewer was that they felt this demonstrated my ability to transfer knowledge and understanding and a willingness to 'find out more'.

Be prepared to describe why you have applied for a particular post. It is worth doing your homework here. Find out about the Trust and the benefits they offer. This may be in terms of CPD opportunities or general support networks. The website is a good starting point for your research.

A number of the interviews I attended asked about my commitment to personal and professional development. At this point I was able to produce my CPD folder and this formed a focus for discussion.

I arranged a visit to the department beforehand. Some hospitals don't offer this, I know, but it helped me to grasp what the job was about and gave me a feel for the place. Feedback from my new employer was that they were impressed by my enthusiasm.

Reflect on your performance

Immediately after the interview find somewhere for a coffee and treat yourself to something nice. Do not mentally dissect the experience at this point as you are probably too emotionally close to the experience.

When you feel ready, jot down the questions asked and reflect on the answers you gave. Identify what you did well and things you would do differently in the future.

If you have followed the steps outlined in this chapter, you stand an excellent chance of being successful at interview. However, it is probably inevitable that there will be times when the telephone rings and the news may not be quite so good.

Coping with rejection

The first thing to remember if you are unsuccessful in your interview is that there are many factors you may be unaware of and that were beyond your control. The job market is a competitive place and the person who was successful may have had more experience, have been qualified longer or could have worked in the setting.

You may be well aware that for some reason you did not perform at your best and fluffed a few of the questions. This is why it is useful to list the questions and your answers just after the interview while they are fresh in your mind. This way you can revisit these and use them to prepare for your next interview.

The challenge comes if you felt that you answered as well as you could and you are not sure how you could improve on your performance. It is always advisable (no matter how painful) to ask for feedback. Treat the application process a bit like you would an assignment. The aim of this learning experience is to find out how to improve on future interviews so that you can successfully gain the post you want. In the words of one student:

When I learned that I had been unsuccessful in my application I felt devastated and it was then really difficult to telephone to ask for feedback. However, I am so pleased that I did. This was incredibly constructive and really gave me the 'edge' when I went for another interview for a job in a different setting.

🌿 IN A NUTSHELL

This chapter has highlighted that finding and gaining your dream job is an active process. In order to succeed you need to:

- Be clear about the type of job you are looking for

- Identify where posts are advertised and develop a routine of systematically looking in these places

- Apply all you have learned about structuring, writing and using evidence to develop your personal statement

- Use the person specification in much the same way you would use learning outcomes to strengthen your application

- Plan in advance possible questions that could arise at interview and ways to respond to these

- See this process objectively and seek feedback in order to improve on your future performance

References and signposts to further materials and resources

Bright, J. and Earl, J. (2000) *Brilliant CV: What Employers Want To See and How To Say It*. Englewood Cliffs, NJ: Prentice-Hall.

Cottrell, S. (2003) *Skills for Success: The Personal Development Planning Handbook*. Basingstoke: Palgrave Macmillan.

Hodgson, S. (2002) *Brilliant Answers To Tough Interview Questions*. Harlow: Pearson.

Howard, S. (1999) *Creating a Successful CV*. London: Dorling Kindersley.

McErin, A. (2004) *Writing the Nursing CV*. Sale, Cheshire: Edukom.

Zedlitz, R.H. (2002) *Get a Job in Health Care.* Clifton Park, NY: Thomson Delmar Learning.

19

Ending at the beginning: a brief guide to continuous professional development

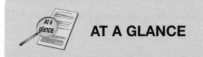 **AT A GLANCE**

This chapter is for you if

- You want to be the best practitioner you can be

- You see learning as a lifelong process

(Continued)

- Your favourite phrase is 'what if...?'

- You enjoy finding opportunities for learning in everything you do

- You are not yet part of a journal club

Picture the scene. It is the day of your graduation. You stand, clad in cap and gown, clutching your certificate, the sum of two/three/four year's hard work. Proud parents, partners, friends and family look on, beaming. You feel on top of the world. This is as good as it gets. You have a wonderful job, a good degree. It was worth every moment, all the hard work, all the anxiety, those nights of revision, the stressful group presentations. You need never engage in another learning activity or look at another textbook or journal article again. It is done. Finished. This is the end. Wait ... or is it? Rewind for just one second.

Your degree is evidence that you have achieved the necessary understanding, skills and competencies required to practise and be a member of your profession. It represents the end of one journey and the beginning of another where you progress from a novice and blossom into an expert practitioner. If we think of the analogy of driving: passing your driving test is the first hurdle, but it is only when you are out on the road that you really learn how to drive.

Standing still is the equivalent of moving backwards. Why CPD?

The process of ongoing learning and development is called continuous professional development (or CPD). It is the key to being an up-to-date practitioner in tune with the latest advances, ensuring that you are following best practice and that your clients are receiving the most current interventions.

The Allied Health Professions Council describes CPD as:

A range of learning activities through which health professionals maintain and develop throughout their career to ensure that they retain their capacity (and capability) to practise safely, effectively and legally within their evolving scope of practice. (Health Professions Council, 2006: 6)

This definition places its emphasis on fitness to practice. However, there are lots of other potential benefits. Here are the top five reasons why you should engage in CPD.

From global to local: five reasons why you should engage in CPD

5   *For your profession and practice*

Practice does not stand still; it continually evolves and develops. Continuous professional development will enable you to play a key role in contributing to the existing body of professional knowledge and will move practice forward. Just imagine, you will be playing a part in moulding the future of your profession. Wow!

4   *For your organisation*

Researching and using the most up-to-date knowledge and practices will inevitably be of benefit to the organisation you work for. Under clinical governance, your organisation has a responsibility to support you in this process and you have a commitment to your employer. In this way it becomes a two-way relationship.

> Continuing professional development should be a partnership between the individual and the organisation, its focus should be on the delivery of high quality ... services as well as meeting individual career aspirations and learning needs. (Alsop, 2000: 6)

3   *For your team*

There is a saying that the team that plays together stays together. Updating and sharing knowledge can bring colleagues together and create a focus that moves beyond professional boundaries.

2   *For your clients*

This is one of the most important reasons for engaging with continuous professional development activities. The Health Professions Council states that registrants must 'seek to ensure that their CPD activities benefit the service user' (Health Professions Council, 2006: 4). Indeed, our clients need to know that we are offering best practice and the highest standard of care possible.

1   *For you*

Continuous professional development will help you to feel confident in what you do. As you deepen and broaden your knowledge base you will expand your expertise and become more efficient and less fazed by new challenges. This keeps things interesting, reduces boredom and leads to increased job satisfaction. The process can open up pathways in your career development, offering you the opportunity to take on additional roles and new specialisms. It is also a professional requirement for registration. I will say a little about this later.

The good news is that the range of learning and reflective processes you have been participating in throughout this book and the course that you have been undertaking means that you already have the basics in place. Many of these will be very familiar to you. The steps to success are just about pulling these different elements together.

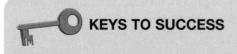

KEYS TO SUCCESS

The keys to successfully engaging in a process of continuous professional development hinge on your ability to:

- Identify your immediate and long-term learning needs
- Develop clear goals and build a strategy to enable you to meet these
- Recognise the resources that can support you
- Continuously reflect on the experience and engage in the process of personal and professional development planning
- Document the process

Identify your immediate and long-term learning needs analysis

The first stage of CPD is to step back and reflect on your current role and identify the gaps in your skills and knowledge base. As a practitioner, you have a number of resources at your fingertips to help you. For example you could:

- Draw on your own reflections and use your ongoing reflective log – your exploration of critical incidents and observations made at formal training events to direct your thinking
- Undertake a personal skills audit and list the skills you require in the setting where you work, rating yourself against each of these
- Work with your preceptor to identify areas for development
- Look to more formal feedback processes such as those provided through appraisal or individual performance review and feedback provided by your supervisor

Ask yourself the question: What am I missing? This will relate to a number of areas, including:

- Knowledge (e.g. there may be gaps in your personal knowledge about particular aspects of practice or the research base for a particular intervention)
- Clinical skills
- Policy and legislation

Answering this question will provide you with your short-term goals. These tend to focus on your current job and the skills and competencies you require to perform at your best. However, once you have settled into your job you might also want to look to the future and think about a bigger picture and your future plans and ambitions.

The following short exercise can be helpful. Use the space to draw or describe what you see yourself doing in:

Six months' time   A years' time   Three years' time   Five years' time

Ask yourself the question: Am I interested in

- A clinical role?

- A managerial role?

- A research career?

- An academic career?

- Being an active participant in the professional association or a specialist interest group?

- A combination of a number of these?

- Something else?

Is success

- Managing a team?

- Seeing my name referred to or on an academic paper?

- Earning lots of money?

- Being valued by my clients?

- Having a part-time post and spending time with my family?

- Something else?

In terms of my career I would be disappointed if...

Imagine that you are introducing yourself to a stranger. What would you like to say about your work role?

What is the most satisfying part of your job? The least satisfying? Why?

My ideal job description would read as...

I currently have the following skills to meet this.

I need the following skills to meet this.

These questions are intended to help you begin to think about your future. You may start work with very fixed ideas about what you hope to achieve or these may emerge as you go along. It is inevitable that your ideas will change. Having a direction for the future will help you to focus your energies, enable you to identify the skills you need and plan your long-term CPD needs.

Develop clear goals and build a strategy to enable you to meet these

After you have identified your short-term and long-term learning needs the next challenge is to transform these into concrete goals and to build a strategy to enable you to meet them. It will be helpful to revisit Chapter 5 on setting and achieving goals to remind yourself about the setting of SMART targets. If you are a visual learner, try this mapping activity.

Begin by listing the skills, knowledge and personal qualities (e.g. patience) you currently possess. You can do this either as a list or as a mind map. Alongside this, make a second list or draw a mind map. This time include the skills you require to fulfil your current role or the skills needed. You may find it helpful to refer to your professional standards here, for example the post-registration education and practice (PREP) standards for nursing. If you are looking towards your long-term aspirations in a different area or specialism, you may need to undertake specific research to look more deeply at what is required.

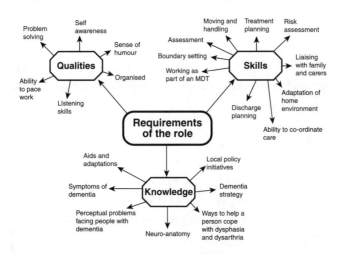

Now marry up the two and create a final mind map which bridges the gap between where you are now and where you hope to be, identifying specific areas for development.

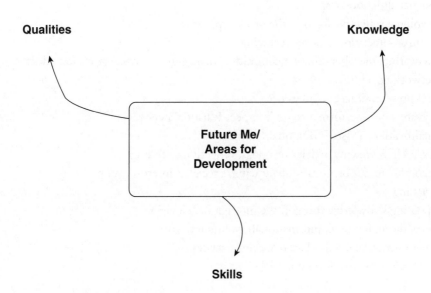

This will form the basis for the goal-setting process. It is probably advisable not to work on everything at once but to focus on specific areas and to develop a strategy to enable you to fulfil these objectives. Again, Chapter 5 will provide a useful starting point.

Recognise the resources that can support you

There are a vast number of resources that can support your continuous professional development. The key is to move beyond thinking about learning purely in terms of formal educational opportunities. Alsop (2000) expresses this well. Continuous professional development, she says, is not confined to formal study programmes but embraces a far broader range of activities 'through which individuals learn and develop their skills and expertise' (Alsop, 2000: 1).

Here is a quick A–Z (incorporating examples identified by the various regulatory bodies) to help you begin to identify the full range of opportunities that exist in the workplace and beyond.

acting up, audit, action learning
books, being a tutor, being an examiner
colleagues, conferences, coaching, consultancy
distance learning, developing specialist skills
educational programmes, exchange programmes, evening classes
formal learning
gaining qualifications
higher education courses
informal learning, in-service teaching
journal club, job swap
keeping a reflective log or a file of your progress
lecturer–practitioner posts, lecturing
mentoring, membership of a committee, management training, masters degree
networking
oral presentations at conference
private work, performance review, peer learning, peer review
qualifications (Msc, PhD), quality circles
research, reviewing articles or books, reflections, reading
secondment opportunities, shadowing, specialist interest groups
teaching
updating knowledge through the internet or television
visits (local, national, international), voluntary work
work shadowing, work-based learning, writing
xpert witness, xpanding your role

Continuously reflect on the experience and engage in the process of personal and professional development planning

If you manage to recognise and access these opportunities in the workplace, you will be well on the way to the process of lifelong learning that is at the heart of personal and professional development planning. However, to really achieve this you need to put into practice those skills covered in Chapter 9 on reflective practice. In this way, you can transform critical incidents into learning opportunities. This will involve dedicating time to recording and reflecting on your experiences, critically evaluating these and identifying how to take this learning forwards. You need to become disciplined and build in time to do this. Again, refer to Chapter 9 to look at tools and techniques that can support this process and help you identify barriers to reflection.

Documenting the process

It is not enough to 'do' CPD. You must also find a way of documenting the process in order to evidence your personal and professional development. There are lots of good reasons why you may want to document your CPD activities:

- Recording your achievements provides you with a systematic way of documenting your progress. This can help you to identify skills gaps and plan future CPD activities to fill these. It is also very satisfying to look back and to recognise just how far you have travelled personally and professionally

- For your future career development. Many employers expect you to bring a record of your CPD activities, usually in the form of a portfolio, along with you to your interview. They will take time to look through this so it is important that you get this right

- As a focus for performance review

For many health and social care practitioners, the process of keeping an accurate record of your CPD activities and your learning is not optional. A number of the bodies governing professional standards have made it a requirement for individuals to maintain a record of their ongoing professional development as a prerequisite for continued registration. For example, nurses and midwives are required to document their learning in order to meet the PREP standards. Similarly, professions governed by the Health Professions Council (HPC), including occupational therapy, physiotherapy, radiography, paramedics and operating department practitioners, are required to submit a profile, on request, of their ongoing professional development as a requirement of continued registration. This profile must:

1. Maintain a continuous, up-to-date and accurate record of your CPD activities;
2. Demonstrate that your CPD activities are a mixture of learning activities relevant to your current or future practice;

3. Seek to ensure that your CPD has contributed to the quality of their practice and service delivery;

4. Seek to ensure that your CPD benefits the service user; and

5. Present a written profile containing evidence of your CPD upon request. (Health Professions Council, 2006: 4)

Interestingly, the emphasis here is on the submission of a *profile*, which is essentially a summary of your learning. This profile is usually based on a more substantive document called a *portfolio*, which can be defined as 'a systematic documented record of the processes and outcomes and learning showing what has been achieved and how new learning will inform future practice' (Health Professions Council, 2006: 10).

Your CPD portfolio

The portfolio can be seen as a collection of documents illustrating the range of professional activities you have engaged in and your learning from these. The good news is that in reading this book and recording your reflections and learning in the classroom and on placement you have the foundations of this document in place and you can then build on it. However, it is not enough to randomly record and include everything. When you begin to assemble your portfolio you will need to spend time considering what you will document and how you will organise it. According to Alsop (2000), a good portfolio should be:

- Structured – divided into identified sections so that it is clear and easy to follow

- Selective – include a range of carefully selected evidence to demonstrate your learning progression and development over time

- Systematic – the portfolio should be methodical in how reflections are recorded and potential actions decided

- Contain an element of synthesis – your portfolio needs to bring your learning together across all areas of your work as well as your professional, academic and personal development

- Suitable for purpose – the portfolio is primarily a document for you. You need to feel comfortable engaging with it and it should therefore reflect something of your personality

What will the portfolio look like?

This is very much dependent on you. When you start to keep your portfolio you will need to make a few simple choices:

- Designed by you or off the peg? There are a range of professional portfolios, which are essentially templates, where you record your observations, reflections and actions. These have the advantage that they are easy to use, but the drawback is that you then need to fit your thinking and writing into a set format which can feel quite constraining.

- Electronic or hand-written? Some practitioners prefer to record their continuous professional development straight on to a computer in electronic format. Other people enjoy the process of writing.

Whatever you choose, the portfolio is made up of basic ingredients. You need to remember that it is a record of your *learning*. It is very personal, not just a collection of certificates. It can include:

- Reflections

- Testimonials written about you by others

- Articles you have written or contributed to

- PowerPoints of presentations you have given

- Certificates with summaries of your learning

- Photographs (presenting at conference, designs you have made)

- Patient leaflets and assessments you have developed

- Case studies (do not forget to make sure that these are confidential – the client's identity needs to be protected)

- Evidence of specialist groups you are part of

- Evaluations of training you have given

- Records of appraisal, individual performance review

There will be a tension between the public and private function of the portfolio, so it is worth dividing it into two sections. The first section can record your ongoing personal reflections and the second section can be used to represent a more public face that can be subject to scrutiny by others. In both of these, remember the importance of confidentiality.

Dividing your portfolio in this way is useful as it will help you to organise your evidence so that if you are asked to submit a *profile* to maintain your registration, it will be easy to summarise and extract the relevant information demonstrating how this has contributed to patient care. Here is one example of a possible structure you might follow when ordering your portfolio. The website accompanying this book (www.skills4

health.co.uk) provides links to additional sites which offer examples of alternative structures. The key is to find a system that meets your needs and works for you.

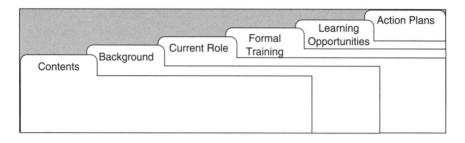

        IN A NUTSHELL

This chapter has provided a very brief overview of continuous professional development. It has highlighted that:

* Being a health or social care practitioner is a lifelong learning process

* Continuous professional development is a core requirement for continued registration

* Engaging in professional development activities enable you to fulfil a range of personal and professional objectives

* It is not only necessary that you engage in CPD but systematically documenting these experiences will be to your advantage

* Gaining your professional qualification is not an ending, it is a beginning

References and signposts to further reading and resources

Alsop, A. (2000) *Continuing Professional Development: A Guide for Therapists.* Oxford: Blackwell Science.

College of Occupational Therapists (2006) *Post Qualifying Framework: A Resource for Occupational Therapists* (Core). London: COT.

Health Professions Council (2006) *Continuing Professional Development and Your Registration.* London: HPC.

Hull, C. and Redfern, L. (1996) *Profiles and Portfolios: A Guide for Nurses and Midwives.* Basingstoke: Macmillan.

Nursing and Midwifery Council (2008) *The PREP Handbook.* London: NMC.

Endings and new beginnings

Learning is a journey for which there is never really an end. As soon as you arrive at your destination you will realise that there is another adventure to look forward to: a new country to navigate, another path to follow. As the final chapter has illustrated, health and social care practice is very much like this. You will arrive at the end of your training, hopefully succeed in gaining your dream job and discover a range of new and exciting challenges you will strive to meet, different places to go, new things to try.

I hope that this book has helped build your confidence and equipped you with skills that will enable you to move to the next exciting chapter of your career, to climb the highest mountains and to go on to wherever you choose.

Fellow traveller, thank you for your company. It has been a pleasure.

Index

The Qualitative Research Kit

Edited by Uwe Flick

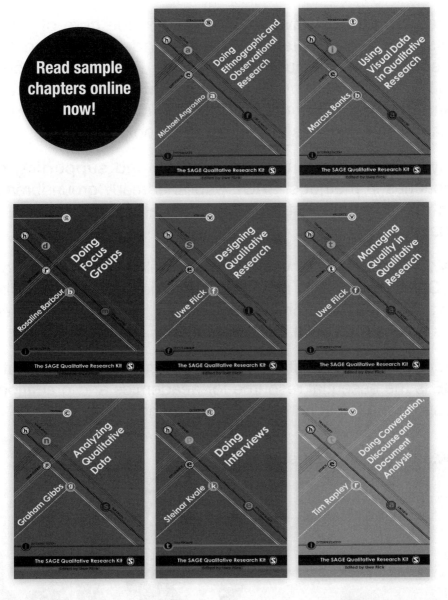

Read sample chapters online now!

Doing Ethnographic and Observational Research — Michael Angrosino — The SAGE Qualitative Research Kit

Using Visual Data in Qualitative Research — Marcus Banks — The SAGE Qualitative Research Kit

Doing Focus Groups — Rosaline Barbour — The SAGE Qualitative Research Kit

Designing Qualitative Research — Uwe Flick — The SAGE Qualitative Research Kit

Managing Quality in Qualitative Research — Uwe Flick — The SAGE Qualitative Research Kit

Analyzing Qualitative Data — Graham Gibbs — The SAGE Qualitative Research Kit

Doing Interviews — Steinar Kvale — The SAGE Qualitative Research Kit

Doing Conversation, Discourse and Document Analysis — Tim Rapley — The SAGE Qualitative Research Kit

www.sagepub.co.uk

Supporting researchers for more than forty years

Research methods have always been at the core of SAGE's publishing. Sara Miller McCune founded SAGE in 1965 and soon after she published SAGE's first methods book, *Public Policy Evaluation*. A few years later, she launched the Quantitative Applications in the Social Sciences series – affectionately known as the 'little green books'.

Always at the forefront of developing and supporting new approaches in methods, SAGE published early groundbreaking texts and journals in the fields of qualitative methods and evaluation.

Today, more than forty years and two million little green books later, SAGE continues to push the boundaries with a growing list of more than 1,200 research methods books, journals, and reference works across the social, behavioural, and health sciences.

From qualitative, quantitative and mixed methods to evaluation, SAGE is the essential resource for academics and practitioners looking for the latest in methods by leading scholars.

www.sagepublications.com